Gender Circuits

MW00813737

Gender Circuits explores whether and how new technologies are reshaping what it means to be a gendered person in contemporary society, through substantive sociological analysis and both historical and contemporary case studies. This book sheds light on the complex intersections between societal gender ideologies, information and biomedical technologies, and embodied identities.

The new edition of *Gender Circuits* contains three new case studies that examine key contemporary technologies: modern beauty norms, Botox and eating disorders; the gender of medicine and reproductive technologies; and gender diversity on social networking websites such as Facebook. These studies, along with the updated and expanded cases from the first edition, offer contemporary, real-world examples of how new technologies are reshaping the embodied lives of individuals.

Dr. Eve Shapiro is a Visiting Research Scholar at the Center for Research on Women and Social Justice at the University of California, Santa Barbara. She received her PhD in Sociology from the University of California, Santa Barbara and has published widely, including in *Gender & Society*, *Sexualities*, and the *Journal of Gay and Lesbian Social Services*. Her current research examines the myriad ways new technologies can be purposefully used to reshape individual and community lives, particularly around gender and sexuality.

Contemporary Sociological Perspectives

Edited by **Doug Hartmann**, University of Minnesota
and **Jodi O'Brien**, Seattle University

This innovative series is for all readers interested in books that provide frameworks for making sense of the complexities of contemporary social life. Each of the books in this series uses a sociological lens to provide current critical and analytical perspectives on significant social issues, patterns and trends. The series consists of books that integrate the best ideas in sociological thought with an aim toward public education and engagement. These books are designed for use in the classroom as well as for scholars and socially curious general readers.

Published:
Political Justice and Religious Values by Charles F. Andrain
GIS and Spatial Analysis for the Social Sciences by Robert Nash Parker and Emily K. Asencio
Hoop Dreams on Wheels: Disability and the Competitive Wheelchair Athlete by Ronald J. Berger
The Internet and Social Inequalities by James C. Witte and Susan E. Mannon
Media and Middle Class Mom: Images and Realities of Work and Family by Lara Descartes and Conrad Kottak
Watching T.V. Is Not Required: Thinking about Media and Thinking about Thinking by Bernard McGrane and John Gunderson
Violence Against Women: Vulnerable Populations by Douglas Brownridge
State of Sex: Tourism, Sex and Sin in the New American Heartland by Barbara G. Brents, Crystal A. Jackson & Kate Hausbeck
Sociologists Backstage: Answers to 10 Questions About What They Do by Sarah Fenstermaker and Nikki Jones
Surviving the Holocaust: A Life Course Perspective by Ronald Berger
Stargazing: Celebrity, Fame, and Social Interaction by Kerry Ferris and Scott Harris
The Senses in Self, Society, and Culture by Phillip Vannini, Dennis Waskul and Simon Gottschalk
Surviving Dictatorship by Jacqueline Adams
The Womanist Idea by Layli Maparyan
Social Theory Re-Wired: New Connections to Classical and Contemporary Perspectives by Wesley Longhofer and Daniel Winchester
Religion in Today's World: Global Issues, Sociological Perspectives, by Melissa Wilcox
Understanding Deviance: Connecting Classical and Contemporary Perspectives edited by Tammy L. Anderson
Social Statistics: Managing Data, Conducting Analyses, Presenting Results, Second Edition by Thomas J. Linneman
Transforming Scholarship: Why Women's and Gender Studies Students are Changing Themselves and the World, Second Edition by Michele Tracy Berger and Cheryl Radeloff
Who Lives, Who Dies, Who Decides?: Abortion, Neonatal Care, Assisted Dying, and Capital Punishment, Second Edition by Sheldon Ekland-Olson
Life and Death Decisions: The Quest for Morality and Justice in Human Societies, Second Edition by Sheldon Ekland-Olson
Gender Circuits: Bodies and Identities in a Technological Age, Second Edition by Eve Shapiro
Migration, Incorporation, and Change in an Interconnected World by Syed Ali and Douglass Hartmann

Forthcoming:
Social Worlds of Imagination by Chandra Mukerji
All Media are Social by Andrew Lindner

Gender Circuits

Bodies and Identities in
a Technological Age

Second Edition

Eve Shapiro

Routledge
Taylor & Francis Group

NEW YORK AND LONDON

Second edition published 2015
by Routledge
711 Third Avenue, New York, NY 10017

and by Routledge
2 Park Square, Milton Park, Abingdon, Oxon OX14 4RN

Routledge is an imprint of the Taylor & Francis Group, an informa business

© 2015 Taylor & Francis

First edition published by Routledge 2010

Library of Congress Cataloging-in-Publication Data

Shapiro, Eve.
  Gender circuits : bodies and identities in a technological age / by Eve Shapiro. — Second edition.
    pages cm. — (Contemporary sociological perspectives)
  Includes bibliographical references and index.
  1. Gender identity. 2. Transgenderism. I. Title.
  HQ1075.S527 2015
  305.3—dc23
  2014028359

ISBN: 978-0-415-63854-8 (hbk)
ISBN: 978-0-415-63853-1 (pbk)
ISBN: 978-1-315-87962-8 (ebk)

Typeset in Adobe Caslon
by ApexCoVantage, LLC

Printed and bound in the United States of America by Edwards Brothers Malloy on sustainably sourced paper

DEDICATION

For Moose and sweet Aviva

TABLE OF CONTENTS

LIST OF FIGURES

PREFACE

Recently, while sitting at a coffee shop writing (and surfing the Web on my smartphone, in all honesty) two men behind me were having a vibrant conversation about cloud computing, smartphones, and about why the Internet connection might be slow that day. While neither worked in the tech industries, each was remarkably proficient at making sense of the intricacies of information technologies, both hardware and software. I was struck by how benign, how taken for granted, the quite remarkable integration of technology into day-to-day life has become. The recent explosion in the "Internet of things" wherein objects are linked, traceable, and usable through the Internet is just one example of how emerging information and biomedical technologies are reshaping our lives anew. From phones, glasses, and watches that allow on-the-go video conferencing and interactive heads-up displays, to biometric devices that track one's physical activity, heart rate, and blood pressure and import all of that information to one's social networking website of choice, human beings are ever more cyborg beings.

In 2008, when I was working on the first edition of this book, I took myself on a writing retreat to get away from my daily distractions. Since it was off-season, the inn at the retreat was empty and I ate my meals, for the most part, alone. During my first meal at the restaurant I was engaged in friendly conversation by my waiter who asked me what I did for a living. When I shared with him that I was a sociologist, he became quite agitated and launched into a long, rather one-sided conversation.

Shifting his weight from one foot to the other repeatedly, Will grilled me about what I thought had caused some of the biggest changes in our society. I was not particularly interested in having a conversation with Will, so I mumbled a response and made motions to get back to my meal. Not to be deterred, my chatty waiter shared with me his take on his own question. He informed me that technology was transforming our world, including individuals. At this point my ears pricked up; I had not mentioned to Will that I was currently writing a book on technology, and here he was lending credence to my ideas. Will went on to explain that, in his view, technology was changing how people acted, what people believed, the nature of interpersonal relationships, and indeed who people were. He also shared that, as a technophobe, he knew that he was missing out on key parts of contemporary life. Without an email account he felt left out with friends, and with no computer skills he felt unable to pursue his true passion: becoming a wine buyer for the inn. What struck me as poignant when talking with Will was that his internal struggle over technology was palpable. He wanted so much to join the fold, so to speak, but simultaneously was afraid of who he might become because of it.

I wonder what Will is doing now, four years later. Did he finally get an email account? It is hard to imagine not having one in this day and age. In fact, many activities—from obtaining social services to applying for jobs and participating in school events—now exist solely online. In California, for example, social services are almost exclusively accessible online. If one has to apply for unemployment benefits, an online application is available and quick, while phone lines are only open for a few hours a day.

Since the first edition of *Gender Circuits* was published in 2010 I have had the immense pleasure of talking with a wide range of people about technology and gender. I am amazed at the places the book and its ideas have reached, from family therapists, doctors, corporate leaders, and students across the United States, to technological innovators, scholars, and politicians. Throughout these diverse conversations, the ubiquity of technological intervention—both welcome and unwelcome—in people's lives was a common theme. No matter who someone is or how they have come to know *Gender Circuits*, individuals describe feeling a connection to the material because of their own complicated relationship to technology in different parts of their lives. Whether it is a complex decision over a medical treatment or an effort to regulate their child's (or their own) time on Facebook, the rewards and challenges of new technologies resonate with people.

Since writing *Gender Circuits* I have felt as if everywhere I turn I find evidence of how technologies are reshaping people's lives and embodied selves. Perhaps I am a magnet for this type of information because I am so attuned to the topic, but I think it is more than that. These conversations have become commonplace in society as a whole. In numerous venues, including in popular media, political debate, and social commentary, attention has been paid to the changing nature of life in North America amid technological innovation. Consider, for example, telephones. While few individuals had cell phones 10 years ago, most teens today cannot imagine a life without them, and pay phones are disappearing from public streets. In fact, smartphones are such "old technology" that young people view emails and voice calls as relics of the past; texting has replaced both as the choice mode of communication. Similarly, we accept as normal the integration of biomedical technologies like implants, contact lenses, pharmaceuticals, and pacemakers into the human body; many of these technologies were the sole purview of science fiction just a few years ago. All to say, trying to make better sense of how new technologies are reshaping contemporary bodies and identities continues to be an engaging and prescient endeavor at this moment in North America.

Technology and technological innovation have a long history. Technologies have been in a dynamic relationship with gendered bodies and selves throughout history. However, the pervasiveness of technology and the speed of change that we are experiencing in this era are impacting modern lives and societies in new and transformative ways. These changes, in conversation with social norms and in line with dominant ideologies, are transforming what it means to be an embodied, gendered person. This is true even if we, as individuals, ignore or resist these processes. Dominant power holders construct some beliefs, norms, appearances, and experiences as prized, normal, and valued, while discrediting others. Normative values and expectations shape individuals in myriad ways even when they do not fit into or abide by them. The inspiration for *Gender Circuits* lies at the intersection of these social forces—technology, bodies, identities, dominant ideologies, and social scripts. I begin and end by questioning how technological change is affecting society and individuals. I hope that this book, born out of my own questions, generates new inquiries and offers new analytical tools to help readers to answer their own questions about their life, community, society, and world.

The new edition of *Gender Circuits* has a number of exciting additions. First and foremost, there are three new case studies that examine key contemporary technologies: modern beauty norms, Botox and eating disorders; the gender of medicine and reproductive technologies; and gender diversity on social networking websites such as Facebook. These cases, along with the updated and expanded cases from the first edition offer contemporary, real-world examples of how new technologies are reshaping the embodied lives of individuals and help to bridge sociological concepts and everyday experience. In addition to the new case studies, all of the chapters have been shortened and updated to reflect the most current statistics, research findings and social changes. This is particularly important for material on transgender and intersex lives because of the significant changes in psycho-medical treatment and social and civil rights that have taken place over the last five years. Finally, *Gender Circuits* includes many more images to help elaborate on historical and contemporary examples, and additional multimedia materials will be available through an online companion site. I hope that these changes make *Gender Circuits* even more readable, teachable, and thought provoking.

A few notes about language. I have endeavored to write in a jargon-free manner. I have, in the process, made a few stylistic choices. First, given my focus on the complexity and historicity of sex and gender categories, I have tried to minimize gendered language. In the absence of common gender neutral pronouns (although I do introduce some in Chapter 1), I use "they" instead of he/she and "their" instead of his/

her. While grammatically incorrect, this approach has the benefit of avoiding gender-specific language. Second, in an effort to engage in conversation with readers' own lives and experiences, I have at times used inclusive language (e.g., "you," "we," and "us"). My intention is not to assume a shared experience or identity with readers or to be condescending. Rather, it is my invitation to you, as readers, to consider whether your own experiences mirror or contradict the examples in this book and how you might make sense of these overlaps and divergences using the analytical tools developed herein.

In addition to text boxes that highlight the definitions of new terms and theories, the notes offer more details about the ideas raised in the book and list many wonderful empirical articles and books on the topics introduced here. They are a wonderful place to learn more about the mechanisms by which particular identities are integrated, technologies are developed, and bodies are shaped. I encourage you, when inspired, to use the notes to find books and articles that elaborate a particular topic and continue your research there.

The analytical approach I adopt in this book can be used to examine many other areas of embodied identity and social change. I hope that *Gender Circuits* can serve as a launching pad for research on a diverse array of other topics. Because of both space constraints and issues of complexity I have chosen to focus on social changes, gender ideologies, and social contexts within North America. However, there is outstanding work that engages these same issues outside of this region and I encourage you to explore this scholarship.

A project such as this cannot be accomplished by one person alone. I had the great joy and privilege of being trained by an incredible group of scholars including Richard Flacks, Jodi O'Brien, Leila Rupp, Beth Schneider, and Verta Taylor, all of whom have, over the years, shown phenomenal generosity with their time and provided me with invaluable mentorship. Many colleagues were generous enough to read drafts of this manuscript. Patricia Drew and Lisa Leitz read every chapter and cheered me on when I needed it most. Kendal Broad, Leah DeVun, Jessica Fields, Mary Ingram-Waters, Linda Kim, Amanda Moras, and many others read chapters, offered support, and otherwise enriched my life. The members of my writing group—Linda Kim, Amanda Moras, Emily Musil, Jen Sandler, Asali Solomon, and Melissa Stuckey—have been the most steadfast of friends, critics, and champions. Many of the strengths and none of the failings in this book are thanks to them. I was lucky to have the research assistance of Jennifer Weekley and Liz Hauck, and to benefit from the wonderful research skills of the University of Connecticut Women's Studies librarian Kathy Labradorf and San Francisco State University Sociology librarian Jeff Rosen. Max Gentry created the wonderful high heels image. Sabrina Matthews edited each and every chapter brilliantly and, like always, made me laugh in the process. This book would never have been possible without the guidance and support of series editors Valerie Jenness, Doug Hartmann, and Jodi O'Brien, and the vision of Routledge editor Steve Rutter and associate editor Samantha Barbaro. Thank you for believing in the project and for more than a few wonderful conversations.

A thank you to the reviewers of this edition:

Mary Ingram-Waters	Arizona Honors College
Ann Hibner Koblitz	Arizona State University
Dana Berkowitz	Louisiana State University
Amy Stone	Trinity University
Courtney Marshall	University of New Hampshire
L. Ayu Saraswati Prasetyaningsih	University of Hawaii at Manoa
Kelly J. Rawson	University of Kentucky
Janni Aragon	University of Victoria

Finally, there are people in my life to whom I owe innumerable thanks and without whom I would never have been able to arrive at this point. Mindy Stevens has brought more joy to my life than I knew it could contain. I cannot imagine a better partner with whom to build a life. My parents and brother made me believe that I could accomplish anything I wanted. And my beloved Aviva has made all colors brighter and all sounds sweeter since her arrival. All of my accomplishments—indeed, all of the good things in my life—I share with them.

PREVIEW
GENDERED BODIES AND IDENTITIES IN A TECHNOLOGICAL AGE

As a child, inspired by science fiction in books, films, and cartoons, I expected the twenty-first century to be run by robots. Humans would live forever as cybernetic humanoids, receiving regular tune-ups, replacement parts, and even body swaps. Our food would be "replicated" at our whim as it was on *Star Trek,* and we would wear clothing made from plastic. We would all be able to communicate with one another on our Dick Tracy phone–watches from halfway around the globe, or even from other planets (so we could let our parents know if we made a quick jaunt to Mars for a party). The giant *Transformers* would be engaged in an epic battle of good over evil, while Rosie, George Jetson's domestic robot, dusted our homes. Now that we have arrived at the beginning of the twenty-first century, predictions such as these seem both hilarious and eerily true. While we do not have regular body swaps, we do have face transplants, plastic surgery, stem cell research, cloning, and in-vitro fertilization. Although we do not yet travel on the daily Mars shuttle, we do have an international space station, Mars rover and science lab, and space tourism. We have cell phones, genetically modified food, clothing made from recycled plastics, drone strikes, and robotic vacuums.

TECHNOLOGY

Technology is anything that humans develop to manipulate the natural environment. From the Greek root word *techne*, "art" and suffix *logia*, "to speak," "technology" means "expression of a craft"; this original definition signifies the breadth of the concept.

Humans have developed a wide variety of knowledge, activities, implements, and processes to alter our material and conceptual worlds. From smoke signals to the smartphone, technology has infiltrated every part of the human experience and continues to change how people experience the world around them, interact with each other, and go about their daily lives.[1] From our daily use of mobile devices and computers to access the World Wide Web and electronic media, to the genetic engineering of our food, bodies, and medicine, technology mediates most of our daily experiences in the twenty-first century and has become the middleman, as it were, between much of our social world and ourselves.[2]

According to my smartphone—on which I took the initial notes for this text—on July 30, 2007 I listened to the car radio while I drove to work. I am sure my Bluetooth earpiece was in my ear even as I listened to a program on my car radio in which Dr. Danna Walker, a journalism professor at American University, described her students' reactions to an enforced media blackout.[3] Walker asked students in her "Understanding Mass Media" course to refrain from all electronic media for 24 hours. Many of the students reacted to the experience with frustration and anger, including one claim that it was "one of the toughest days I have had to endure."[4] Another of Walker's students declared that spending the day without technology made her feel homeless: "I was walking down the street literally with nowhere to go, and I just did not know what I was going to do." This is a phenomenal statement about the centrality of technology in our twenty-first century lives; then again, should that have been so shocking, given how encumbered by technology I was at that very moment?

Think about the speed with which we go about our days, days filled with the multi-tasking, double-booking, and phone calls made while traveling to the next place our physical presence is required. A leading scholar of identity and society, Jodi O'Brien, writes about how in our modern world we come to "lean forward" in time, always paying attention to the next thing we have to do, spurred on by our increasing ability—and increasing expectations—to speed up our lives by using modern technology. Regardless of all of the time-saving devices introduced to our life in the last 20 years, or maybe because of their introduction, people feel more "short on time" than ever before.[5] The many news articles on the increasing speed of life—more than 50 in major U.S. newspapers alone in 2013—are testament to the feelings of being overwhelmed by technology, and to our ambivalence about this phenomenon.

While technology obviously impacts our lives on a practical level, it also affects our attitudes and our everyday behavior. Cell phones are a familiar illustration of this; they give us a way to contact others at any time we choose, but the other edge of the sword is that we are expected to be reachable at every moment of the day. I am personally engaged in an ongoing tug-of-war with my father. If I do not return his phone calls within an hour, he will call again . . . and again . . . and again. When I was in college, before the pervasion of mobile phones, I could go for days ignoring his phone calls, but now, although I am older and more independent, along with my cell phone comes his expectation, even demand, that I be available at all times. It is very likely that my father feels that he is equally on-call.

It is incontrovertible that technology is ubiquitous in the everyday life of most North Americans.[6] Those individuals with means enough to have ready access to technology use electronic devices no longer just to gain information, but to perform tasks and to communicate with a multitude of acquaintances, online or off. Even for those of us who lack economic privilege, technology has come to play a prominent role; food stamps are electronic and computers are required for many social and economic tasks. Unequal access to technology exacerbates existing social inequalities. And, even when economic, racial, sexual, gender, or age status (to mention only a few defining characteristics) puts access to certain types of information or medical technology out of reach, those individuals without access are affected by the social changes that the technologies bring about.

Technology is not just the means through which we increasingly shape the world around us, but it also acts as an instrument to shape *how* we interact. The technological tendrils that permeate our lives have not stopped with accelerated communication or medical advancement. New technology is changing everything about our lives and world, including our bodies and identities. Many contemporary social debates center on questions of technology and its impact on the human experience, and scholars have begun to ask questions about how this increasingly technological world is changing who people are.[7] Some social theorists argue that technology will supplement the limitations of nature, and expand possibilities for humanity.[8] Others contend that technology will constrain and imprison civilization.[9] Regardless of whether scholars take a utopian or catastrophic view, most agree that technology raises the question of "whether humanity could become a new order of being."[10] A social scientific approach, as taken up in this book, views people as products of both nature and society. This vantage point is likely to prompt a range of additional questions about whether societal changes are interdependent with technological development and, if so, how this affects who people are, and can be, in our society.

Making Sense of Human Diversity

Human beings are phenomenally diverse. Individuals look, act, move, and think in dramatically different ways. For all of our variety, however, these differences are also patterned; people who share a culture, country, or social identity (e.g. race, gender, or ethnicity) tend to be more similar to each other than they are to others. Making sense of this diversity and its origins has consumed a great deal of human attention.

Theories of Difference

Some explanations suggest that human difference is due fully to differences in biology, genetics, and evolution.

BIOLOGICAL DETERMINISM

A theory that human life, including behavior, appearance, and personality, is fully determined by biological factors. This theory posits that the essential features of human lives, features such as gender, sexuality, and race, are fixed and inherited and not learned.

Theories rooted in biological determinism often locate the source of patterned differences in our evolution. For example, they might explain contrasting relationship behaviors between men and women, such as men's perceived tendency toward promiscuity versus women's toward fidelity, as deriving from divergent evolutionary drives: i.e. stability for women as opposed to producing a maximum number of offspring for men.[11]

Other explanations for human variation are based on social constructionism, a theory that asserts that human difference is the product of differences in socialization and lived experience.

SOCIAL CONSTRUCTIONISM

A theoretical approach which states that societal structures (at the individual, interactional, and institutional levels) are the product of social processes and are not biologically or naturally inevitable. This theoretical paradigm is often contrasted against essentialism, which states that social reality is the product of ahistorical, inevitable forces such as "natural law" or "divine will."

Social constructionism posits that the forces that shape the lives of individuals (e.g. gender, race, law, and governance structures) are created, defined, and redefined over time out of social interaction and guided by reigning worldviews in a society. These theories assert that gendered self-concepts are fully the product of learned social (gender) roles. Finally, some theories work to marry these two perspectives, suggesting that social structures are written on top of biological forces to produce human behaviors. According to these hybrid theories, personality differences between men and women are both the product of hormonal differences and of social expectations for communication. These efforts to find middle ground between essentialist and constructionist theories rely on the assumption that each individual lives in a fixed biological state, which is a rigid precursor to social influence.

Preeminent gender scholar Raewyn Connell argues that none of these models adequately capture the dynamic and mutually constitutive relationship between material bodies and social forces. Connell describes these three approaches as "body as machine" (biological differences drive gender differences), "body as a canvas" (social structures drive gender differences), and "two-realms model" (social structures lie on top of body differences to create gender differences), respectively.[12] If biological models alone could explain human diversity, researchers would find significant differences between men and women. Instead, study after study finds more similarities than differences in aptitude, ability, and function.[13] Of course, it is illogical to assume that the body and its internal structure do not play any part in shaping the lives of individuals. Indeed, the question of whether nature or nurture is the source of differences between men and women is simply the wrong question to be asking. First, the question presupposes only two kinds of human beings—men and women—and ignores the incredible variation that exists in sex and gender. More significantly, the question assumes that biology (aka nature) and socialization (aka nurture) are separate and static forces. These assumptions belie the complexity of human experience and development. As Anne Fausto-Sterling, the well-published biologist who pioneered an integrated theory of biology and society cautioned, "don't get stuck trying to divide nature from nurture . . . living bodies are dynamic systems that develop and change in response to their social and historical contexts."[14]

Contrary to the early scientific conception of the embodied self as the untainted reflection of biology, social and biological scientists in the last 25 years have explored how social beliefs shape physiology and biology. What their research has shown is that social beliefs and practices influence the human form both externally (e.g. grooming and body modification) and internally (e.g. genes and hormones). Consider, for example, a prime marker of femininity in North America: the high-heeled shoe. As a rule, women wear them and men do not. Most members of our society see wearing them as a symbol of femininity and assume that it is natural for women to be drawn to wearing them, while most men are repelled. Connoisseurs of high-heeled shoes often remark on how they show off women's natural curves, highlighting their femininity—that is, according to our society's definitions of femininity.

Objectively, however, the culturally and historically specific fashion practice of wearing these shoes actually creates some of the femininity that is assumed to be natural. Over time, wearing high heels will change the shape of a woman's feet and the arch in her back, alter her gait, and strengthen particular muscles in her legs. These changes result in a body comportment that highlights breasts and buttocks, a gait that incorporates swaying hip movements, and legs with long, lean muscles (see Figure 0.1). In other words, while there is no chromosome that regulates the wearing of high heels, following this social expectation changes women's physiology and produces or accentuates many of the feminine characteristics that we attribute to genetics and assume to be natural.

Our body both informs and responds to the society we live in. All social dynamics are embodied, experienced by and through the body of individual, and changes in society inevitably produce changes in the body—and vice versa. How, then, do we make sense of the complexity of human life if bodies and social forces are in constant interaction, each shaping the other? Connell theorizes that:

> [B]odies are both *objects of* social practice and *agents in* social practice. The same bodies, at the same time, are both. The practices in which bodies are involved form social structures and personal trajectories, which in turn provide the conditions of new practices in which bodies are addressed and involved. There is a loop, a circuit, linking bodily processes and social structures. In fact, there is a tremendous number of such circuits. They occur in historical

Effects of High Heels on the Skeletal Structures of the Body

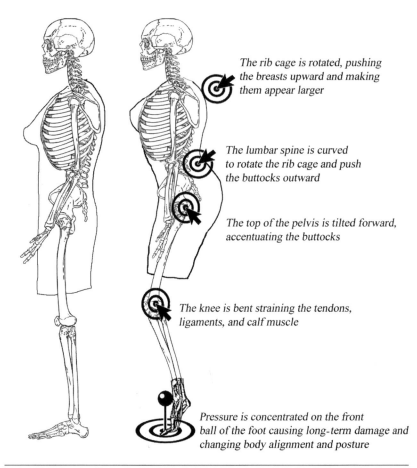

The rib cage is rotated, pushing the breasts upward and making them appear larger

The lumbar spine is curved to rotate the rib cage and push the buttocks outward

The top of the pelvis is tilted forward, accentuating the buttocks

The knee is bent straining the tendons, ligaments, and calf muscle

Pressure is concentrated on the front ball of the foot causing long-term damage and changing body alignment and posture

Figure 0.1 Drawing illustrating the impact of high heels on the body. Illustration by Max Gentry.

time, and change over time. They add up to the historical process in which society is embodied, and bodies are drawn into history.[15]

Connell refers to this process as "social embodiment." The way that individuals experience the world is through their bodies and, in the process, bodies are transformed.

> ### EMBODIMENT
>
> A state of being in which the body is the site of meaning, experience, and expression for individuals in the world. Embodiment also refers to the internalization of cultural norms, and the expression of these social elements in the form and function of individual's bodies.[16]

Some of these changes are physiological, affecting how the body moves and functions. Some are conceptual, shaping how people make sense of and experience the body. Yet others occur at the cellular level affecting when and how our genes are activated—what scientists call epigenetics.[17] Whether we look at how the social world affects physiology or self-concept, it is clear that there is much to gain from thinking about how society, the self, and the body continuously interact with one another.

Understanding the Embodied Self as a Social Product

Making sense of the body from a social perspective requires confronting our own understanding of biology as fixed, innate, and natural. Through empirical studies and gender theorizing, scholars have demonstrated how embodied identities (such as race, class, and gender) are not just physical realities but also social institutions that shape individual lives.

> ### SOCIAL INSTITUTION
>
> An established path for achieving particular social or individual needs or goals. Institutions can be physical structures or societal concepts and are imbued with social power. Social institutions are the means by which social order is established and upheld.

The meaning and importance of the body are as much social products as they are biological. For example, the significance of one's skin color has everything to do with racial inequality and racism and very little to do with levels of melanin in the skin. Some people are under surveillance by the staff of fancy stores, while others are not, based upon a set of assumptions about each as conveyed through their embodied gender, class, and race. One could, with certain resources, dress up, act differently, or otherwise attempt to shape one's identity to change other people's responses, but this would alter one's own embodiment. Most embodied ways of being are difficult to modify, however, and the very act of policing some types of people and not others is one of the many ways that powerful social norms and social inequalities are reinforced. When working-class people or people of color are monitored in stores, it sends a message about who is welcome and who is not—about who the right kind of person is, and who is a problem, and this both follows and reinforces dominant stories about who is "normal" and who is "different."

NORM

A norm is an informal or formal rule for behavior, belief, appearance, or attitude, within a society or community. Norms can be formalized as laws, such as marriage laws that dictate who can form families. Norms can also be mores: societal expectations that have a moral judgment attached to them, such as rules about cannibalism. Finally, informal expectations that are not highly punished when violated (such as greeting a neighbor when passing on the street) are a type of norm called folkways. Beliefs, norms, and values are components of culture that we learn and internalize in the process of everyday life.

Historically, prejudice and discrimination have been legitimized on the basis of claims about biological or "natural" differences between groups of people. Eugenics movements were early twentieth century social campaigns that advocated for the active cultivation of particular characteristics in society by encouraging some people to reproduce and curbing (by influence or force) the reproduction of others. Seeking a scientific basis for the racial superiority of its proponents, eugenics drew on Darwin's concept of "survival of the fittest" and asserted that only the fittest members of society (i.e. white, Western, Christian, and able-bodied) should bear children. By claiming that biology was the reason that whites were economically, politically and socially better off, eugenics movements shifted attention away from the very real discriminatory practices that led to racial inequalities. Beginning with late nineteenth century race and gender rights movements, and accelerating in the wake of the Holocaust's reliance on race science, numerous philosophers, scientists, and scholars have argued against eugenics and the biological basis of social inequalities.

The body, which is the human means of connection to the world, is viewed according to the values, norms, and socially specific meanings dominant in any historical era, but the relationship between society, identity, and the human body is even more complex. Not only does society shape how others see our bodies, but social forces also shape the most basic meanings we make about who we are and what the experiences we have as embodied selves mean.

How we analyze and assign meaning to our body and its sensory experiences is shaped by social context, expectations, and our definition of the situation. The physiological responses to excitement and fear are remarkably similar, but it is our interpretation of the situation that helps us to know what we are "really feeling." Even something as simple as distinguishing pleasure from pain is based upon the meaning we give to an experience. Consider a study that tested sensory perception. Researchers Bryant Anderson and James Pennebaker rubbed an emery board across participants' skins to see how they interpreted the sensation. They found that when they told participants that this experimental manipulation might cause pain, the individuals were far more likely to describe pain as a side effect of the experiment than those who were not told it would be painful. Conversely, when other participants were told that the same manipulation might cause pleasurable sensations, they were more likely to describe the experience as pleasurable.[18] This and other studies have shown that a wide range of external factors shape the internal experience of the body.[19] That is, the process of analyzing and assigning meaning to our body and its sensory experiences is a learned one that is shaped by cultural beliefs, expectations, norms, interpersonal dynamics, and personal values.

As the social meaning of the body changes throughout history, these changes affect how individuals make sense of their own physiological experiences. Socially constructed gender beliefs in the early 1900s painted "good" women as lacking sexual desire, and forbade public distribution of educational materials about sex and sexuality. These social conditions meant that discussions of women's sexual needs were absent from most public or private discourse, denying women any positive explanations for their experiences. My own grandmother had no exposure to reproductive biology or sex education at home, in school, or through popular media. When she began to menstruate—in the 1930s—she truly believed that something had burst inside of her and that she was going to bleed to death. This reaction and explanation may seem ridiculous to modern ears, but my grandmother made sense of this event using those tools at her disposal; this meaning-making reflected her socio-historical context. In turn, this context and my grandmother's experience shaped her understanding of her body in significant and enduring ways.

The body is the intermediary between our internal mind and the external world as well as the visible component of who we are. In contemporary society, we assume that identity and personality characteristics reside in the body to the extent that we believe what we look like tells the world something about who we are. Not only do we assume gender, race, and often, social class based upon what someone looks like, but also we deduce all sorts of other social values.[20] In contemporary North American societies, we evaluate fat people as lazy, blondes as stupid, and masculine women and feminine men as gay; such designations go on and on. Each person experiences and internalizes social beliefs and norms through the body as well. In turn, the body is assumed to reveal to the world the individual's identities, values, and moral character, making a statement about an individual before they ever utter a word.

Making Sense of Embodied Identity

Over the past 500 years, scholars of the self and society have tried to make sense of how individuals come to understand who they are. For many centuries leading up to the 1600s, Judeo-Christian theology guided Western pre-Enlightenment philosophers to the belief that the self was a reflection or product of a god, and that human lives followed a pre-ordained path set out to follow a god's will. With the rise of empirical study and a shift of social power from religious institutions to scientific ones, however, Enlightenment philosophers began to argue that while the "self" was a pre-formed, fixed mind, this mind was unique to individuals, and not the product of divine will. In 1641 René Descartes argued that we know our "self"—our stable, internal, answer to the question, "who am I?"—as we know our thoughts: *cogito ergo sum* ("I think, therefore I am"). In general, philosophers during the Enlightenment viewed the definition of who someone was as a static, inborn set of identities and traits.

Building on Enlightenment philosophy, but extending a more interpretive perspective, early twentieth century pragmatic sociologists argued that the self was a social entity, not an independent one.[21] Instead of something pre-formed within a bodily shell, the self was theorized as the product of social interaction. They argued that, as individuals, we develop who we are by knowing (or imagining) how others see us.[22] George Herbert Mead, among others, suggested that people make sense of who they are through interactions with others, and this has been the dominant approach to identity within the social sciences for the last 50 years.[23]

IDENTITY
An individual's sense of self. The answer to the question, "who am I?"

An interpretive theory of identity highlights the interaction between society and the individual. Consider for a moment how you know who you are: are you *really* kind or cruel? Gentle or gruff? Forthright or dishonest? Both personal experience and social psychological research suggest that who we are is due, in part, to whom we spend time with, and how they evaluate us. Unlike eye color, height, or age, our minds and identities are not quantifiably observable; instead, we learn to make sense of who we are (and should be) through our interpretation of our interactions with other people. If others see us as kind, for example, we are more likely to feel that we are kind. This is what scholars mean by a "social self."

How Social Scripts Shape Selves

Navigating the social world is an endeavor that, on a daily basis, includes multiple interactions with individuals, groups, and institutions; part of how people manage this is by learning and adopting socially accepted patterns for interaction. Instead of going through life having to interpret each experience or interaction anew, members of society develop patterns of behavior that they learn and use as signposts to guide everyday experiences. These blueprints or recipes for meaning-making—what sociologists call social scripts—help us to define our situation and figure out what to do next.[24]

SOCIAL SCRIPT

A learned "cultural scenario" for behavior, belief, interaction, and/or identity.[25]

Just as a play has a script for the actors so that they know what to say and do from Act 1 to the final curtain, social scripts guide each of us, and our behavior, through the scenes of everyday life.[26] We learn cultural expectations and guidelines for social endeavors through socialization, apply them in interactions with others, and ultimately integrate them with our own psychological self-conceptions and desires.[27] Once we learn these scripts, however, they become so automatic that we forget that we had to learn them in the first place. In fact, these patterns and interpretations begin to feel so natural that they come to feel like self-initiated responses to events and not social scripts for behavior. This does not mean that we abide by them all the time, of course. Individuals inadvertently breach, or choose to defy, expected patterns for behavior all the time, in the same way that actors add improvisational components to personalize scripted material. That said, social scripts for behavior are transmitted and enforced ubiquitously through social interaction, and contravening them inappropriately often has real-world consequences.

Consider Shari Dworkin and Lucia O'Sullivan's interviews with men about sexual activity within heterosexual relationships. Dworkin and O'Sullivan found that different sexual scripts for men and women shape who initiates sex and how these acts are understood. Their interviews revealed that "men in relationships feel comfortable if women initiate 'once in a while' or 'more' than currently, but 'not too much.'"[28] That is, dominant social scripts for sex normalize men asking for sex, but make it problematic for women to do so; these scripts shape how men and women interact and make sense of their own sexual selves. Moreover, as men and women engage in sexual activity, they learn these rules and experience reward or sanction for rejecting or abiding by them.[29] Social scripts shape even the most intimate of behaviors, and they do so in ways that feel like authentic expressions of personal will.

Social scripts become more easily visible when they are performed incorrectly. My mother, an émigré from Romania, used to amuse me with stories of funny things she said or did right after she arrived in the United States, when she knew little English and even less of American social scripts. My favorite was her "How Are You?" story. Each morning a neighbor used to greet her in the hall of our apartment building with a friendly "How are you today?" and my mother would answer, honestly and at length, despite her limited English skills. She would share with them how she was feeling physically and emotionally, what she was excited to do that day, and what she was missing about home. At this point in the story I would always laugh, as would my mother. The American script for greeting a casual acquaintance differed from anything with which she was familiar. Asking "how are you?" is not a way that friends or strangers greeted one another in Romania, and so my mother defined the situation based upon her native social scripts, and answered the question literally. While her neighbor never actually *said* anything about these detailed replies, my mother soon deduced from her neighbor's uncomfortable reactions that hers was not the appropriate response to the question. We all learn how to define new situations and the scripts for behavior that go with them as we interact with others in society. Quickly my mother adjusted her response to fit the social script of the United States and now answers "How are you?" with a cheery "Fine!"

Social scripts guide far more than how to greet friends and acquaintances in the hallway. We also have social scripts for identities and bodies. These scripts affect not only what social status someone can hold in society (e.g. what gender, race, or sexuality), but what this group of people is expected to be like, and how they are evaluated by others. Social scripts—these cultural scenarios—tell us how to make sense of our own embodied selves and the bodies and selves of others. They help us to understand expectations associated with the categories we are placed into, as men, Latinos, heterosexuals, etc., and help us understand ourselves and others through those lenses. Likewise, we assume that different social statuses such as gender, race, and sexuality can be determined based upon how bodies look (shape, size, and coloration) and move (gestures, poise, and dress) and we assign individuals to different categories when we interact with them. When a status characteristic is attached to an individual we apply the relevant social scripts for attitudes, behaviors, and appearances and expect them to live up to those scripts.[30] Moreover, we apply those scripts to ourselves as well.

When individuals are reminded of social scripts for their gender, race, or other social status, they unconsciously fall back on those expectations. For example, in one study Asian women performed better on a math exam when their Asian identity was made salient versus when their identity as woman was primed. Social scripts for women devalue their math ability, while those for Asians elevate it, and these social scripts for race and gender affected individual performance and self-evaluation.[31] All told, the social scripts we learn and internalize affect our own identities and behaviors as well as how we see others (and how others see us). While our evaluations of ourselves and others feel individual and personal, they are in fact shaped by social scripts that we have learned and internalized through processes of socialization. When social scripts are unequal—and they are—the outcome is that we assume different things from people based on their social status and this reproduces inequality.

In North American societies, social scripts for gender teach us that individuals will always be one of two genders—woman or man—as determined by the unchanging physical and physiological features of their female or male body. We then follow these gender scripts to determine who someone is based upon the style of their clothing, hair, and their body movements, and from this we assume many things about them, their body, and their life. Young children still learning the rules often get scripts "wrong." Children make firm plans to grow up to be a dog, marry their cat, or become another gender. Firm correction from others starting at a very young age, however, helps children to quickly adopt the social scripts for the set of identities that they are permitted to grow into. By age three or so, children display a rigid set of rules for gender and go about enforcing them on everyone around them.[32] If you have ever been around small children, you have likely been firmly scolded about your gender presentation or behavior. Perhaps you were told you couldn't be a boy with long hair like that, or that real girls don't drive trucks. For young children, once learned, the rules are rigid. This process of scripting gender continues throughout life. As teenagers go through puberty they are taught (through sex-education, media, religion, and family, among other forums) the range of sexual selves they can and are expected to be. Adulthood brings gender rules and norms regarding marriage, child rearing, and aging.

Why Gender is a Good Vantage Point for Inquiry

One of the primary ways that we know ourselves is by identifying with a gender and embodying the behaviors and characteristics associated with that gender. Because gender is one of the main ways that we *all* organize ourselves in society and experience the world, it is a strategic vantage point from which to examine the changes that new technologies are bringing about.[33] And, embodied gender conveys more than just born sex; it also conveys and gives meaning to other socially significant identities such as race, class, sexuality, nation, age, etc.[34]

GENDER

A social status and personal identity, defined in North America as woman or man.[35] As a social status gender is a set of values, beliefs, and norms that are created and enforced by society and assigned to individuals on the basis of birth sex.[36] As a personal identity, gender refers to an individual's sense of self as a man, woman, or yet other gender.

Gender, like race, class, age, and other social categories, is both a personal identity and a culturally specific set of behaviors, beliefs, and values. Each society has a particular interpretation of what it means to be a "real" man, a "real" woman, and, in some societies, "real" other genders. These particularities are what inspire men and women to dress, talk, act, and look different in different places and during different eras. These gender social scripts include everything from our perception that we have a gender, to those norms that advise whom and how it is appropriate to desire because of this gender. And, like all social scripts, those for gender are perceived as being innate and fixed. Gender scripts—stories for who we can be—are one of the main resources that individuals use to construct socially legible lives. They structure our everyday interaction and shape each of us, regardless of how much or how little heed we pay them. They are far more complex than molds from which each of us is stamped out, however. Scripts are not deterministic but they do guide who and what we are by offering a range of possibilities for gendered selves from which individuals construct authentic embodied lives. This book explores the dynamic relationship between dominant beliefs, social scripts, and emerging technologies (both information and biomedical) by focusing on gender in order to elucidate the complexities of these dynamics.

By examining the social histories of gender and by exploring contemporary examples, we can elaborate how technology, social beliefs, and gender scripts are in dynamic relationship to individual bodies and identities. Much like a circuit requires connections between each component part to allow the flow of electricity, each of these components is necessary to make sense of contemporary bodies and identities.

By taking up unique case studies to observe these phenomena, we can learn a great deal about how we all navigate everyday experiences, social interaction, and technological change. Before we begin, however, we must develop a shared understanding of what phenomena we are focused on, namely embodied identity, gender, and technology. Let us begin by reviewing in more detail the social construction of gender.

Gender is a Social Endeavor

Gender is regarded by most people, institutions, and governments as a fixed descriptive characteristic of individuals based upon each one's born sex: as a trait that is outside of the realm of social construction. We are taught that our bodies are shaped by chromosomes, hormones and physiological structures into male and female and that our lived experiences as men and women are also outgrowths of these innate differences. This dominant understanding—what we will come to call a gender paradigm—treats both sex and gender as if they were natural, ahistorical facts and naturalizes differences between male and female embodiment and men's and women's experiences. There is incredible variation in the natural world, however. In many species of animal there are more than two sexes and/or male and female characteristics are fundamentally different (e.g. which sex bears offspring). In some species animals change their sex over their lifespan, sparked either by biological or *social* changes, such as too many or too few members of the same sex.[37] Contrary to popular understanding, both the sex of our physical bodies and our genders are shaped by the complex interplay between biological and social forces. It is a dynamic system in which physical, emotional, and cultural experiences interact with the body's nervous, muscular, and emotional systems to produce the sexed and gendered body.[38]

SEX

Socially interpreted meanings of chromosomes, genitalia, and secondary sex characteristics. In contemporary North America sex takes the form of male, female, and intersex.[39]

This approach is far better at explaining the complexities of human (and animal) experience and embodiment. Even though people have long been looking for differences in the body to explain differences between men's and women's behaviors and abilities, scientific research has not been able to locate these preformed differences. Instead, study after study (in both mice and humans) has found little evidence of sex-based differences in the brain and instead has documented the myriad ways that environment and experience shapes how gendered bodies and brains develop.[40]

What evidence seems to suggest is that human beings are neither born fixed to a particular gender because of sex (in any of its forms—chromosomal, hormonal, genital, etc.) nor are they blank slates. Quasi-experimental studies show that differences in biology, physiology and hormones play a part in the gender development of children. And research suggests that children begin to learn gender differentiation, starting with voices, when several months old. This learning process continues through childhood as children learn to distinguish men and women, masculine and feminine activities (specific to each cultural and familial environment, of course), and eventually come to articulate a sense of themselves as a boy, girl, or other gender.[41]

Like sex, gender is *not* a direct product of biological forces, but rather a set of values, beliefs, and norms that are created and enforced by society in conversation with biology.[42] We experience gender in what our bodies look like, how we move them through space, how we interpret physical and physiological input, and how our bodies interact with other bodies, both socially and sexually. Gender is also an experience of the mind—a sense of who we are, and of what we are "like" and "not like." Our gendered bodies and our gendered identities are neither solely biological nor social manifestations. Gestures and behaviors, such as batting one's eyelashes or spitting, supplement information regarding one's embodied identity already broadcast by bodily appearance, clothing style, and choice of words.[43] Consider, for example, how you "know" what someone's gender is. Can you articulate each characteristic that communicates this information? Gendered ways of conducting, dressing, and carrying oneself, like other types of norms, are not assumed by chance; individuals learn, adopt, and are compelled to conform to these scripts through the systems of reward and sanction that underlie social conduct—a system, itself, that is so entrenched in our society that most of us think of these social scripts as innate.

People quickly learn that failing to adopt the proper gendered body scripts has consequences. Take a moment to think about how often in the last year you were told that your portrayal of gender was unsuitable. Were you told that something you wanted to do was "unladylike" or "girly," that you were acting "like a sissy girl" or "too butch," that you did not walk, talk, or act like the gender you were supposed to be? Chances are you and most people you know have had this experience. When I ask this question in classes, I see only one or two people, out of perhaps 150, who do not raise their hands to show they have had an experience in which their gender was policed. If our gender flowed directly from our genes, then the vast majority of humans would all produce the correct gender attributes perfectly and consistently, the same way the majority of us have two ears and ten toes. Moreover, gender expectations and behaviors would only change when our biology changed; considering that 99.9 percent of the DNA in all humans is identical, humans all over the world would "do gender" nearly the same way.[44]

The idea that sex and gender are the products solely of biological processes is so ingrained in how we understand the world that it is hard to imagine it being any different; furthermore, it is hard to think about gender, which our whole society treats as natural, as being shaped and defined by different societies. This is what scholars mean when they talk about hegemonic gender.

HEGEMONY

Domination without force. Hegemonic ideas are those beliefs that urge us to participate in a system that dominates us, even when we do not benefit from doing so. Hegemonic beliefs are taken for granted as natural and eternal, and therefore hold incredible power in society to shape individuals' lives, possibilities, and freedoms. For example, the hegemonic belief that gender is a direct product of biology carries with it the conclusion that there are natural and eternal differences between men and women, which in turn justifies treating women differently from men. Systemic inequality is built on these beliefs of divergence between genders.[45] Because hegemonic beliefs are understood as natural and timeless, imagining change is difficult.

However, gender is far more variable than most people take into consideration, with vastly different expectations for what defines men and women across time and place. In different places around the world, ideal masculinity may be characterized as tall or short, thin or stocky, quiet or domineering, gentle or gruff, sexually aggressive or stoic and subdued.

The fact that the "ideal" body changes over time also rebuts the concept of gender as fixed, defined simply by biological reality. Fashion is one excellent illustration of the continuously changing concept of an ideal body. Styles for men and women come in and out of fashion, all the while shaping what we consider as traits of femininity and masculinity. Through the late nineteenth century young boys in Europe and North America were dressed in skirts and dresses into early childhood. The advertisement in Figure 0.2 shows the Siegel Cooper Company of New York advertising the same dress for boys and girls. We can contrast this to contemporary norms where dressing even infant boys in dresses is perceived as gender-bending.

Similarly, as explored in the second case study, in the late nineteenth century, wearing pants was unthinkable—at least for feminine, "good" women. Social scripts of that day dictated that women were curvy, and overdressed to the point of near immobility. In contrast, in the 1920s the stylish woman's body was petite, small breasted—even boyish—and clothed in light form-fitting dresses or even pants. In the 1980s both men's and women's fashion rebelled against the long hair, platform shoes, and bell-bottom pants of the 1960s and 1970s. Business suits, men's leisure suits, and acid-washed jeans refocused men's fashion on the qualities that then defined masculinity, such as business acumen and ruggedness. Women's clothing became tighter fitting, following what

Figure 0.2 Advertisement for Siegel Cooper Dresses for Boys & Girls, 1904.

was then established as feminine. Recently, the rise of the "metrosexual" man who pays attention to his hair, clothing, and style is reshaping what it means to be masculine, as opposed to earlier decades where North American men were expected to ignore their looks: in fact, such attention to appearance may well have called a man's masculinity or even sexual identity into question. With the understanding that social trends and norms shape embodied gender, it is possible to make sense of these changes over time and place.

While scholars have studied and theorized how gender is a socially constructed category shaped by social norms, hierarchies, and power relationships, most of us have continued to treat it as something that is a natural and fixed part of who we are, and always have been. In part we do it because gender is such a pervasive and fundamental social institution. It shapes our lives, our experiences, and even our bodies consistently and dramatically. Gender helps to determine what clothes we wear, what toys we play with as children, our school experiences, what we think we can be when we grow up, how we fall in love (and with whom) and who we should desire sexually. In many times and places gender determines what political rights we have, the jobs we can obtain, and what roles we are expected to take on in our own families.[46]

Gender as Socially Constructed but Meaningful in Our Lives

The contradiction posed by the reality that gender is socially constructed while also significant in shaping our lives is one of the most challenging aspects of understanding gender and its importance. If delineations of masculinity and of femininity are variable by locale and historical moment, if gender is truly intangible, created by society, then how can gender be a foundation of so many decisions and processes? The first way to approach this contradiction is to understand gender as something that "does not exist (in nature)" but is "real (in terms of life consequences, including various structural inequalities, physical violence, etc.)."[47]

Even though gender rules and norms are things that are created by society, and therefore not facts of nature, the repercussions of following these rules—or transgressing them—are concrete and meaningful, and are experienced mentally, emotionally, and physically by individuals.[48] For example, contemporary North American gender norms suggest that "real" men are naturally well muscled and athletic. These socially constructed beliefs about what it means to be a man affect how boys and men prioritize working out, learning sports, and building muscle. The investment of time and energy into this type of transformative physical activity (lifting weights, running, etc.) leads to boys and men who are more muscular and skilled in athletic activities, which completes the circle and reinforces the idea that men are naturally big and strong. In fact, the demand for muscles is high enough that increasing numbers of men, and even professional athletes, use steroids to accomplish the task.[49] What is particularly ironic about steroid use is that it can lead to a number of bodily characteristics that undermine normative masculinity, including breast growth, shrinking of the penis, and increased emotionality.

Meanwhile, this focus on muscularity and athleticism—adherence to a set of socially informed gender beliefs—also shapes men's own beliefs about gender, how they function within and interact with the world, and on what they spend their time. Ultimately, the masculine body is not simply an outward expression of male XY chromosomes, but also a reflection of the social norms and values around male masculinity within the United States. This is a clear example, not only of how social beliefs about bodies prioritize some characteristics over others at different times, but also of how these social beliefs shape both our bodies and our identities.

Because we have been socialized with the beliefs that gender exists naturally, and that there are natural differences between men and women, the social forces that create, uphold, and reproduce gender are invisible. Yet, the "*cultural messages* that form our expectations and 'rules' about gender determine the gendered experiences of our bodies—our *embodied knowledge,* and these messages and our resulting gendered practices help to shape our physical bodies as well."[50] Throughout this book we will examine how new technologies are changing social scripts, or what gender scholars Crawley, Foley, and Shehan call "cultural messages," for whom individuals can be in the world, with a focus on how this is allowing people to shape their gendered bodies in new ways.

Accounting for Gender Variation in Society

There is more variation in gender than we acknowledge as a society, and in recent years there has been increased public attention paid to individuals who are living in a gender different from that assigned to them at birth. From talk shows to TV documentaries to movies to newspaper articles, there has been an explosion of coverage about trans* individuals and lives.

TRANS*

The term "transgender" is often used as an umbrella term that refers to the broad range of individuals who live in a gender different from that assigned to them at birth. Historically this term has referred to individuals who sought social but not somatic (bodily) transition.

"Transsexual" is an older term that refers to individuals who transition (or who want to transition) from male to female or from female to male. This can involve both social and biomedical interventions (e.g. hormones and surgery). Historically, transsexual was understood to mean individuals who desired or employed gender affirming surgeries to bring their body into alignment with their gendered sense of self.

"Trans*" is a newer term used to encompass all gender diverse identities, including but not limited to transgender, transsexual, genderqueer, androgynous, and gender fluid. The asterisk is taken from database/Internet searching convention in which the asterisk denotes a wildcard search that will pick up any terms that begin with the preceding letters.

A quick LexisNexis newspaper search pulls up more than 3,000 U.S. newspaper articles in 2013 on trans* individuals, rights, and communities. We can compare this to 1,000 articles between March 2002 and March 2003, and only 320 fifteen years ago.[51] Not long ago, trans* individuals were portrayed only as the brunt of jokes in movies like *Sorority Boys*, or relegated to appearances on Jerry Springer-like talk shows.[52] Now, however, their lives and experiences garner increasing attention and more favorable coverage by mainstream media. In the past few years there have been a number of television shows about trans* youth and adults including features on *20/20*, *Oprah*, *Katie*, and *Our America with Lisa Ling*, and many documentaries by channels such as National Geographic, the Sundance Channel, and the Discovery Channel.[53] Trans* characters have been included on TV shows like *Orange is the New Black*, like *Ally McBeal*, *Nip/Tuck*, *South Park*, *Ugly Betty*, and *All My Children*, while talk shows and news programs alike have done stories/episodes on trans* lives, experiences, and challenges. In addition, quite a few memoirs have been published, including the best sellers *A Queer and Pleasant Danger* by Kate Bornstein, *She's Not There: A Life in Two Genders* by Jennifer Boylan, and Renee Richards' *No Way Renee: The Second Half of My Notorious Life*. A number of major newspapers such as *The New York Times* and *The Boston Globe* have profiled gender diverse children and the need for social and psycho-medical support structures for trans* youth and their families.[54] *Time* magazine declared 2014 the "transgender tipping point."[55]

Increased attention to gender diverse individuals both reflects change in society and spurs further change as well. School, work, and government policies about gender diversity have become increasingly common, and a number of states have enacted non-discrimination policies with respect to gender presentation. Some states have made further strides; California is one which requires that health insurers cover transgender-related healthcare. In the last few years, significant changes have taken place at the federal level as well, including revision of Social Security policy to allow transgender people to change the gender designation on their records without providing documentation of surgery (a policy requiring this documentation had been in force until June 2013). In a landmark 2012 decision, the U.S. Equal Employment Opportunity Commission (EEOC) extended Title VII protections from discrimination in the workplace to trans* workers. In 2014 U.S. President Barack Obama included gender identity protections in a LGBT employment nondiscrimination order for all federal workers and contractors.

Across the board we have seen more attention paid to trans* lives, and both media and public discussion about how people can be gendered have increased awareness and affected how most people in North America think about gender. If who we are is shaped by our society, then wider social understanding of trans* lives challenges our social and personal beliefs that there are only two genders that flow directly and innately from two types of sexed bodies. One way that we see the effects of this social broadening is in responses to trans* people. Most students in my college courses have some understanding of gender nonconformity, as opposed to my own limited exposure as a young person in the 1980s and 1990s. Moreover, there are clear generational changes in how people make sense of trans* lives.

Consider the recent case in Largo, Florida, where the city manager, Susan Stanton, was fired in 2007 after coming out as transsexual.[56] Although she had been highly praised throughout her previous 14 years of service, city commissioners voted five to two that Stanton should be fired after she came out. According to Commissioner Andy Guyette, Stanton's decision to come out and change her public identity and body—what is often referred to as "transitioning"—from male to female, showed that she lacked "honesty, integrity and trust."[57] Susan was called sick, deviant, and a "weirdo" by city leaders, abandoned by friends, and ridiculed on national television. Stanton shared in a newspaper article a year later that: "I was totally unprepared for the reaction and rejection of [sic] almost everyone who'd been close to me."[58] While she was taken aback by these retaliations, such responses are, unfortunately, too common; the marginalization of trans* individuals in our society is an attendant consequence of breaching gender social scripts.

If, however, you look at the response of Stanton's 14-year-old son, Travis, you see an understanding of gender in general, and of trans* individuals more specifically, which differs greatly from the norm. In a school essay Travis wrote the following about Susan:

> Throughout my whole life, I thought my dad was a really tough guy. He went out with the cops and busted bad guys. He shot guns, fought fires. He was an aggressive driver. He liked football and lots of sports.
>
> Then one day my thoughts changed about him when we had a family meeting and he told me how he felt about himself. He said he felt like a woman on the inside and was going to change into one. He said he tried his best to be a manly guy, but he couldn't stop his feelings to become a girl.

At first, I thought I was in a dream. I thought he was 100 percent manly man, more manly than most guys.

After a few days, I thought about it. I knew he was making the right choice to become a girl. Although I cannot relate to his feelings, it must be really hard to hide something like that . . . I think that everyone should be who they are and not try to be the same as other people. If you ask me, this has got to be the most manliest thing he has done in his whole life. It takes a real man to come out of his shell and say, "Hey, I am who I am."[59]

Travis essay is not only deeply moving; it also reflects a flexible understanding of gender and identity. He almost takes for granted that one's sex and/or gender can change, and recognizes that he now makes sense of gender differently than how other people viewed it. In an interview, Travis Stanton reflected, "everyone thinks my dad has hurt me and my life is ruined. But that's not how it is at all. I just think I get things more now . . . We do stuff together all the time. It is like being with my aunt or something, only he's still my dad."[60] What this example suggests is that exposure to new gender norms and social scripts has transformed the ways that some young individuals make sense of gender and gender nonconformity; the possible ways of choosing gender in the world are changing, and these changes are affecting younger generations in transformational ways.

Many people rallied around Susan. In fact, 230 supporters, most of whom were young, trans* activists and allies, showed up to her hearing with city commissioners, and national trans* and LGBT organizations took up her case. Susan was profiled in numerous media outlets, was featured in a documentary by CNN, and was eventually hired as city manager in Lake Worth, Florida and most recently in Greenfield, California. These positive responses go hand in hand with the new meaning-making that Susan's son, Travis, is engaged in.

The Impact of Challenging Gender Norms

Gender nonconformity is not a new thing. It has existed throughout recorded history, and across all cultures and ages. Chapter 1 explores how gender has been understood over time. Before scientific medicine became the authority over our bodies, most individuals were treated as their desired gender if they took on the corresponding social roles and responsibilities.[61] In more recent times, psychology has offered the diagnosis of Gender Identity Disorder, or GID, which has been listed as a mental illness in the *Diagnostic and Statistical Manual* since 1976. Recently renamed Gender Dysphoria (GD), individuals who express dissatisfaction with their assigned gender or sex are considered to be manifesting a psychological disorder warranting psychological or medical intervention. Some contemporary psychological theories treat the desire to change sex or gender as a product of a disordered sense of self. Most recently, in the last 15 years, trans* activists have pushed for new understandings of gender nonconformity, unfettered by medical definition, and have challenged the pathological categorization of GD/GID. These challenges are forcing scientific and medical practitioners to rethink the treatment of gender nonconformity. Contemporary engagement with trans* lives and issues, along with other examples of gender variation and flexibility, call our view of gender as an unwavering reflection of biology into question.

Just as Susan Stanton's son (and the other individuals who rallied around her) reflect a new, broader set of beliefs, other groups are also challenging the idea of a fixed, determinate gender. These challenges happen more in some groups and communities than in others. This raises the question: what would cause a group of people to think of gender as something that can be changed, or moreover, as something that they could think about changing within themselves? Furthermore, what does it mean when whole *groups* of people assert that questioning gender and changing how they understand their gender identity is not just a possibility, but also a legitimate endeavor?

I encountered a community like this when I studied a drag performance troupe several years ago.[62] Drag has traditionally been understood as the theatrical performance of one's "opposite" gender for entertainment, but in the group I studied, the Disposable Boy Toys (DBT), drag meant any gender performance. DBT was comprised of female-bodied people performing as men (drag kings), trans* performers performing masculinity or femininity, some in accordance with and others differing from their chosen, self-defined gender (trans* kings and queens), and women performing femininity (bio-queens). Members of this group were endowed with a variety of body types, possessed a range of masculine and feminine qualities, and identified as both men and women. While all of the members were born into female bodies and raised as girls who were to become women—in other words, individuals that society would likely consider to be female women—the members themselves would not all characterize themselves as such. In fact, no member's constellation of sex, gender, and sexual identity aligned the way that social norms dictate, norms so taken-for-granted that they are usually unexamined, even unnoticed. These variations from hegemonic gender were not the case before individuals participated in the troupe, however. Almost everyone in the group defined their own gender differently after performing together for a few years than they did before they joined DBT.

The ability for members to embody gender differently led the group as a whole to view gender as a chosen and evolving identity. Time spent together in rehearsal, performance, and socially, created an environment in which participants were able, and even encouraged, to try on, practice, and embody different genders. Any given performance crossed gender lines, claimed new gender definitions, or portrayed trans* lives. Because drag in DBT was inherently about gender play, it enabled members to experiment with a variety of gendered elements, and this changed how members felt they could embody gender in their everyday lives.

Members of DBT felt able and empowered to define their gendered selves in a new way. Many of these performers went from referring to themselves as simply "female" to claiming a radical femininity, described as "chosen," "proud," and "transgressive." Others came to take on male or masculine gender identities including butch, ambiguously masculine, masculine female, female-to-male transsexual, and transgender male. A number of participants came to resist singular gender classification altogether and prefaced naming their gender with phrases such as "if I have to choose," or "I guess I am." Regardless of identity, members described gender as a conscious act and explained these gender shifts as outcomes of their participation in DBT. One performer, Summer's

Eve, a feminine woman who performed an exaggerated femininity on stage, noted,

> We joke in DBT about drag being the gateway drug for gender regardless of what that gender is. Some members came into a masculine butch, some members came into a female-identified butch, and some members came into fiercely femme.

This example reveals what other research on identity also suggests, that our sense of our self is shaped by the world around us, who we spend time with, and what we do.[63] The possible ways of being gendered (e.g. having a female body but dressing, behaving, and identifying as a man) expanded for members of DBT. The group encouraged its performers to play with gender and supported them through identity change, and this expansion of social scripts for how one could be defined changed members' gendered identities.

A New World Order: Life in a Technological Age

If social scripts for gender drive how individuals experience their gendered lives, then changes in hegemonic gender norms and associated societal scripts will change who individuals are and how they understand their embodied selves. And what is true for gender is true more broadly; social structures and norms are in dynamic relationship to embodied lives—each informing and transforming the other. Social change impacts individuals not only in how they interact with each other within social institutions and structures, but also in terms of who they are as human beings. In fact, some of the most pressing contemporary social debates—such as concerns over the nature of humanity in an age of information technology, the sacredness of the body in the face of cloning and stem cell research, and the changing self in an increasingly global society—are about this relationship between embodied individuals and social change. And social change itself begs the questions: Who are we? And how are we changing? One of the ways to examine how social changes have affected us as modern individuals is to look at cases where new technologies are changing social beliefs about who we are and can be. In our technologically saturated age, individuals have access to more information, more real and virtual communities, and more medical intervention than ever before. By examining how these new technologies have created new physical and social possibilities for gender we can learn a lot about *how* our modern technological world is changing who we can be, and allowing us to change who we are in fundamental ways.

Scholars have traditionally examined the development and acquisition of gendered social scripts through face-to-face interaction within social institutions such as school, family, and religion. In our contemporary, fragmented world, however, it is becoming increasingly routine to come to know others and ourselves through technology. Many factors including race, class, gender, and age shape each person's access to and use of medical and information technologies—and their relationship to dominant social scripts and ideologies. Technological, social, and physical conditions all interact with one another within a specific social context and through a variety of institutions. As technology advances, each new set of body and identity possibilities is interpreted through dominant social scripts and beliefs, and these things work together to shape our identities and bodies. For example, medical technologies that allow us to see, alter, and treat the body in ways that were previously impossible precipitate changes in social norms and embodied lives.

Biomedical Technology as Mediator between Physical and Mental Life

In our modern medical age we learn and experience our own physical bodies through technology. We have become a society that relies on science to keep us healthy and uses technology to overcome nature; we may have some intuitive sense, fever, or stomachache, but know we are *really* sick only because a medical test tells us so. When we miss class or work we must legitimate illness through a note from the doctor, rather than through some personal accounting of how we felt or how our body manifested an illness. This socially sanctioned need for scientific proof of illness further authenticates the authority of medical technology over our own instinct.

BIOMEDICAL TECHNOLOGY

Technology that maintains and/or transforms the human body. Bio-medical technology includes, among other practices, genetic testing and manipulation, pharmacology, surgery and micro-surgery, imaging, cloning, synthetic drugs, hormones and vaccines, prosthetics, and implants.

In our new biotech world, we can get full-body medical scans that will tell us everything that is—or will be—wrong with us. Armed with this knowledge, and some disposable income, we can treat ourselves with new pills and lotions for ailments we never knew we had. Are we sick, then, because of how we feel or because of what technology tells us? Do we trust our bodies as sources of knowledge less as we trust technological intervention more?

In 1985, feminist philosopher Donna Haraway wrote an article foretelling the encroachment of technology into human bodies and identities. In it Haraway argues that we have all become cyborgs—a combination of machine and organism—in this modern technological world.[64] Our bodies are no longer left in their natural state to grow, age, and die, but instead are modified with and by machines. We modify and reconstruct our bodies using lifestyle and daily maintenance drugs, contact lenses, tattoos, tanning salons, hair dyes, prosthetics, and plastic surgery. Haraway argues, "communication technologies and biotechnologies are the crucial tools recrafting our bodies."[65] In this techno-world, the body comes to be an ongoing production of society, constantly changing through technological intervention. These are significant changes. Media studies scholar Anne Balsamo argues that these changes are shaped by and, in turn, shape the individual attributes that society inscribes onto the body—elements like gender and race.[66]

Take the double eyelid surgery called blepharoplasty as an example of society's technological re-production of the body. The surgery, which uses sutures to create rounder looking eyes with a creased eyelid typical of white features (but atypical of Asian ones), is the most popular cosmetic surgery for Asian American women, and a hotly debated issue within Asian American communities. While the surgery itself is more than 100 years old, its popularity has exploded in recent years as medical advances have made it less invasive, safer, and more affordable. While men can and do get the surgery, it is overwhelmingly pursued by women.[67] It is no surprise that women make up the overwhelming majority of plastic surgery patients, given the beauty demands that society focuses on women. While it is overly simplistic to assume that individuals accessing this plastic surgery are doing so out of racial discontent (indeed the surgery has long been popular outside of a North American cultural context), blepharoplasty is a clear example of using technology to change the body in both a gendered and racialized way. Indeed, the use of this surgical intervention is tied to social norms and expectations within North America and plays out differently in other nations. In many Asian countries men utilize the surgical intervention at much higher rates, and the cultural meaning of the surgery is different given the minority status of white individuals.

In her critique of plastic surgery as the erasure of race and bodily difference and disability, feminist philosopher Sara Goering notes, "the fact that most of the practices aim at one specific kind of body [creating white features] suggests that much more than personal preference is at issue."[68] We can make sense of unnecessary surgery designed to create "Western-looking" eyes as a product, at least in part, of specific *cultural beliefs about beauty* in North America and the gifts of ease and access offered by advancing medical technology.[69] And the meaning of such a surgery is different within a culture that privileges white embodiments (i.e. North America) than it is in Asian contexts where different cultural beliefs about beauty dominate and different systems of stratification shape society. Within North America these interventions change the perception of what Asian women should look like by changing what some actually do look like, and in the process they both reinforce and challenge social scripts about what it means to be a woman in the twenty-first century.

These examples—illness, cyborgs, and plastic surgery—are just a few of the myriad ways new biomedical technologies are reshaping who people are and can be in society. As technologies enable new forms of body modification, social norms and scripts change. So, too, come the development of new body practices and embodied experiences. And, ultimately, these new individual practices and self-conceptions reshape social norms and scripts. Of course, biomedical technologies are only one part of how technological development is reshaping modern society.

Information Technology as Mediator between Physical and Mental Life

Changes in the values of a society and the lived, embodied experience of individuals can also be the product of information technologies that allow us to discover, meet, and interact with people and their ideas in new ways.

INFORMATION TECHNOLOGY

Technology that facilitates communication between individuals through computer-based hardware and software, Internet access and networking. Information technology includes, among other practices, email, virtual communities, online social networking, and online games.

We communicate with friends and strangers over email and through online social networking sites like Facebook, MySpace, and Instagram. Online forums are sites for community development, romantic relationships, and sexual experimentation. More and more, online social spaces have become places to "be yourself" and online depictions of ourselves have the ability to shape our offline behavior and identity. These dynamics can be seen in the increasingly popular virtual worlds such as Second Life®, World of Warcraft, and the child-focused Habbo Hotel.

The Second Life virtual world is a copycat world where individuals build schools, businesses, and governments, and interact in virtual copies of real-world places (see Figure 0.3). Since its inception in 2006, Second Life has attracted more than 34 million users (there were 13.5 million active users as of July 2013) who have created "avatars":

Figure 0.3 Murray Infohub, one of many islands in Second Life.

two- or three-dimensional virtual depictions of who they are and what they look like, or want to look like.[70] You can see some examples of newly created avatars in Figure 0.4. Not only do individuals create visual representations of the self; they use these virtual bodies and identities to have real-time experiences with other people, all mediated by the technological interface of computer networks.

Users spend billions of hours in the Second Life world where "residents" go to school in virtual classrooms (while earning real-life college credits), go to dance clubs, participate in charity races, and even date. Realtors facilitate the buying and selling of virtual land (for real money), and contractors offer their services to help people to build avatars, virtual houses, and businesses. Offline businesses have virtual stores where individuals can try on, buy, and sell real-world goods, conveying those transactions between virtual world and the physical world. Virtual bars and restaurants offer places for individuals and groups to eat virtual food, drink virtual drinks, and interact with one another through virtual representations (accurate or not) of their physical bodies. Comedians and musicians have gone on tour in Second Life, and the men's magazine *Maxim* voted "Second Life Girls" number 95 in their list of "100 Hottest Females of 2007."[71] Second Life offers a whole new set of

Figure 0.4 Second Life avatars.

social spaces to develop and assert one's personal identity, and you can "do" all the things virtually in Second Life that you can with your physical body offline, plus a lot more.

These online interactions have meaning for people offline. In September 2007, 2,000 real Italian union workers spent 12 hours in virtual protest over stalled contract negotiations, outside of IBM's virtual headquarters in Second Life. Their avatars gathered outside of IBM's virtual island and voiced their grievances, and these virtual protesters took advantage of the real-world possibilities offered in Second Life, as well as more fanciful ones; alongside the anticipated union activists in union shirts and employees carrying protest signs, a large yellow banana held a sign that read, "Fair work, fair pay, please don't take our money away," as a green triangle stoically stood by. And this virtual protest had real-world import; the Italian CEO of IBM resigned soon after, and union contract negotiations were reopened. Within days, 9,000 real-life union workers had a new contract.

As Second Life demonstrates, people are using online spaces in complex and varied ways to mimic and even carry out social, political, and community activities in step with, or instead of, activities in the offline world. Just as offline interactions shape what we think about who we can be as individuals, these technologically mediated spaces offer new experiences and definitions of who we are and new forums in which to work on ourselves. If biomedical and information technologies have the ability to reshape not only social structures and norms but also individual embodied identities, then any effort to understand contemporary society must consider the dynamic relationships between dominant norms and scripts, technologies, and the individual.

Investigating the Impact of New Technologies

The following chapters will investigate how gendered bodies and identities are changing in a society that is being reshaped by technology. In between the substantive chapters are short case studies that explore specific examples of how people use technology to produce bodies and identities in line with dominant gender ideologies and social scripts, as well as how they challenge them with alternative bodies and identities. The first, which follows this preview, examines the technological innovation of tattooing and its relationship to masculinity in North America.

Chapter 1 develops a more nuanced understanding of technology and examines how the social histories of gender and technology have been intertwined. After exploring how gender has been understood and shaped by the technologies developed in different historical eras, we will examine how a sociological approach best recognizes the connections between gendered bodies, identities, social scripts, ideologies, and technologies, including how online interactions can alter individuals' sense of self and their embodiment. This type of approach will be instrumental for understanding nineteenth century battles over dress reform, which are highlighted in the second case study, following Chapter 1. The third case study takes up twenty-first century beauty norms and body modification.

Chapter 2 uses a sociological approach to make sense of how new information technologies are reshaping gendered bodies and identities. Through examples such as virtual interactive worlds, online support groups, and trans* discussion boards, we can ask whether and, if so, how information technologies are offering people new social scripts for gendered bodies and identities and changing the real-life experiences and identities of individuals. The significance of these dynamics is profiled in the fourth case study on trans* social movement organizing and the Internet, as well as in the fifth case study on social networking websites.

Chapter 3 examines how technological advances in plastic surgery, body modification, and medicine help individuals to shape their physical bodies in new ways. By focusing on the dynamics at play in surgical and hormonal interventions, steroid use and plastic surgery, we can examine whether and how social scripts and individual identities are changing as part of biomedical technological innovations. The last two case studies examine biomedical technologies and gender by focusing on reproduction and on the treatment of sex and gender diversity in North America. Finally, the Review returns to the questions with which we began: How are new technologies changing who we are and how can we be defined as gendered beings? And where are these changes leading us as individuals and as a society?

Notes

1 Bijker and Law 1992; Franklin 2007; MacKenzie and Wajcman 1999; McGinn 1991; Turner 2007.
2 Kleinman 2008.
3 "Professor Assigns Students to 'E-Fast'." 2007.
4 Walker 2007.
5 O'Brien 2005: 502–503.
6 Many scientists, philosophers, and scholars have been thinking about how new technologies are shaping our world. See, for example, Adas 1989; Alkalimat, Gills, and

Williams 1995; Bijker and Law 1992; Cowan 1997; Featherstone and Burrows 1995; Hacker 1989; Lyon 1995; Morley and Robins 1995; Rheingold 1993b; Shields 1996; Turkle 1994 and 1995; Webster 1996.

7 Bryant 2007; Futter 2006; Holstein and Gubrium 2000; Kendall 2002; Rheingold 1993b; Shilling (ed.) 2007a; Turner 1997; Zipern 2001.

8 McLuhan 1994.

9 Heidegger 1977.

10 Turner 2007: 23.

11 Trivers 1972.

12 Connell 2009.

13 Hyde 2005.

14 Fausto-Sterling 2012: xiii.

15 Connell 2009: 67.

16 Williams 2004: 73.

17 If our genetic code is like the hardware of the body, determining its capacities and function, then epigenetics are like the software—telling the genes what to do, when, and how. The study of epigenetics has revealed how environmental and experiential factors affect the behavior of our genes. For example, an individual may have a gene that predisposes them to cancer but whether it gets "switched on" is determined (scientists think!) by environmental and experiential factors (Brower 2011; Carey 2012).

18 Anderson and Pennebaker 1980.

19 Blitz and Dinnerstein 1971; Buss and Portnoy 1967.

20 Gimlin 2002.

21 Pragmatism is a theoretical tradition focused on the process of how ideas, meaning, and truth come to be, and how they work in practice.

22 Cooley 1902; Goffman 1959; Mead 1934.

23 Mead 1934. For scholarship on situational identity theories see: Becker 1953; Blumer 1969; Denzin 1987; Fine 2001; Sandstrom, Martin, and Fine 2006. For scholarship on identity development through narrative practices/discourses see: Charmaz 1994; Collins and Blot 2003; Gimlin 2007; Holstein and Gubrium 2000; Reagan 1996; Ricoeur 1991; Sandstrom 1998.

24 Kimmel 2007; O'Brien 1999.

25 DeLamater and Hasday 2007.

26 Goffman 1959.

27 Shapiro 2013.

28 Dworkin and O'Sullivan 2007: 115.

29 Dworkin and O'Sullivan 2007.

30 Nosek and Hansen 2008; Ridgeway and Erickson 2000; Shapiro 2013; Wagner and Berger 1997.

31 Shih, Pittinsky and Ambady 1999.

32 Archer 1992.

33 Fausto-Sterling 2000.

34 Lamb and Watson 1979.

35 Lorber 1996.

36 Connell 2009.

37 Fausto-Sterling 2012.

38 Fausto-Sterling, Coll, and Lamarre 2012.

39 Preves 2003.

40 Fine 2001; Jordan-Young 2010.

41 Fausto-Sterling 2012.

42 Kessler and McKenna 1978; Lorber 1996.

43 Lamb and Watson 1979.
44 Pääbo 2003.
45 Gramsci 1971.
46 Clothing (Turbin 2003), toys (Messner 2000; Schwartz and Markham 1985; Zammuner 1987), schooling (Jacobs 1996; Orenstein 1995; Thorne 1993), careers (Padavic and Reskin 2002), love and desire (Kimmel 2005; Tolman 1994), political participation (McGlen and O'Connor 1998), employment (Reskin and Roos 1991), and family (Brines 1994; Coltrane 2004; Hochschild 1989).
47 Crawley, Foley, and Shehan 2007: 4.
48 Crawley et al. 2007; Lorber 1996.
49 Cafri et al. 2005; Stanford and McCabe 2005.
50 Crawley et al. 2007: 1, emphasis theirs.
51 Lexis Nexis search March 11, 2013, for "transgender" and "transsexual" in U.S. news sources.
52 Gamson 1998.
53 The documentaries *Transgender America*, *TransGeneration*, an eight-part documentary about transgender college students, and *Changing Sexes: Female to Male 2003*, respectively.
54 Padawer 2012; English 2011.
55 Steinmetz 2014.
56 DeGregory and Helfand 2007.
57 Stratton 2007.
58 DeGregory 2007.
59 DeGregory 2007.
60 DeGregory 2007.
61 Fausto-Sterling 2000; Feinberg 1996; Foucault 1990.
62 Shapiro 2007.
63 Holstein and Gubrium 2000.
64 Haraway 1991.
65 Haraway 1991: 164.
66 Balsamo 1996.
67 In the United States 86 percent of eyelid surgeries are performed on women according to 2008 statistics (American Society of Plastic Surgeons 2009a).
68 Goering 2003.
69 Bartky 1988.
70 Active participants are participants who have logged in at least once in the past 60 days. See www.gridsurvey.com/economy.php for additional metrics.
71 "Maxim's 2007 Hot 100."

CASE STUDY: FOCUS ON TATTOOING AND MASCULINITY

In contemporary North American society, tattoos are viewed as meaningful acts of identity building and personal expression. A number of reality television shows are set in tattoo studios and document acts of narrative identity formation, often profiling the personal stories behind a client's tattoo. In daily life, individuals are both asked to account for the significance of their tattoos, and report to others that their tattoos communicate who they are and commemorate significant experiences.[1] When called on to narrate the meaning of a tattoo for themselves and for others, individuals do so using the social scripts available.[2] As sociologist Mary Kosut explains:

> Although tattooing is a way to construct one's body and self in one's own desired image, it is also a phenomenon that reflects cultural influences. An important characteristic of the tattoo as a form of communication is that it largely "speaks" through non-verbal transmission.[3]

Both the non-verbal stories communicated by tattoos and the stories that individuals tell about their tattoos are the product of the internal self and embodied experience, and are shaped by the dominant beliefs and scripts of the day. Personal and societal meaning-making about tattoos come from the interaction of a number of social forces: dominant ideologies for bodies, social scripts for gender and other identities, technologies of tattooing, and the bodies and identities of individuals within a group or society.

Tattooing is a technology that creates an obvious transformation in the natural body. Because tattoos are pictorial and/or word images literally written on the body, they alter the embodied landscape of individuals. And, because of the body–identity connection assumed in contemporary body ideologies, these inscriptions are assumed to have significance for the individual.[4] Yet the social meaning of tattoos has changed over time, most drastically over the past 150 years, and these changes have concurrently shaped the significance of tattoos for individuals. In different eras, social scripts in North America have labeled tattooed bodies as beautiful or deviant, military or criminal, aristocratic or working-class. Tattoos have been used by individuals as accessories, badges, and to symbolize, among many other things, social status, rites of passage, community affiliations, personal triumphs and tragedies, and racial, ethnic, political, sexual, and gender identities. Moreover, expectations about the meaning and import of tattoos shape the tattooed experience.

Tattooing dates to 6000 BCE (Before the Common Era), and has been present in many cultures around the world. Save for one significant innovation in the late 1890s, when the tattoo machine was invented, the principles and basic methods of tattooing have changed very little over its long history. A tattoo is created by inserting ink (natural or synthetic) under the dermis layer of skin using needles, which have been made of a variety of materials such as shells, bone, quills, and metal. Early European explorers came into contact with tattooing practices among the Moors (North African peoples), within indigenous communities in Central and South America and on the Pacific Islands. In the mid-eighteenth century, European sailors and merchants began acquiring tattoos during their travels; the practice became more widespread in the West after Captain James Cook returned from his first voyage of discovery with a Tahitian person, and the account of his ship's travels was published, including references to the "tattaw." As trade and colonization accelerated, tattooing was increasingly practiced in Europe and the North American colonies.

Tattoos themselves carried with them symbols and information related to a man's trade and life history—adventurer, merchant, rebel, or sailor—and in the process reinforced the meaning that tattoos had within the society. Because the European men (and it was, almost exclusively, men) who donned tattoos in the 1800s were from a social stratum associated with social nonconformity and even radical politics, these characteristics came to be associated with tattoos as well. Tattoos conveyed ideas not only of the specific gendered and classed identity of the subject, but also his social and political affiliations. For these very reasons men who were free thinkers, radicals, and outlaws embraced the tattoo and its associations. This type of mutually constitutive process is at the heart of how new technologies reshape bodies and identities in conversation with other social forces.

For a brief period of time (from the late 1800s to the early 1900s) the European gentry was enamored with tattoos. Formerly the purview of sailors (by choice) and criminals (by force), tattoos became all the rage among upper classes in these few decades. This trend was part of a larger fascination with all things "native" and "primitive," sparked by the expanding European colonization of Pacific and American lands. Elite individuals used tattoos to inscribe markers of aristocratic status on the body. A number of European royalty were tattooed including Prince Waldemar of Denmark, Grand Duke Alexis of Russia, Queen Olga of Greece, and King Oscar of Sweden.[5]

It was in the midst of this tattooing fad that the practice came to North American white communities (it had been prevalent among some indigenous groups long before then). An article that appeared in the *Boston Morning Journal* in 1897 emphasizes the very classed nature of the tattoo fad of the late 1800s:

> Have you had your monogram inscribed on your arm? Is your shoulder blade embellished with your crest? Do you wear your coat-of-arms graven in India Ink on the cuticle of your elbow? No! Then, gracious madame and gentle sir, you cannot be *au courant* with society's very latest fad—the tattooing fad. It has just reached New York from London and Paris. It may develop into a mania.[6]

By emphasizing its European roots and suggesting that individuals inscribe their crest or monogram, the article makes clear that this type of tattoo was associated with both cosmopolitan fashions and aristocratic genealogies in the late 1800s. Both poor and wealthy men (and some women) were tattooed but these tattooing practices and motifs differed from one another. These differences were the product of differences in social scripts and embodied identities available to men and women of different social classes.

By the early 1900s tattooing had once again become highly contested and over the next several decades lost social status and became reassociated with marginal subcultures. This shift was due in part to the increased access working-class individuals had to tattooing. Tattoos had long been a way for poor and working-class men to compensate for their compromised masculinity; because many of the socially sanctioned markers of successful masculinity (e.g. a high-paying job, material wealth, and social power) were out of reach for poor men, they drew on tattooing and its related masculine social scripts to bolster their sense of manhood. In 1891, when Samuel O'Reilly patented the tattoo machine, the tattooing process became more efficient, more affordable, and less painful. The more accessible tattoos were, the less elite they became.[7] In addition, while forced tattooing of prisoners in Europe had fallen out of fashion, criminal connotations persisted and voluntary tattooing was seen as proof of deviance.

At the turn of the twentieth century, a number of criminologists began to hypothesize that tattoos were proof of criminal intent or propensity. Public health campaigns linked tattooing to sexually transmitted diseases, and some doctors went as far as to claim that tattoos were external representations of sickness and deviant proclivities. According to criminologists, the tattoo was a stigmata of as-yet uncommitted crimes, and according to medical experts, the tattoo was a symptom of as-yet undiagnosed diseases. These hegemonic beliefs about tattoos, criminality, and bodies compelled individuals to turn away from this form of body modification and, as they did, its marginal status increased.

This connection between tattoos and both mental and physical pathology remains in some current social science and medical research, as well as in popular culture.[8] These enduring legacies continue to shape the meaning of tattoos and the social scripts that govern their significance for gendered embodiments. For example, tattoos are often used in literature and film as shorthand for a man's shady past, questionable character, or ill intent, and a for woman's lack of femininity or morality. In the 1951 Tennessee Williams' play *The Rose Tattoo* (made into an eponymous film in 1955) a truck-driver who smuggles contraband has a rose tattooed on his chest. When he is shot and killed by the police, his wife discovers not only his illegal activities but also his adultery. By the play's end, the tattoo of the title symbolizes the husband's duplicity and deception.

In the post-World War II political and social climate in North America that stressed conformity to white, middle-class values, tattoos were increasingly disparaged. By mid-century, tattooing had been taken up by prison and motorcycle gangs and came to symbolize violent, rebellious masculinities.

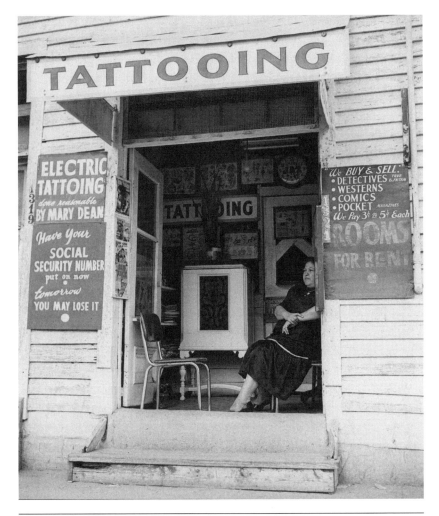

Figure 0.5 Mary Dean, one of only a few women tattoo artists, in front of her tattoo parlor in 1950.

The historical legacy of tattooing that links the act to archetypical masculinities remained, however; in the 1950s and 1960s Marlboro cigarette advertisements featured cowboys, musclemen, and suave debonair men with Marlboro eagle tattoos on their hands.[9] Even though tattoos were held in distaste, their connection to idealized masculine figures in these advertisements created a tattoo craze. Concurrently, the conventionalized form of these tattoos, drawn from media or trademark imagery, tended to reinforce dominant paradigms of masculinity, such as rugged independence and physical strength. It was only in the midst of the 1970s' social change movements that tattooing began to be revived as a socially acceptable form of bodily manipulation. In this era of anti-establishment attitudes and rejection of authority, the tattoo was reclaimed, and many counter-culture musicians and celebrities sported highly visible tattoos. The tattoo was burnished with rock-and-roll glamor.

Since then both the number of individuals soliciting tattoos and the stigma associated with the practice have shifted considerably. A recent national survey conducted by the Pew Research Center estimated that 36 percent of the U.S. population between the ages of 18 and 25 and 40 percent between 26 and 40 had at least one tattoo. Estimates for Canada are similar.[10] Not only is this figure a large proportion of the North American population, but it also points to a dramatic increase in the use of this particular body technology; in the same survey only 10 percent of individuals between 41 and 64 years old reported ever getting a tattoo.[11] Charting the same generational shift, survey data from the early to mid-1990s estimated that fewer than 10 percent of the U.S. population had a tattoo, while a 2006 survey found that 24 percent of individuals under 50 had one.[12]

Tattoos have also been, and remain deeply gendered; historical data points to a dramatic disparity in rates of tattooing between men and women, and the stigma attached to tattooed women has been much stronger than that attached to men. Although tattooing was on the rise in Western society during the 1800s, it was almost exclusively practiced on men. Tattoos are linked to qualities of masculinity, and these qualities are available to men regardless of social class. Women in other societies, such as the Ainu of Japan, practiced tattooing, but in the West, tattooed women tended to be part of extremely marginalized social groups. In a 1950s account of tattoo culture and its gendered nature, tattooist Samuel Steward recounted that he personally refused to tattoo women unless they were 21, married, and had permission from their husbands.[13] Statistics suggest that women accounted for a small minority of tattoo clients up until the 1970s. By the late 1990s, Copes and Forsyth estimated that while between 10 percent and 20 percent of men in the United States were tattooed, only 7 percent of women were.[14] This is rapidly changing, however. Several surveys conducted in the early 2000s found no significant differences in rates of men and women clientele; women were requesting tattoos at rates even with those of men.[15]

Once almost exclusively male, men and women are now equally likely to obtain tattoos, yet the gendered legacy remains. The increasing parity between men and women tattooees does not erase the gendered aspects of tattooing or the particular function tattoos continue to play in relation to masculinity. A number of scholars have documented how tattoos on men and women are interpreted in vastly different ways: boosting masculinity while threatening femininity.[16] Research suggests that women choose tattoos to both reinforce and challenge gender normativity and sexism. Regardless of intent, however, the social meaning and import of a tattoo for women is shaped by larger gendered structures. As Kang and Jones summarize: "Even when women seek freedom and power over their own bodies, the meanings women attach to their tattoos are 'culturally written over' by the larger society."[17] There are also significant differences in the placement and imagery of tattoos between men and women. Women are more likely to situate a tattoo on a part of the body that is easily covered; men are nearly twice as likely as women to have visible body art (23 percent versus 13 percent).[18] Moreover, men often select a highly visible area that is associated with male secondary sexual characteristics, such as biceps and forearms.[19] The imagery in women's tattoos tends to be artistic or fanciful, while that in men's is often chosen to represent—and reinforce—masculine traits such as toughness, individuality, and bravery. The scale of men's tattoo designs tends to be larger as well.

In their study of young British men, Rosalind Gill, Karen Henwood, and Carl McLean found that men turned to tattooing in part as an effort to publicly stake claim to particular identities.[20] In a historical moment when men's bodies are under increasing scrutiny but, simultaneously, men are not supposed to care about their looks, body work is fraught with tension for men. Young men "must simultaneously work on and discipline their bodies while disavowing any (inappropriate) interest in their own appearance."[21] As a result of these constrained social scripts for acceptable masculinity, Gill, Henwood, and McLean argue that young men make sense of tattoos as identity and community-focused endeavors. Moreover, they found that the available social scripts for young men's masculinity were so limited that, although all the young men interviewed espoused personal reasons for getting a tattoo, their narratives were surprisingly uniform.

Tattooing has been most common among young and working-class men since the mid-twentieth century in North America. Tattoos have primarily featured military, death, and pinup imagery, and small tattoos are often used like badges to mark significant events. The tattooing session itself is one such event. Withstanding the pain of tattooing is viewed as evidence of machismo or manliness; willingness to accept this pain has historically situated tattooing as a rite of passage for men (often at puberty or adulthood) within a variety of cultures worldwide.[22]

In the West this has been particularly true within military groups. The first professional tattooist in the United States was Martin Hildebrand, who traveled around during the American Civil War tattooing both Union and Confederate soldiers in what was likely the first widespread use of tattoos by soldiers. Hildebrand's tattoos were primarily political and patriotic images that made explicit for which side, North or South, the soldier fought.[23] The practice of tattooing in the armed forces continued into the twentieth century. "Fighting men want to be marked in some way or another," according to tattooist Charlie Wagner, profiled in the *New York Times* in 1943. "High-class fellas, too—men from West Point and Annapolis. Sailors used to be my big customers, but now it's soldiers."[24]

Today, different branches of the military claim particular symbols, tattoo locations, and rituals such that the whole experience, from the act of getting the tattoo (which symbolizes bravery) to the images inscribed (symbolizing dedication to the group) connect an individual to his military "brothers." Sociologists Coe, Harmon, Verner, and Tonn interviewed military college cadets and found that, for these men, getting a tattoo was a social bonding act done in groups and was used to mark their membership in the community.[25] Not only do they select a single, often very specific, design in common, these men will be tattooed as a group, adding a ritualistic quality to the tattoo process. Both the cost and the pain of the tattoo were sources of pride and of the men's sense of masculinity.

Research suggests that tattooing is a significant social practice within other men's groups and communities in North America as well.[26] Tattoo scholar Janine Janssen argues that, for many men:

> A tattoo is not only a form of establishing an identity (e.g. as a sailor or biker), there is also a relationship between tattoos and male bonding. By wearing a specific tattoo they can show each other and the rest of the world what kind of men they are (e.g. gang members or soldiers). Not only the final result—the tattoo—but also the process of "inscribing" the body can be a manner for expressing one's masculinity.[27]

Within gangs (a particular social context with its own social scripts for behavior), tattoos take highly regimented forms as a way of communicating to others an individual's personal experiences within the group, such as their history of violence, loss of loved ones, or sense of loyalty. Each element of the tattoo holds a range of meanings, information that is further supplemented by its location on the body and the symbols contained therein.

In North America, masculinity has intertwined with tattooing in a variety of ways including in its historical legacy and enduring social meanings, and in the process of acquiring a tattoo, its location, and the imagery it contains. Many of the qualities defined as central to masculinity within dominant social scripts, including bravery, endurance, and immunity to pain, are qualities tested in the act of acquiring a tattoo.[28] As these varied examples suggest, the technology of tattooing, informed by the social norms and scripts of an era, has and is used in the service of gendered body and identity work.[29]

The technology of tattooing has simultaneously shaped and influenced social scripts for masculinity and individuals' embodied experiences. Sociologist Paul Sweetman summarized that:

> As corporeal expression of *the self,* tattoos and piercings might thus be seen as instances of contemporary *body projects* (Shilling 1993): as attempts to construct and maintain a coherent and viable sense of self-identity through attention to the body and, more particularly, the body's surface (Featherstone 1991).[30]

As body projects, tattoos carry with them legacies of social signification about men, masculinity, and social class. Whether upper-class men in the 1900s tattooing their elite lineage, or 1850s sailors charting their travels, men have purposefully used tattoos to establish and reinforce their masculinity. These legacies, built out of dominant ideologies about the gendered body and self, have in turn shaped the use of this technology by different groups of men over time.

Notes

1 Kang and Jones 2007.
2 Kosut 2000.
3 Kosut 2000: 80.
4 Giddens 1991.
5 DeMello 2000; Fisher 2002; Sanders 1989.
6 "The Tattoo Fad" 1897.
7 Fisher 2002.
8 Armstrong and Pace Murphy 1997; Braithwaite et al. 1999; Koch et al. 2005.
9 Fisher 2002.
10 Hawkes, Senn, and Thorn 2004.
11 Pew Research Center for People and the Press 2007.
12 Armstrong and Pace Murphy 1997; Laumann and Derick 2006.
13 Steward 1990.
14 Copes and Forsyth 1998.

15 Laumann and Derick 2006; Pew Research Center for People and the Press 2007.
16 Hawkes et al. 2004.
17 Kang and Jones 2007: 44.
18 Pew Research Center 2010.
19 Fisher 2002: 100.
20 Gill et al. 2005.
21 Gill et al. 2005: 38.
22 Janssen 2005.
23 Govenar 2000.
24 Cumming 1943: 38.
25 Coe et al. 1993.
26 DeMello 2000.
27 Janssen 2005: 185.
28 Halnon and Cohen 2006.
29 Phelan and Hunt 1998.
30 Sweetman 1999: 53.

1

A Social History of Technology and Gender

Just a few minutes into the movie *Kinky Boots*, Lola curses her biggest obstacle as a drag queen. Holding up her boot to display its freshly broken heel, she laments: "Like most things in life, it cannot stand the weight of a man."[1] With this remark, Lola pinpoints a key barrier in her ability to successfully dress as a woman. Lola's problem (and that of her real-life compatriots) is the construction of women's shoes: they are not built to support most male bodies. High-heeled shoes are not typically constructed to accommodate the average male's heft, foot size, or gait. All high-heeled shoes, particularly extremely thin "stiletto" heels, require technical acumen in their design because the structure of the shoe focuses immense pressure on a very small area; a petite woman in stilettos can exert 20 times the pressure of a 6,000 pound elephant under her heel.[2] It was only in the 1930s that the manufacture of stiletto heels became possible at all, when the specialized design of inserting thin metal tubes into the heel structure of shoes was developed. The standard construction of heels can withstand only a certain amount of pressure, and more often than not male bodies exceed these limits. This structural problem, combined with norms for high-heel shoe size and width, makes finding and wearing high-heeled shoes very difficult for those born into male bodies.

In *Kinky Boots*, the based-on-real-life story of a rural British shoe factory struggling to survive in a global market, owner Charlie Price recognizes his niche market—after being literally hit over the head with the problem: shoes for "drag queens" (aka men who perform dressed as women). He works with Lola to design shoes that will allow male bodies to successfully function in women's high-heeled shoes. As fanciful as the film is, the problems it centers around are genuine. A 2006 *New York Times* article inspired by the film featured interviews with a number of drag queens, trans* women and shoe designers regarding the real-life challenges posed by lack of footwear for male bodies.[3] What the interviewees make clear is that, without footwear that fits their feet, male-bodied individuals struggle to perform femininity as drag queens, or embody it as trans* women. High-heeled shoes are one of the few items of clothing that remain strictly gendered in this age of increasingly androgynous fashion; if one is to portray normative femininity—regardless of birth sex—one must have access to the appropriate footwear. The solution to this shoe problem is the creation of new approaches to, methods for, and products targeted at male-bodied individuals who want to successfully produce normative femininity. In other words, successfully "dressing the part"—a key component of embodying gender—requires the development of new technologies. What is true for shoes is true more broadly with respect to gender; what defines it, how gender is manifested in the body, and what social scripts are available to individuals are often shaped by technology.

Building on our understanding of social scripts as culturally specific blueprints for behavior that shape social and individual expectations and productions of gender, this chapter examines how technologies prevalent at different historical moments have been used to make sense of gendered bodies, to police gender ideologies and scripts, and to create or inhibit space for diversifying gender norms and defying expectations. Investigating how the histories of gender and technological innovation fit together suggests that how people understand, conform to and contest embodied gender changes from era to era as technologies advance. People use the technologies available to them at any given time to produce both normative and nonconforming gender, and in turn, the resulting gender scripts, bodies, and identities shape technological development.

NORMATIVE GENDER

Individual gender expression that is in line with dominant social scripts for masculine men or for feminine women. Another way to refer to this is gender conformity.

NON-NORMATIVE GENDER

Individual gender expression that conflicts with dominant social scripts for masculine men or for feminine women. Another way to refer to this is gender nonconformity.

For example, twenty-first century women can employ plastic surgery to create more curvaceous bodies while nineteenth century women used corsets and girdles, and these new technologies allow women to embody socially scripted feminine qualities while enjoying an increased range of physical motion; technologies have allowed scripts for what a feminine body is capable of to change. Over time, as technological innovation transforms ways of knowing and shaping bodies and identities, social knowledge of and scripts for gender change as well.[4]

A Sociological Approach to Analyzing Gender and Technology

Making sense of technological innovation and its relationship to bodies and identities is no easy feat. Exploring how gender identities and bodies are transformed within the context of changes in dominant paradigms, social scripts, and through technological intervention requires new analytical tools that can recognize the complex and layered nature of social life. Instead of existing in one-directional relationship to each other, as if technologies change social scripts but social scripts do not affect technological innovation (or vice versa), dominant ideologies, scripts, technologies, and gendered bodies and identities appear to be mutually constitutive, each component interacting dynamically with the others. High-heeled shoes would not have been developed for people born into male bodies without new technologies and shifts in dominant gender scripts; in turn, these new technologies led to new social scripts and norms for gendered bodies. That is, all of these components are engaged in a complex interplay with one another, each shaping and being shaped by the other constituent parts. To understand how new technologies reshape the lives of individuals we can draw on a sociological analysis that examines all of these social forces in interaction.

SOCIOLOGICAL ANALYSIS

An analytical approach that takes into account individual, interactional, and structural/institutional dynamics within a particular social context.

Social forces are not directly observable, but rather something that individuals experience in the process of interacting in society; dominant social scripts, transmitted through interaction with socializing agents like parents, teachers, peers, and media, disappear under the guise of everyday interaction. Because of this, it is difficult to see how gender ideologies and social scripts have shaped each of us as individuals; our own embodied gender feels—and *is*—very real. The impact of new technologies on our bodies and identities is rendered invisible by the mundane nature of social life. It is only when we turn our analytical attention to these social structures and mechanisms for change that we can truly understand the complex forces that shape our gendered lives.

There are five aspects of social life that we will focus on throughout this book: paradigms, scripts, technologies, bodies, and identities. These aspects of social life are intricately interconnected and, we will see, mutually constitutive. A sociological analysis that accounts for this complexity, and makes sense of how new technologies are transforming gendered lives, looks at individuals' embodied experiences (individual level), the impact of social interactions in subcultures, groups, and communities on the choices people make (interactional level), and on how social norms and institutions (such as medicine or education) guide and structure our ability to manifest gender in our bodies and identities as we so choose (structural level).

This approach is not a conceptual theory or empirical model but rather a way of taking into account a broad range of social forces. This allows us to make sense of how social and individual changes are intertwined, and reveals how different gender paradigms and social scripts are both shaped by the actions of individuals and are constitutive of them. Ultimately, our sociological analysis charts a path toward answering whether and how information and biomedical technologies can have real-life effects on bodies and identities as well as on society at large.

Feminist scholar Bernice Hausman suggests that technologies of the time shape what and who people think they can be, both physically and ideologically. Hausman's research traces how the development of medical technologies in plastic surgery and endocrinology (the science and medicine of hormones) led to the development of contemporary transsexual identities. The social changes brought about by technological innovation expanded existing scripts and created new ones for embodied genders. This is not to say that gender nonconforming individuals, i.e. males who identify as women, or females who live as men, exist only as a modern phenomenon, but rather that the creation of a pathologized medical identity, "transsexual," is new.

These and other similar changes are the product of ideological and theoretical innovation (e.g., the idea that sex is different from gender) as well as tangible technologies (such as the example of shoes for drag queens), all of which allow individuals and society as a whole to imagine and manifest new ways of existing in the world. Technology interacts with dominant ideologies, scripts, and embodied identities to produce an array of socially legible gendered identities and bodies, from which individuals construct their lives. As Hausman summarizes: "The development of new technologies (especially those where contact with the body is most intimate, such as medical technologies) also effects the production of new subjectivities [aka identities]."[5]

Neither technological innovation nor changes in gender identity are modern phenomena, even though people often assume they are products of contemporary social, political, economic, and scientific changes. In fact, both have very long histories. Throughout history, gender scripts, ideologies, bodies, and identities have been shaped by the technologies of the time.

Making Sense of Technology

While technology is often defined in terms of machines, its linguistic origins, meaning "the expression of a craft," suggest its scholarly use to refer to anything that people develop to manipulate the natural environment. Technology is a complex amalgam of objects, knowledge, activities, and processes, all of which manipulate our material environment. Anthropologists trace technology back to the point when early humans harnessed the power of fire.[6] From this distant innovation to the development of the most recent supercomputer, technological development has been an integral part of the lives of human beings.

> **TECHNOLOGICAL INNOVATION**
>
> The leading transnational institution in charge of encouraging and monitoring technological innovation is the United Nations Educational, Scientific, and Cultural Organization. UNESCO defines technological innovation as the development of "know-how and creative process that may utilize tools, resources, and systems to solve problems, to enhance control over the natural and man-made [sic] environment to alter the human condition."[7]

Technology does more than alter our material world, however, as these changes give rise to changes in the behavior of individuals and even entire cultures.[8] Our very bodies and identities have been shaped by technology in profound and dramatic ways. The advent of clothing included the development of sewing, the harvesting of plants and animal skins for cloth, and the creation of methods and processes for production. Further evolution of these processes and the changing designs of the clothes themselves allowed migration out of Africa around 200,000 BCE. Clothing provided warmth and protection from the environment such that individuals could migrate into colder climates.[9] These technological developments changed where and how people lived on Earth from that point forward, allowing geographical expansion, cultural differentiation, and accelerated social change. The relationship between technology and society is a reciprocal one; as people create technology,

technology shapes people and the societies they live in, which leads to the creation of new technologies ... and the cycle continues.

A Brief History of Technology

While the first technological leaps occurred when humans began to use or control natural resources as tools to shape their environment, technological advancement gained momentum with the rise of scientific inquiry in the 1400s. Prior to the fifteenth century, when scientists or laypeople approached the natural world as an area of inquiry, they did so in ways informed by a religious system of thought.[10] This channel of thinking—what sociologists might call a paradigm—shaped how individuals made sense of the world around them, and how they asked and answered questions about the physical and social world.

PARADIGM

A system of thought or theoretical framework that structures how a group or community makes sense of the world around them. Paradigms are comprised of ideas, beliefs, assumptions, and ways of knowing. Paradigms provide a particular perspective on the world and are so pervasive as to seem natural or even invisible without examination.

Beginning in the 1400s, with the popularization and professionalization of science, individuals began to privilege knowledge of the natural world that was developed through empirical research and the application of the scientific method. The rise of science afforded people the idea that it was possible—even obligatory—to understand the natural world through observation and analytical reasoning. This encouraged and facilitated the development of new technologies to shape and manipulate the natural environment. As society fell under the jurisdiction of science, a shift in social, political, and economic power followed; where world views guided by religious doctrine had pointed toward church leaders and divinely chosen royalty as the legitimate authorities in society, science naturally pointed to scientists and logicians.[11]

> ## ONTOLOGY
> A worldview; a grand theory about the nature of the world and existence. An ontology is a group or community's answer to the question, "what exists in this world?"

More than a simple shift toward empirical study of the natural world, this transfer of influence from theocratic to scientific ontology altered the whole structure of society and granted social and political power to a variety of scientific institutions. Medicine (rather than religious institutions) came to be the authority over ill and healthy bodies, logic-based legal institutions (instead of royalty) over crime and punishment, and biology, chemistry, and physics over the natural world. In all aspects, a focus on new technologies was part of this change, and since this ontological shift in the fifteenth century, technological innovation has been a key component of scientific and social change.

Challenging Technological Progressivism

As tech-savvy modern individuals in North America we have a tendency to think of technology as always moving society forward—what Daniel Kleinman calls *technological progressivism*.[12]

> ## TECHNOLOGICAL PROGRESSIVISM
> A paradigm that suggests all technological innovation produces beneficial social changes.[13] A sociological analysis contradicts this paradigm and suggests, instead, that technological innovation is shaped by myriad social institutions and that its benefits are accompanied by a multitude of unforeseen—and sometimes unfortunate—consequences.

While technology often creates new possibilities, it is important to remember that new tools and methods are sometimes developed with the intent of maintaining the status quo. Innovations in weaponry, such as automatic rifles or nuclear bombs, have been developed and refined by countries in order to maintain their global dominance. Similarly, medical techniques have historically been employed to maintain "racial purity" and perpetuate existing racial inequalities. As new biological technologies were developed in the nineteenth and twentieth centuries, they were immediately deployed to find "true" differences between whites and people of color. These studies were often referred to as "race science," and the subsequent findings were used to justify slavery, colonialism, and genocide. Many technological advances, such as embryonic sex selection (selectively implanting embryos cultivated in-vitro on the basis of desired sex), reflect social debates and tensions over power, morality, and social structure. It is important to remember that technology is always driven by, shaped, and understood through individual and societal values. The topics that innovators choose to focus on (or choose to ignore), the methods they employ (or dismiss), and the items they produce (or choose not to produce) are decisions shaped by personal and social paradigms and values. Technology, while often construed as inevitably progressive, is in reality intimately shaped by dominant beliefs and other social forces. The development of new technologies is tied to social paradigms in a myriad of ways; technology is always already a social endeavor.[14]

Theorizing Technology

The meaning and significance of technological development has been a central theme for social theorists of the past 200 years. Some scholars view technology as dehumanizing; Max Weber, one of the founding thinkers of sociology, for instance, argued that technological innovation would only exacerbate the increasing rationalization and bureaucratization of society, which were already stripping people of their creative life force.[15] Other similar dystopian perspectives represent technology as making people less unique, less free, and less happy.[16] On the other hand, theorists such as Karl Marx, the social and political theorist, saw technology as the path toward an egalitarian society.[17] Although the technological innovations of the Industrial Revolution had led to short-term inequalities, Marx argued that science and technology would ultimately offer liberation by moving society beyond capitalism.[18] Other technological utopianists also argue that new technologies will transform institutions, values, and culture, to create a more perfect society.[19]

Technology as Social

One of the most comprehensive social theories of technology was formulated by twentieth century philosopher and historian Michel Foucault. Foucault was interested in how systems of knowledge shaped society and individuals, and he developed a complex definition of technology in an effort to grasp how and to what ends technologies shape everyday individuals and lives.[20] Foucault argued that technological innovation takes many forms, including the creation of new products, new words and meanings, new means of shaping one's body, and new ways of controlling members of society.[21] He advanced the idea that these technologies are both shaped by and shape individuals and society as each new innovation goes through the inevitable processes of upholding and challenging social paradigms and structures.

Consider, for example, body modification. The technologies that enable body modifications reflect deeply entrenched gendered body scripts in North American societies.[22] Some individuals fit "naturally" within hegemonic norms of beauty and attraction, but the majority of people seek an approximation of these body expectations through one or more forms of technological intervention that allow them to alter the appearance, shape, and function of their body. From clothing choices to tanning, from treatments for baldness to major plastic surgery, individuals change the form and function of their bodies in efforts to achieve socially valued body shapes, facial features, and standards of beauty. People create new measures for altering their physical appearance, and as more people make use of these measures, society at large begins to more often approximate—and subsequently more often expect approximation of—an accepted ideal. As Foucault theorized, technology (as guided by social paradigms and scripts) created by people changes people and society.

Foucault's theory of technology captures the ways in which technology is intertwined with social ideologies, scripts, bodies, and identities.

In his *History of Sexuality*, Foucault argues, "the biological and the historical are not consecutive to one another ... but are bound together in an increasingly complex fashion in accordance with the development of the modern technologies of power that take life as their objective."[23] For example, as feminist activism challenged the dominant ideologies about gender in the middle of the twentieth century, new technologies were developed that called into question the naturalization of male and female social scripts. One consequence of this trend was the differentiation of the meaning of *sex* from that of *gender*. This differentiation allowed feminist scholars to distinguish bodily traits (sex) from the social status (gender) attributed to individuals because of their sex. The language of sex and gender is an intervention into the natural world—a technology—since it changed how individual behaviors and social practices are interpreted and rendered significant.

Technologies can also be used to reinforce social inequalities and hegemonic norms.[24] Foucault examined how individuals' sexual expression and identity were shaped and policed throughout history by use of what he calls "technologies of power." He employed this phrase to refer to the means used by those in positions of influence to control the behavior and beliefs of individuals. He asserted that regulatory systems, such as obscenity laws about sexual conduct, were developed and used in concert with the field of psychology to define and to enforce "normal" versus "deviant" sexual behaviors, desires, and identities.[25]

Technologies have often been used to police gendered bodies and identities in line with prevailing gender ideologies and social scripts; this can be seen in the contemporary lack of gender-based workplace protection for individuals, or the psychological definition of Gender Dysphoria (formerly Gender Identity Disorder) as a mental illness. These are logical products of technologies of power that reinforce normative gender scripts and marginalize non-normative genders; by pathologizing gender nonconformity and legitimating discrimination on the basis of gender, power holders maintain and reify existing gender ideologies. Gender theorists Epstein and Straub explain, "the 'normative' and the 'transgressive' in our sense of our bodies, our sexual practices, our erotic desires, and our gender identities exist in and through the cultural discourses that construct and enforce them."[26] What people think of as appropriate or transgressive gender, and how each individual presents their own gender, is therefore a product of the technologies of power wielded during their historical era.

Technology and the Individual

Direct interventions into the body are theorized by Foucault as technologies of the self.

TECHNOLOGIES OF THE SELF

The way in which individuals shape their self (body and identity) to their own (and society's) liking.[27]

In addition to working in dynamic relationship with other social forces such as dominant ideologies, technologies are used by individuals to change their bodies and identities.[28] Technologies of the self are ways of shaping and reshaping who and what we are; for example, bodybuilding can be viewed as an example of a technology of self that allows individuals to change their physical body to achieve a particular shape, identity, or aesthetic.

From the historic Muscle Beach in Venice, California, and numerous men's fitness magazines, to the increasing attention to film actors' muscle definition in mainstream media and the presence of weightrooms at most schools, gyms, and recreation centers, immense pressure is exerted on boys and men to develop and exhibit highly developed muscles. North American cultural expectations very clearly tie muscular definition to masculinity and over the past 25 years men's attention to muscle mass has steadily increased. In national U.S. surveys only 18 percent of men expressed dissatisfaction with muscle definition in their upper bodies in 1972, while 38 percent did in 1985, and by 1994, 91 percent of college men surveyed reported a desire to be more muscular.[29] These are dramatic numbers. In an effort to embody socially valued masculinities, many men engage in time-consuming and often painful workout regimens to achieve the type of musculature associated with hegemonic masculinity. Some of the technologies of the self that are utilized toward this end include nutritional supplements, exercise regimens, and weight-lifting machines. The extensive work many men do on their bodies can be interpreted as a response to gender paradigms that define men as naturally strong, and to dominant scripts for masculinity that connect strength to manhood.

At the same time that individuals use technologies to achieve particular aesthetics, social scripts for bodies shape the use and development of new technologies. Changes in men's bodies and musculature in

Figure 1.1 Babe Ruth playing baseball, 1920. Reproduction made from an original at the Library of Congress. © Sporting News via Getty Images

Figure 1.2 Mark McGwire playing baseball, September 1997. © Bettmann/CORBIS

social institutions such as media and sports shape what individual men imagine their own body should look like and the kind of technologies they employ to manifest this embodiment. The two greatest baseball home-run hitters of all time, Babe Ruth and Mark McGwire, built their careers on mastery of their masculine bodies—bodies that were very different from each other's.

While both were large men for their time, they had very different images of athleticism; at the height of their careers, Babe Ruth (1926) had 12½ inch forearms and 15½ inch biceps.[30] In contrast, in 1998 Mark McGwire's biceps were 19 inches and his forearms an astonishing

17½ inches.[31] Not only did the athletic body change over time, but the technologies employed to manifest these bodies changed as well. Exercise technologies, such as weightlifting, changed dramatically over the 70 years between their careers and steroids were in widespread use in 1998 compared to 1926.

Embedded in social gender scripts are assumptions about technologies of the self. The belief that men are naturally stronger is built on the fact that boys and men are encouraged to be more physical from birth, which increases their muscle mass and strength. Similarly, the contemporary gender norm of women's bodies as hairless relies on the fact that women use razors, waxes, and lasers to achieve this aspect of gender. Technologies of the self, however, can be used to construct both normative and non-normative gendered selves. In contemporary North American culture, dance, particularly classical forms such as ballet, are considered feminine endeavors. Men who dance are often assumed to be effeminate gay men who failed at normative masculinity (when used in this manner, homosexuality is intended as a slur to signify de-masculinization).

This is such a common trope that the story of a boy dancer, Billy Elliot, was easily turned into a blockbuster movie and Broadway show. In *Billy Elliot*, a young boy struggles to take ballet lessons in the face of significant and violent resistance from friends and family.[32] While the moral of the story is that Billy should, and did, eventually do what he loved—dance—the film gets its humor from the incongruity of a young working-class boy in England becoming a professional ballet dancer. Billy's interest in dance is blamed on the death of his mother and on the failing of his father, but never attributed to an innate talent or a love of dance; these things are seen as incompatible with "normal" (aka normative) masculinity. Technology plays a part in both enforcing normative gender (e.g. delineating dance as feminine) through technologies of power, and in non-normative gender. Men who pursue dance use new technologies to help to train for and choreograph performances, to strengthen and treat injuries, and to maintain particular body size and shape norms particular to dance subcultures. In the process, men dancers use technology to produce masculine bodies and identities that are non-normative.

As with any aspect of technology, whether and how individuals participate in technologies of the self depends on a multitude of personal, social, and embodied factors. Some people pursue counter-hegemonic technologies, others normative ones, and others engage in a combination of both. The technologies of the self that are demanded of people in order to conform in one situation may be unacceptable when attempting to conform to norms in another, for example, the way one dresses for work as opposed to what one wears out for a night on the town. The paths that individuals take to navigate this complex terrain are determined by the social scripts at their disposal. The rest of this chapter explores how standards for gender normativity have changed over time, shaped by technologies of the day, and how these changes have affected what was expected of individuals in order to be appropriately—or inappropriately—gendered in society.

Theorizing Gender and Technology Together

Gender paradigms in a society set out the core beliefs about gender, and shape how individuals and institutions structure gendered lives. Social scripts establish what is appropriate for men and women in our society, and shape how each of us "does" gender on a daily basis. Social theorists Candace West, Don Zimmerman, and Sarah Fenstermaker discuss this production of gender as "doing gender."[33] Their theory explains why the accomplishment of gender feels effortless and inevitable unless we go against the grain, do it wrong: until we somehow do not conform.

> **DOING GENDER**
> A theoretical approach that makes sense of gender as an accomplishment and not as a set of individual characteristics. Gender is something that individuals "do" in interaction and which is imbedded in all parts of social life.

West, Zimmerman, and Fenstermaker argue that gender is a trait *produced* in interaction, rather than one *possessed* by individuals. Doing gender in the process of social interaction is inevitable; because it is a primary organizer of everyday life, it is inescapable and produced in virtually all interactions. We learn social rules about how to behave in both formal and informal ways, in institutions and through everyday trial and error.[34] Beginning in infancy, these processes of self-regulation are learned through social interaction. Children learn, through family, media, and other institutions, what it means to be a boy or girl, and then practice these distinctions with themselves and others. These rules, expectations, and underlying gender scripts are not deterministic, however; we engage in behaviors or resist engagement, whether normative or nonconforming, as we see fit. While the technologies of any age shape how individuals can make sense of and intervene in the gendered body, and the available gender scripts constrain the choices they have about gendered identities, individuals are still agents of their own lives.

Gender nonconformity has been documented throughout history, from Greek mythology to contemporary studies of trans* youth.[35] Philosophers, historians, and, more contemporarily, anthropologists and psychologists have all documented gender nonconformity, often because these individuals fell outside of the normative gender scripts of the day. Attention has always been paid to individuals we would now call transgender, as technologies of power have been used to police what constitutes normalcy.

Social norms are defined through dominant paradigms and enforced through technologies of power; Western scripts designate cisgender as normal and transgender as abnormal.

CISGENDER

A word used to describe individuals whose gender identity matches the expected norms for their sex (for example, a masculine gender identity and male sex). The prefix "cis" means aligned with or on the same side of. Cisgender, then, means a gender identity aligned with one's ascribed sex (i.e. non-transgender individuals). The term has been taken up by many in the trans* activist and scholarly community in an effort to resist the normalization of non-transgender individuals and the simultaneous pathologization of trans* people. Instead of defining sex/gender alignment as "normal" and other sex/gender pairings as abnormal, a cisgender/transgender framework establishes both as legitimate ways of being in the world.

The process of setting up normal and deviant sex and gender categories was abetted by social, political, and scientific technologies of the self that defined and subsequently attempted to treat and cure deviant behaviors and individuals. Examples of gender nonconformity were used as foils against which "normal" gender identity could be elevated. Historical studies of gender nonconformity in anthropology, psychology, medicine, and science were part of this social negotiation of sex, gender, and sexuality. Reflection on these historic cases also offers what Susan Stryker calls "transgender effects," moments where "the spectacle of an unexpected gender phenomena illuminates the production of gender normativity in a startling new way."[36]

While we cannot necessarily predict how an individual will respond to their particular combination of life experience, socialization, scripts, and technologies, we can—and should—examine and theorize how these dynamics function in general, what their consequences are, and how they have played out in people's lives. Even if an individual chooses to defy guidelines set by existing gender norms and scripts, they will use the technologies available at any given time to do so. One way to trace a history of gendered body and identity norms through time is to look at how evolving technologies have helped individuals to make sense of and transform gender according to their own needs and circumstances.

How Technology Has Shaped Gender and Gender Nonconformity

What makes a man a man? What defines a woman as a woman? We often assume the answers to these questions are obvious, but when we look at definitions of sex and gender both historically and in this contemporary moment, a clear-cut distinction is elusive. Although we think of modern biological science as providing definitive answers, numerous scholars have explored the ambiguity of the sex and gender binary. While the technologies of our age have provided more insight into the body than ever before, including the specifics of sex and gender, social beliefs about gender continue to shape what scientists, doctors, and scholars observe, and how they interpret these "facts."

Judith Lorber, one of the foremost contemporary gender theorists, puts it this way:

> When we rely only on the conventional categories of sex and gender, we end up finding what we looked for—we see what we believe, whether it is that "females" and "males" are essentially different or that "women" and "men" are essentially the same.[37]

Whatever criteria we use—chromosomes, genitalia, secondary sex characteristics, or hormone levels—the lines between male and female bodies are blurred. Sex categories may appear stable, but the fact is that there is more variation than we are aware of. The biological "facts" that we use to distinguish and divide bodies into two sexes are based on entrenched social beliefs depicting gender as binary, and they do not necessarily reflect an underlying natural or truly objective sexual dimorphism. The use of binary categories to "prove" that two sexes equals two genders is a cultural construct and a circular argument.[38]

Technologies of Sex and Gender Formation

Competing debates and ideas about sexual differentiation emerge in the earliest biomedical texts, persist through the Middle Ages, and continue up to contemporary times. From their earliest iterations, philosophical and medical texts in the West offered explanations for a diversity of sexes or genders. Two dominant philosophical traditions, Galenic/Hippocratic and Aristotelian, produced conflicting ideas about the body, and these manifested in fundamentally different ideas about male and female bodies and selves. For example, Hippocrates' *On Regimen*, (one of the earliest medical texts, dating back to the fifth century BCE), explained six sex/gender possibilities based on outward bearing: manly men, manly women, feminine men, feminine women, "hermaphrodite" men and "hermaphrodite" women.[39] In the fourth century BCE, Aristotle contravened Hippocrates' definition by asserting that women were differentiated from men in status, morality, and physiology, because of the coolness of their humors.[40] According to Aristotle, women's humors were cold and wet compared to those of men, which were hot and dry.[41] In the Roman period (129–200 CE) Galen argued that women's and men's bodies were the same, save for women's genitals, which were "turned inside out." Scholars built on Galen's theories through the fifteenth century. In contrast, Patrick Geddes, an eighteenth century professor of biology, asserted that the very cells in women's and men's bodies were different, claiming that men's cells gave off energy while women's cells stored it.[42] The variety of competing theories of sex difference fell by the wayside in the late eighteenth and nineteenth centuries in the light of new medical technologies that provided greater access to and more detailed information about biology and physiology than ever before. These different paradigms for sex led to radically different "truths."[43] Throughout history, different dominant ontologies and attendant gender paradigms have responded to and in turn affected the social structures and hierarchies of the day, and technologies were key participants in this process.

In 1796, Samuel Thomas von Soemmerring claimed to be the first anatomist to document a female skeleton (see Figure 1.3).[44] While Soemmerring likely exaggerated his case, it is true that drawings of female bodies were not included in anatomy texts until the 1730s.[45] During some periods prior to this, differences between male and female bodies were seen as insignificant. In others, women's bodies were not considered an intellectually important subject (while men's bodies were).

Soemmerring's illustration was part of a concerted effort within eighteenth century science and medicine to locate sex differences literally within every part of the human body.[46] On top of this, challenges by early feminists to reigning gender paradigms and scripts raised the importance of locating gender difference—and inequality—in the body in order to maintain the status quo. If men's and women's bodies really were different in every aspect, then gender inequality was biologically proscribed. These new gendered body paradigms, built on the foundation of new, socially guided biomedical technologies, allowed a reinterpretation of gendered bodies and identities. One of the key outcomes of this effort to find biological sex differences was a dramatic shift in the interpretation and treatment of gender nonconformity.

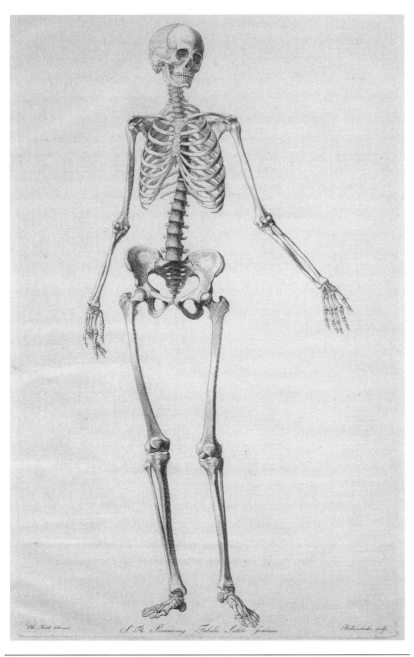

Figure 1.3 Drawing of a female skeleton from *Tabula Sceleti Feminine* by Samuel Thomas von Soemmerring. Reproduction made from an original at the Boston Medical Library in the Francis A. Countway Library of Medicine.

Beginning in the mid-nineteenth century with the rise of the scientific and medical investigation of sex, gender, and sexuality, authority over gender shifted from community agreement, law, and the state to medicine.[47] As the medical fields of sexology, endocrinology, and psychology developed, individuals who expressed gender nonconformist desires and/or identities were labeled by doctors with the revival of pre-modern terminology like real or psychological "hermaphrodite," and through the minting of new terms, such as "gender invert" and "eonist." These new technologies did more than name pathologies; they defined appropriate ways to manifest, identify, and treat gender nonconformity. Gender nonconforming individuals whom medical practitioners had previously left to their own devices were suddenly subject to medical diagnosis and treatment.

Technologies of Gender Conformity

The late nineteenth century marked the inception of medical authority over sex, gender, and sexuality, and attendant medical technologies shaped more than just gender nonconformity. Technologies are used to naturalize normative body scripts and render them invisible. Take the ubiquity of the corset for women in nineteenth century Western Europe and North America. Corsetry was more than fashionable dress; prevailing gender ideology of the day demanded corsetry, as it was understood to construct and enforce appropriate, hegemonic, womanhood.[48] While corsets have a long history (corset-like garments have been documented in ancient Egypt and were commonly worn in Europe since the Middle Ages) they were most important socially and in terms of shaping gender scripts between the nineteenth and early twentieth centuries. Almost all women, of all races and class divisions, wore corsets through the 1800s due, in part, to the belief that, as the weaker sex, their body (and mind) needed to be supported. Gender ideologies that defined ideal women's bodies produced technologies that reshaped how individual women looked and identified.

Consider the Chicago Corset Company's advertisements for the "Ball's Health Preserving Corset" and the "H.P. Misses' Corset" (see Figure 1.4). Implied in both of these 1881 advertisements is the necessity of corsets for women. One of the two, "Ball's Health Preserving Corset," asserts

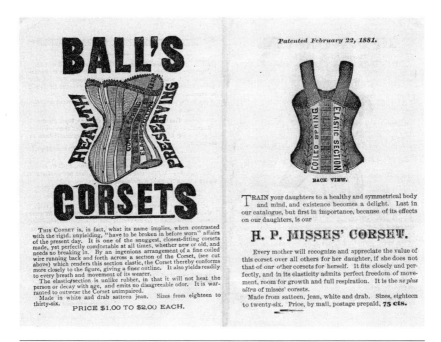

Figure 1.4   Advertisement booklet for Ball's Health Preserving Corsets and the H.P. Misses' Corset. Chicago Corset Company, 1881.

that its newly patented technological innovation—the coiled wires—made corsets more comfortable and healthier than "traditional" boned corsets (which used rigid stays made of bone to keep their shape). Creating the hourglass, "feminine shape"—what we may think of as the normatively gendered body of that era—was considered more important than the medical problems that corsets often caused. The solution to the "unhealthy" consequences of traditional corsetry was not to stop their use, but rather to develop new technologies to make corsets less harmful to the body.

The dominant ideology and the associated scripts for normative womanhood are even more explicit in the second advertisement for a corset intended for girls. The "H. P. Misses' Corset" advertises that wearing the corset will shape young girls' bodies and *minds* appropriately. In fact, the corset's description begins by admonishing women: "Train your daughters to a healthy and symmetrical body and mind, and existence becomes a delight."[49] The implication here is that girls' and women's bodies need corseting to develop both physically and morally, and that adhering to normative values will bring them joy.

The corset was seen as a medical and moral necessity for women in the nineteenth century, and came to signify normative femininity.[50] Simultaneously, and perhaps more significantly, the ways that it shaped women's bodies and affected their movement through the world reinforced social beliefs about womanhood.[51]

Tight lacing damaged women's organs and led to fainting and restricted movement, which was viewed as clear evidence of women's fragile natures, rather than the result of wearing a corset. The 1903 drawing, "Nature versus Corsets" (Figure 1.5) from an anti-corset treatise, illustrates some of

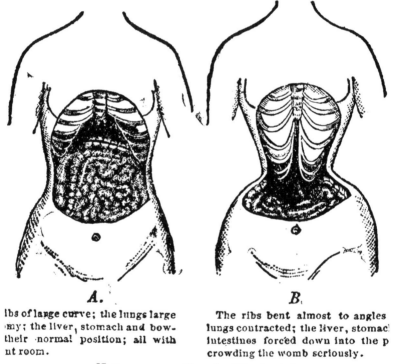

A.

lbs of large curve; the lungs large
my; the liver, stomach and bow-
their normal position; all with
ut room.

B.

The ribs bent almost to angles
lungs contracted; the liver, stomac'
intestines forced down into the p
crowding the womb seriously.

Nature versus Corsets, Illustrated.

Figure 1.5 A 1903 illustration of the effects of corsets on women's bodies from *Golden Thoughts on Chastity and Procreation* by John William Gibson. Reproduction made from an original at the Library of Congress.

the effects of corsetry on women's skeleton and organs. Corsets dominated women's fashion through the early 1900s until social and technological changes led to new gender norms that, among many other social alterations, displaced corsetry. Women's increased participation in the paid labor force and consequent need for less restrictive clothing meant that fabric bras and girdles became more practical than corsets, while advances in the mass production of clothing and elastic made bras and girdles less expensive. Subsequently, gendered clothing norms and scripts changed when flappers hit the scene after World War I.

The rise of the flapper aesthetic in the 1920s was an intentional, pointed, and dramatic rejection of Victorian femininity and female domesticity. As young women cast off their corsets and long skirts, they turned toward a new modern womanhood characterized by independence, urbanism, and youthfulness. These new gender scripts were shockingly masculine compared to the accentuated curves and delicacy cultivated by corsets and late nineteenth century feminine gender norms. As part of these new gender scripts women cut their hair into short bobs, and bound their breasts with cloth to create more youthful, boyish appearances.

All of this gender-bending caused social uproar and gender crisis. Gender scripts for women changed swiftly and dramatically. This shift was tied up with women's newly acquired right to vote (1918 in Canada and 1920 in the United States), and their increasing presence in the public sphere.[52] New technologies including jazz music, mass produced cigarettes, suffrage, and short skirts radically transformed the available gender scripts for women. The body practices associated with flapper femininity—dancing to jazz music, drinking alcohol, smoking, voting, working, and embracing single womanhood—went against the Victorian gender scripts that had dominated society before World War I, and transformed who young women could be. That is, technological innovation in the early twentieth century, in concert with shifting gender paradigms, revolutionized normatively gendered bodies and identities. The meaning of gender nonconformity was also being renegotiated as part of and resultant to these paradigmatic shifts.

Technologies of Gender Nonconformity

Neither the complexities of people's lived genders nor ideologically driven theories of sex and gender are modern phenomena. In every historical era, the technologies of the day have been used to delineate the boundaries between male and female and between men and women, and these technologies have shaped how individuals and societies at large make sense of sex, gender, and their diversity. Evidence that individuals have lived cross-gender or gender nonconforming lives can be found in almost all cultures; there have been gender nonconforming pharaohs, kings, queens, Catholic Popes, soldiers, musicians, governors, criminals, and everyday people. It is difficult to talk about trans* individuals before the development of modern sexual and gender identities, in part because sexuality and gender have often been intertwined.[53] We can, however, look to historical and cross-cultural examples of gender nonconformity as evidence that these practices, and their contemporary corollaries, are not new or unique. In addition to individuals who have lived cross-gender lives, in many times and places still other possibilities were available. While Western societies have not often offered third (let alone fourth or fifth) gender options, many other societies have, and some still do. Some cultures not only accommodate alternate genders but also see them as legitimate, or even embraced as powerful and important to the society at large.[54] These third genders are named in many cultures including in some Native American tribes and Canadian First Nations (e.g. Two Spirit), in Indian society (Hijras), in Albania (Sworn Virgins), and in Maori communities (Takatapui).

In the process of recording gender nonconformity, historical research has also documented the ways that the rigid binary categories of male/female and man/woman have been constructed, reinforced, and defied across time and place.[55] How gender nonconformity has been defined and understood reflects the prevailing ontology, social scripts, and technologies of the time, making it difficult for contemporary scholars to know exactly how to talk about and make sense of gender nonconformity from the past. It is important to both recognize histories of gender nonconformity and keep in mind that we make sense of these stories from the past from within contemporary ontological viewpoints, theories of gender and sex, and vocabularies of gender difference. Some scholars have argued that we can make sense of past gender noncon-formity using contemporary concepts, transcribing current identities onto historical gender diversity. Others have argued that, because sub-jectivities are the product of the ideologies and technologies of the time, ascribing ahistorical identities onto experiences from the past obscures the complexity and historical specificity of gender nonconformity.[56] As historian Elizabeth Reis asks, "can we really compare Joan of Arc's cross-dressing and militarism in fifteenth century France with Sarah Emma Edmonds, who lived as a man and fought in the American Civil War" without eliding the specificity of their historically situated experiences?[57] This dilemma is not unique; gay and lesbian scholars have struggled with the same issues when deciding how to make sense of historical sexual diversity in the absence of contemporary sexual identities.[58]

Understanding past gender nonconformity is also complicated by the histories of colonialism. One of the reasons that gender noncon-formity was documented in cultures around the world was because white Western explorers sought evidence to prove that their own cul-tures were more advanced than "primitive" ones. Almost everything that we know about gender nonconformity within Native American tribes and Canadian First Nations comes from the notes of white explorers who viewed the New World through a lens that justified colonial rac-ism. The word used to describe individuals living cross-gender lives in some Native American tribes and Canadian First Nations, "Berdache," is not a Native word, but one adopted by Europeans from a pejorative applied by French missionaries and explorers.[59] The naming of alterna-tive gender schema in these Native nations, then, reflects the ideology and gender norms of the white men who "discovered" them, rather than indigenous meaning-making. Documentation of non-Western histo-ries of gender nonconformity reveals as much about Western norms and beliefs as it does about indigenous gender diversity; unfortunately, this can make it difficult to comprehend precisely the attitudes of those cultures toward gender nonconformity, or to compare them to contem-porary views. As gender scholar Vic Muñoz argues, the pathology of

Western gender and transgender paradigms have been mapped onto diverse indigenous gender and sexual identities.[60]

While gender nonconformity throughout time cannot necessarily be called transgenderism, we can see that individuals have used the technologies available in any given era to construct gendered bodies and identities in both normative and non-normative ways. The act of substantiating sex and gender has changed over time in concert with technological innovation and dominant gender paradigms. Contemporary gender status for both cisgender and transgender individuals is judged primarily through visibility—whether one's body (inside and out) reflects one's chosen gender according to biomedical criteria and as judged by medical authorities. In contrast, before the rise of medical intervention into gender, the ability for an individual to choose how to do gender was more often rooted in social or legal agreement. This often meant that power holders, legal authorities such as kings, governors, Congress, or judges, claimed a need to confirm an individual's chosen gender.

The colonial Virginia case of Thomasine/Thomas Hall illustrates the different body scripts and technologies at play in the 1600s; in 1629, Hall was called before the General Court in Virginia because their gender was unclear—they wore both women's and men's clothing. It was the *clothing* that was key here; as the primary gender code of the day, clothing inscribed gender. Ultimately the courts ruled that Hall's refusal to "choose" a single gender had to be reflected in their clothing; they had to wear clothing that reflected this duality. It was not the truth of biology or even body that mattered, but rather social presentation vis-à-vis clothing.

In other places and eras as well, taking on a gendered social role and appearance was sufficient to claim one's desired gender.[61] The term "eonist," coined by early sexologist Havelock Ellis, pays homage to Chevalier [Knight] d'Eon (Charles Geneviève Louis Auguste André Timothée d'Éon de Beaumont), a famous eighteenth century ambassador (and spy) for French King Louis XV. While serving Louis XV, d'Eon lived as both a man and a woman; the Chevalier's "true" sex was hotly debated throughout their life: at one point betting took place on the floor of the London Stock Exchange. After a series of espionage-related fiascoes in London, d'Eon petitioned Louis XVI to be able to return to France from exile. The king agreed on the condition that d'Eon live and dress as a woman for the rest of her life. It was only after her death in 1810 that her male birth sex was revealed.[62]

In the early 1900s the dominant paradigms for sex and gender shifted away from the 1800s model that constructed male and female bodies as dramatically different. Instead, male and female bodies were viewed as having the same core biology and physiology but shaped by different "sex hormones" both in-utero and throughout one's lifespan. This led to psycho-medical redefinition of sexuality and gender. Early efforts conflated sexuality and gender, mixing all gender or sexual nonconformities under the umbrella term "inverts," and attributing the roots of sexual and gender variation to physiological and hormonal differences. Over time, sexologists and scientists came to differentiate between sex and gender, shifting toward an identity/mental model instead of a physiologically centered one, and these new technologies opened up new scripts for gender nonconformity. This paradigm shift entitled people to treat gender nonconformity with hormonal and surgical intervention; if the structure of male and female bodies was essentially the same, then biomedical technologies could allow individuals to move from male to female or vice versa. The shifts in scientific gender paradigms opened up the possibility for gender change in the early 1900s, and it is then that we see the definition of transsexuality emerge as the desire to transform one's body *through hormones and surgery*.[63]

These new biomedical technologies were accompanied by an increase in the quantity and selection of information technologies, such as newspapers, magazines, radio, and eventually television, which disseminated information about sex research, transsexual individuals, and other forms of gender nonconformity. Both new information about and language regarding gender nonconformity were in themselves new technologies of meaning-making, and exposure to them opened up new identity and body possibilities for individuals. As historian Joanne Meyerowitz suggests, "stories in the press allowed a few American readers to imagine surgical sex change and seek it for themselves."[64] Meyerowitz describes what was perhaps the most significant media coverage of transsexuality in North America, when in 1952 the *New York Daily News* broke the story that an "ex-GI" had just undergone a "sex-change" to become the blonde, beautiful, Christine Jorgensen. Jorgensen's return to the United States in 1953 was covered in every major domestic news outlet, propelling her successful nightclub act for several years. "Jorgensen was more than a media sensation, a stage act, or a cult figure," Meyerowitz concludes. "Her story opened debate on the visibility and mutability of sex."[65] In that historic moment, one person telling her story in the public realm catapulted transgender issues into everyday society. Jorgensen's story, and the repercussions of it being publicized, reinforces how new technologies, in this case information and biomedical technologies, participate in significant social and individual change. These technologies are responsible for instigating paradigmatic changes as well as new social scripts, all of which allowed new body and identity possibilities for individuals.

The trend toward classification and treatment of gender nonconformity in North America continued through the 1950s, 1960s, 1970s, and 1980s. Medical and psychological diagnoses were introduced and used to classify, pathologize, and treat gender nonconformity. Harry Benjamin, building on the theories of Magnus Hirschfeld and other early sexologists, worked with transgender individuals in North America in the 1950s. Regarded as the father of modern transsexual "treatment," Benjamin wrote the groundbreaking book *The Transsexual Phenomenon* in 1965, thus opening the formal genre of transsexual medical literature. While there had been a handful of articles that dealt with gender nonconformity before, Benjamin's was the first comprehensive analysis and medical treatment guide for transsexual individuals.[66] The guidelines that Benjamin laid out in this and subsequent texts still inform trans* psycho-medical treatment through the World Professional Association for Transgender Health, formerly known as the Harry Benjamin International Gender Dysphoria Association.

Gender Identity Disorder (GID) was introduced as a mental disorder in the American Psychiatric Association's *Diagnostic and Statistical*

Manual (DSM) in 1980. As part of the medicalization of transsexuality, GID was defined as a "strong and persistent cross-gender identification" that causes "significant distress or impairment in social, occupational, or other important areas of functioning."[67] This mental diagnosis remained in the DSM for 33 years until it was replaced in 2013 with Gender Dysphoria (GD). One of the consequences of this process of medicalization has been the construction of a specific gender script to which trans* individuals need to adhere in order to access gender affirming surgery. As gender nonconformity became pathologized and the science of sex came to rule the "truth" about gender, access to gender affirming surgery was restricted and required a significant series of diagnoses, tests, and commitments from the individual. Under the rules set out in the DSM, to be cleared for surgery an individual had to state that they had always felt trapped in the wrong body, wanted to be normatively gendered after going through gender affirming surgery, and aspired to a "stealth" (i.e. keeping secret one's transgender status) heterosexual life. The required statements also implied that individuals would leave behind any transgender identity, community, or activism. While many people genuinely held the obligatory feelings, beliefs, and outlook, and still others may have come to experience them as genuine, others were forced to name their experience in this way to access care. The prerequisite adherence to these dictums is enmeshed with hegemonic gender paradigms. By requiring a very specific transgender script, psycho-medical gatekeepers were able to reinforce hegemonic gender scripts and beliefs in the process. The advent of modern medical technologies not only changed how science and medicine made sense of gender and gender nonconformity; it created new technologies of power that influenced how individuals experienced and made sense of their own gender nonconforming bodies and identities.

We also see a symbiotic relationship between hegemonic gender paradigms and transgender treatment in the public response to gender nonconformity. Hand in hand with the demand for a particular and restrictive narrative for "treatable" gender nonconformity has come criticism of transgender individuals as dupes of the gender system.[68] Scientists, scholars, and people at large have held transgender individuals to more stringent standards of gender-norm resistance than cisgender people such that transgender people have essentially been held responsible for maintaining the entire gender system through their own "normative" masculinities or femininities, while simultaneously being required to produce hegemonic gender to access medical services.[69] They have simultaneously been accused of maintaining hegemonic gender norms and inequalities, of destroying gender diversity, of failing to be gender nonconforming at all times, and of being too flamboyant, radical, or militant. Applying these disproportionately rigorous standards to those who practice gender nonconformity is a technology of power used to downgrade the social status of trans* people. While all members of a society conform to, uphold, resist, and rewrite normative gender scripts through day-to-day interactions, holding trans* people accountable for both the conservation of hegemonic gender norms and the preservation of gender diversity has let cisgender individuals off the hook. In reality, the process of "doing gender" is one in which we all participate and therefore all have the ability to use technologies of the day to challenge, rewrite, and expand socially available gender scripts.

New Technologies, New Genders

The rise of medical science to the peak of social influence is the technological development that has offered the greatest threat and greatest possibility for the creation of new and more diversely gendered physical bodies. Individuals are now able to choose a variety of medical interventions to produce new and varied gendered identities and bodies. These interventions include hormone therapies to produce masculine or feminine secondary sex characteristics and various plastic surgeries, ranging from procedures to remove or implant breasts in order to mimic established gender characteristics, to gender affirming surgeries that create differently gendered genitals. Medical science has simultaneously opened the door to these new possibilities while policing gender and sexuality through the pursuit of pathological diagnostic and curative models and treatments. While pathologization of gender nonconformity has been contested over the past 25 years, reducing its dominance, these scientific standards continue to hold sway over, and have very real impact on, the lived experiences of trans* individuals.

Neither technologies nor scripts are deterministic; they do not lead to one outcome, one set of gender scripts adopted by everyone, or one product, power dynamic, or self. Their resonance and impact are mediated by particular social contexts and personal histories. To fully consider how technologies have shaped gender historically and in our current society, one must keep in mind the complexity of these relationships. The use of medicine as a technology of power is not unique to gender; medical science has been used to enforce the racial and class-based status quo throughout history.[70] Science is automatically the most legitimized knowledge source within a scientific paradigm, and the attendant scientific and medical technologies are used to uphold and defend established social inequalities and prejudices. For example, the application of gender curative therapies are disproportionately directed at young boys while we have much more tolerance for gender nonconformity in girls. This asymmetry is predictable given our societal privileging of masculinity and its attendant traits; to value the desire to be a boy is much more understandable than the reverse.

Even when new gender scripts are put forward, as in cases of trans* social movements, their legibility to others remains constrained by hegemonic paradigms. Leslie Feinberg has been a transgender author, activist, and transgender pioneer for the last 40 years. Ze has written numerous fictional and nonfiction books about transgender lives and has toured the country speaking at activist, educational, and political events.

GENDER NEUTRAL PRONOUNS

Gender neutral pronouns have been suggested by some activists as new ways to refer to individuals that transgress the gender binary. Ze is an alternative pronoun used by some trans* individuals to express the fact that they identify neither as a man nor a woman. Similarly, hir is used instead of his or her. Other individuals have advocated using they as a singular pronoun (referencing an individual and not a group). Common practice within trans* and trans* ally communities is to ask individuals what their chosen pronoun is.

In hir trans* history, *Transgender Warriors*,[71] ze shared a story common to hir experience.

> "You were born female, right?" The reporter asked me for the third time. I nodded patiently. "So do you identify as female now or male?" She rolled her eyes as I repeated my answer. "I am trans-gendered. I was born female, but my masculine gender expression is seen as male. It's not my sex that defines me, and it's not my gender expression. It's the fact that my gender expression appears to be at odds with my sex. Do you understand? It's the social con-tradiction between the two that defines me." The reporter's eyes glazed over as I spoke. When I finished she said, "So you're a third sex?" Clearly, I realized, we had very little language with which to understand each other. When I try to discuss sex and gender people can only imagine woman or man, feminine or masculine. We've been taught that nothing else exists in nature.[72]

Leslie Feinberg's reflection about hir own illegibility points to how our ability to make sense of an individual's sex and gender rests in part on the gender scripts available to us. Try as she might, the reporter could not understand what Feinberg meant by transgender, in part because she had no corresponding gender script on which to draw.

As Feinberg's experience of invisibility renders visible, the stakes are obviously high for trans* people, but these controversies also affect cisgender individuals. We are all influenced by, and involved in, the creation of gender(s). The creation of new gender scripts can benefit all people, not just trans* individuals. One set of new scripts might validate a wider range of emotions for men, allowing them to express themselves more freely; other new scripts could change expectations for women's body size, moving us from a society where most women dis-like their bodies to one where most women hold positive body images. As Cressida Heyes concludes, "a wide range of gendered subjects stand to gain from challenges to enforced binaries within the nexus of sex, gender, and sexuality."[73] Still, our ability to recognize and legitimate new gender scripts remains limited by the dominant ideologies and technologies of the day. But as new technologies emerge, the ability for individuals to transform their own bodies and identities, and to share new gender scripts and ideologies expand.

Engaging in Sociological Analysis

People continue to refuse to conform to gender norms, of course, just as they have throughout history. Alongside social changes in technologies and normative definitions, gender nonconformity has manifested differently as well. It is continually shaped by the technologies available for the production of gender as well as by the social gender scripts of the era. Trying to make sense of gender nonconformity by isolating it, either by viewing it solely as a biological hiccup, or entirely as a product of social experiences and choices, elides the complexity of trans* experience. Only when we examine gender as a product of the varied, complex interplay of biology, social scripts, dominant ideologies, personal histories, and technology can we develop an understanding of gender that reflects the diversity found in society. Approaching the analysis of gendered lives and technological innovation together reveals how they are mutually constituted alongside dominant ideologies and scripts.

The first two chapters of this book have focused on the complex relationships between gendered bodies and identities, dominant ideologies, social scripts and technological innovation. The examples and case study reviewed thus far point to technology as a dramatic axis of social change that has historically shaped, and continues to reshape, who we are as people. The case studies also reveal that technological innovation is always tied up with dominant paradigms, social scripts, and embodied lives. Sociological theories of identity reveal that identity formation is a social, interactive process that responds to and participates in social change. Moreover, social scripts—the stories for who we can be—work alongside dominant paradigms to shape who we are and who we think we can be as individuals.

A sociological analysis allows us to see how all of these forces contribute to everyday gendered life. This sociologically based gender framework allows us to examine how individuals make sense of their gendered bodies and identities, how gendered forces are transmitted, learned, adopted, and contested through interaction, and how social institutions produce and challenge gender scripts and gendered technologies. Such an analysis sheds light on the myriad configurations produced by ever-changing relationships between body, identity, social script, technology, and dominant paradigms, and renders visible the social forces that produce the complex reality individuals experience.

Research on technology and gender in the social sciences suggests that bodies and identities change as new technological processes emerge, informed by the realm of possibilities offered in dominant paradigms and social scripts. New technologies interact with social scripts and gender paradigms to produce particularly gendered identities within different contexts. Dominant beliefs and paradigms combine with the diverse array of bodies and identities within a particular context to shape our vision of who we can be as embodied individuals.

Notes

1 *Kinky Boots* 2005.
2 Strauss 2004.
3 Carr 2006.
4 De Lauretis 1987; Halberstam 1991; Hausman 1992; Irvine 1990.
5 Hausman 1992: 275.
6 Derry and Williams 1993.
7 Gebhart et al. 1979, as cited in UNESCO 1985: 4.
8 Borgmann 2006.
9 Cordaux and Stoneking 2003.
10 Park 2006.
11 The dominant ontology of Western societies through the mid-sixteenth century sug-
    gested that royalty was divinely chosen by God to lead hand-in-hand with the church.
    This ontology granted legitimacy and omnipotence to rulers.
12 Kleinman 2005: 4.
13 Gibson 1903.
14 MacKenzie and Wajcman 1999.
15 Ritzer 1993; Weber 1947 and 2005.
16 Ellul 1964; Heidegger 1977.
17 While Karl Marx saw the Industrial Revolution as devastating for workers, the problem
    lay not with the technological developments that led to the Industrial Revolution,
    but in the economic system (capitalism) that put new technologies to particularly
    exploitative uses.
18 Hughes 2004; Marx 1977.
19 Kling 1996; Segal 1986.
20 Foucault 1965 and 1979.

21 Foucault names these: technologies of production, technologies of sign systems, technologies of self, and technologies of power (Foucault 1988).
22 Gimlin 2002.
23 Foucault 1990: 152.
24 Foucault 1988.
25 Foucault 1979.
26 Epstein and Straub 1991: 17.
27 Foucault 1979.
28 Rooney 1997: 403.
29 Thompson 1999.
30 McGovern and Goewey 1926.
31 Copeland 1998.
32 *Billy Elliot* 2000.
33 West and Fenstermaker 1995; West and Zimmerman 1987.
34 Bourdieu 1968.
35 Feinberg 1996.
36 Stryker 2006: 13.
37 Lorber 1993: 578.
38 Fausto-Sterling 2012.
39 Epstein and Straub 1991: 19.
40 Park and Nye 1991: 54. The doctrine of humors was the dominant ontology from the 400s BCE (theorized by Hippocrates) through the 1700s. It posited that all matter was comprised of fire, earth, water, and air, and that each of these humors had specific qualities—hot and dry, dry and cold, cold and wet, and wet and hot, respectively. The doctrine fell out of favor with the development of cell-based pathological models and microbial sciences in the mid-1800s. See Arikha 2007 for more information on the doctrine of humors.
41 Laqueur 1990.
42 Laqueur 1990: 4-6.
43 Lorber 1993.
44 Soemmerring 1796.
45 Stolberg (2003) argues that this estimate is off by several hundred years, and offers evidence that the first drawing of a female skeleton was published in 1583.
46 Schiebinger 1987.
47 This is similar to the shifts in how mentally ill individuals were treated, which Foucault documented in *Madness and Civilization* (1965). His study began by asking why, over fewer than 100 years, insane individuals went from being tolerated and included in society, to being confined within asylums. What Foucault found was that as medicine gained authority over illness and the body, madness came to be seen as a social failure and consequently individuals were observed, diagnosed, confined, and treated.
48 Summers 2003: 2.
49 Chicago Corset Company 1881: 3.
50 Summers 2003: 7.
51 Gibson 1903: 107.
52 Freedman 1974.
53 As many scholars have argued, an identity based on sexual practice is a relatively new phenomenon that emerged in the nineteenth century alongside the rise of capitalism, urbanization, and "regimes of normalization" (Foucault 1990) (Katz 1996). Before this, sexual practices were acts devoid of an associated identity category. Terms like homosexual were not invented by Kertbeny until 1869 (Stryker 2008: 35).

54 See, for example, Feinberg 1996, who includes detailed histories of non-binary gender possibilities around the world, including Xanith of Oman, Mahu of Tahiti, Travesti of Central and South America, Sworn Virgins of Eastern Europe, and Hijras of India. See also, Blackwood and Wieringa 1999.
55 Epstein and Straub 1991: 19.
56 Bullough 1975; Hausman 1992.
57 Reis 2004: 168.
58 Rupp 2001.
59 Coming, a number of scholars suggest, from a derogatory Persian term for slave boy (Reis 2004: 169–170).
60 Muñoz 2009.
61 Bullough 1975.
62 For a more detailed discussion, see De Beaumont et al. 2001.
63 Meyerowitz 2002: 5.
64 Meyerowitz 2002: 5.
65 Meyerowitz 2002: 1.
66 For a review of Harry Benjamin's work and roots see Pfäfflin 1997.
67 American Psychiatric Association 1994.
68 Jeffreys 2003.
69 Vidal-Ortiz 2002 and 2008.
70 Stryker 2008: 35.
71 Feinberg 1996.
72 Feinberg 1996: 101.
73 Heyes 2003: 1094.

Case Study: Focus on Bloomers and Nineteenth Century Womanhood

In mid-nineteenth century North America, a social battle raged over clothing in general, and over upper-class white women's attire in particular. The fashions of the day kept these women covered from head to toe in long sleeves, corsets, and multiple layers of skirts. While these styles highlighted their race and class status, they severely hampered these women's ability to move freely; corsets restricted breathing and layers of skirts made running and jumping almost impossible. While sports (in particular bicycling) were becoming popular, women were unable to participate fully because of their clothing.

Most women of color and poor women were exempt from these dress norms, not because they were free of hegemonic pressures, but because they were viewed as different kinds of women (if they were viewed as human women at all). The fragility, domesticity, and purity said to characterize upper-class white women's femininity was not considered part of poor women's character; how could it be when working-class women were responsible for the household labor from which wealthy white women were being protected? Even when poor women and women of color took on styles of dress and body codes in line with norms for affluent white femininity, their race and class identities made hegemonic gender unattainable.

From the mid- to late nineteenth century, both men's and women's clothing began shifting dramatically. Highly specialized class- and profession-based clothing was moving toward less formal and less regimented styles, due in part to the Industrial Revolution and attendant social changes. More people were needed in factory work, and one of the technological innovations of the Industrial Revolution was the sewing machine. Developed in the late eighteenth century and in widespread use by the mid-1800s, this new technology made more clothing accessible to more people across social class lines. Whereas most working class and poor individuals had owned only one or two sets of clothing before, the sewing machine (and quick-to-follow technologies of mass produced clothing) allowed most individuals to afford a larger wardrobe. Previously held safely within the domain of the upper classes because of its expense, fashion was now within reach of a much broader range of individuals. Most significantly, the sweeping social changes (in paradigms and social scripts) provoked by the rapid technological innovation of the era were reflected in and played out in its fashions. Look at the change in trends between 1900 and 1924.

In the 1900 advertisement for Easter suits from the National Cloak Company, women are covered from head to toe and neck to wrist (Figure 1.6). Like Victorian fashion in general, these suits focused attention on the tiny waist created by corsets and were sure to cover women's sensuous ankles.[1] Women wore bonnets over long, styled hair. In contrast, just 25 years later, the spring dress fashions profiled by Sarnoff of NYC (Figure 1.7) centered around short skirts, flat breasts, and uncorseted waists. Women's hair was cut short in shockingly masculine styles. Flapper style dresses came to women's knees and were cut to create a uniformly flat appearance from breast to hip. It is interesting to think about what beliefs about women and men must have shifted alongside these fashion changes. For men from the mid-1800s onward, clothing grew less ostentatious and increasingly homogenous across social class lines. For upper-class white women, there was a fight over pants.[2]

The movements for and against "dress reform" took shape in the late 1800s, sparked by a number of social changes including women's increased participation in public life (as teachers, college students, writers, and abolitionists), feminist movements advocating for the right to vote, to work, and to lead alongside men, and post-American Civil War politics. These social changes produced new social scripts for womanhood, challenging dominant gender paradigms that made sense of women as innately maternal but otherwise weak in mind and body and in need of men's moral and intellectual guidance. As these social scripts changed, Amelia Bloomer and others, drawing from styles they observed among Native American women, advocated for the rights of women to wear a female version of pants called "bloomers."

Figure 1.6 Advertisement for ladies $5.00 Easter suits by the National Cloak Company, 1900.

NEW GOWNS FOR AFTERNOON TEA AND DINNER
for Madame and Mademoiselle

The Latest Mode and The
Latest Shop Greet Spring Together!

AUDREY—Renée combines tiny pleats with insertings of thread lace, and adds a lace edged pleated scarf to complete this adorable gown of Crepe Elizabeth. In Bisque, Blonde, Pervanche Blue, Titian, Navy.

69.50

ELAINE—New coat-model dress of finely pleated crepe Elizabeth over printed Foulard Crepe. The smart scarf extending from shoulders ends in silk fringe. Obtainable in Navy, Black or Cocoa.

69.50

AND the last shall be first—in Fifth Avenue! That is both the rule of the modes and the unique experience of the latest shop to present them. The Sarnoff Shop is literally a debutante in an avenue of dowagers! It was actually opened only a few months ago, but its recognition was immediate because women found that it was animated by an artistic and creative spirit rather than by the purely emulative instincts of trade. Instead of commercialism they found *chic* and instead of sameness, dissimilarity. And it is so in the new Sarnoff modes for Spring. Each possesses the artistic gusto of a Paris original.

CLAIRE—Lanvin creates a new smartness in this exquisite Gown of Silk Chiffon with Crepe Satin underskirt. Insertions of Venice lace lend attractiveness. Shown in Bisque with undeskirt of Blonde, Pervanche Blue, Golden Brown or Black.

69.50

MURIEL—Renée inspires this Gown of tucked Crepe Elizabeth with touches of Venice lace medallions at yoke and circular flounce. Bisque, Pervanche, Grey or Madeline Rose.

69.50

Sarnoff & Co.

34th Street— **362 Fifth Avenue** —35th Street
NEW YORK

Figure 1.7 Art Deco flapper girl spring dress fashions from the Sarnoff and Company department store in New York City, 1924.

Instead of confronting the issues raised by social change head on, both advocates and critics of the changing women's role in North American society focused the debate on the idea of women's pants. In an effort to control women, power holders—including doctors, politicians, and religious leaders—weighed in on the importance of women's "traditional" dress.

This cartoon (Figure 1.8), titled "Woman's Emancipation," which was published in *Harper's New Monthly Magazine* in 1851,[3] parodies "a strong-minded American woman." Women dressed in bloomers are seen taking on the social tasks and styles of men: smoking, dog owning, and escorting women in public. The tension over women's place in society vis-à-vis men is made clear; bloomers were seen as a catalyst for gender upheaval in society. The fear was that if women were able to wear pants, they would also want to take on all of the other gendered

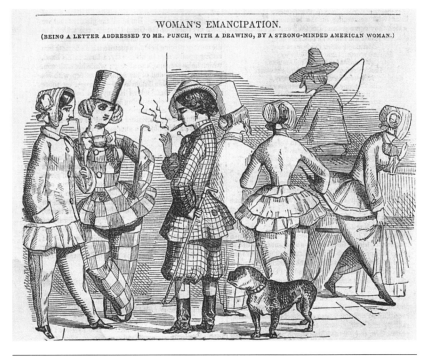

Figure 1.8 A cartoon drawing from *Harper's New Monthly Magazine* in August, 1851, depicting the social consequences of allowing women to wear bloomers.

behaviors associated with men, such as smoking or cavorting in public, or even those activities previously assumed to require men: escorting women, for instance. We, as viewers, are intended to be aghast (as is the woman in the background). As a pastor in Rochester, NY declared in 1852 at a Temperance Society meeting, bloomer-ites were "a hybrid species, half-man, half-woman, belonging to neither sex!"[4] A similar sentiment was expressed in a *New York Times* editorial, alongside a telling assertion that dress reform would compromise the very gender of white women: "This generation has long been aware of the existence of *alleged* women who insist that it is the right and duty of the sex to wear trousers."[5] Many suggested that bloomers (and the bicycle riding that they were affiliated with) "destroys the health of women, and unfits them for the important and sacred duties of motherhood," as stated by a Kansas District Representative in January 1897 when he introduced a bill to the Kansas State Legislature that would outlaw both bloomers and public bicycle riding for women.[6]

This battle over women's dress had far more to do with the social tensions over first wave feminist activism and the shifts in men's and women's social roles that were taking place than with any innate need for women to wear skirts. Its manifestation with concern to clothing, however, was sparked by new clothing technologies like bloomers and factory-made clothes.

As part of the early nineteenth century advent of mass-produced clothing, Elizabeth Smith Miller designed the first women's pants in 1851.[7] While bloomers did get some use as bicycle-wear in the late 1800s, their everyday use was weighed down with controversy and power struggle. Ultimately, pants did not take hold as everyday fashion for women until almost a century later, due in large part to the social and political tensions tied to them. The development of new technologies— bloomers—as part of feminist advocacy and dress reform, provoked new technologies of power in an effort to maintain the existing gendered power structure of the day. Not only were women who donned them viewed as uncouth, but bloomers called into question the gendered— and presumably natural—social order upon which daily life was built. Indeed "bloomer-ite" became a name with which one could ridicule a woman who advocated for social and civil rights.[8] Technologies of power, such as laws against bloomers and bike riding, were deployed to maintain the status quo. These innovations, alongside the new language and aesthetics that were part of feminist activism for women's participation in the public sphere, were met with new rules about women's dress that were, in fact, attempts to restrict women's increasing public social power. Many of these dress rules, such as the requirement that women wear skirts or dresses to class at the college/university level, remained in effect through the 1960s, at which time a new wave of feminist activism again challenged them. While few Americans today would suggest that a woman wearing pants was a blatant example of gender nonconformity, 150 years ago doing just that called into question a woman's actual gender identity. Technological innovation (bloomers) was intertwined with changes in gender ideologies, social scripts and embodied womanhood. This is just one of many examples of how technologies have been used to construct new gender possibilities, delimit normative gender and sanction gender nonconformity throughout history.

Notes

1 Crane 2000.
2 Crane 2000.
3 "Woman's Emancipation" 1851.
4 Gattey 1968: 85.
5 "Divided Skirts" 1881. Emphasis mine.
6 "Against Bloomers and Bicycles" 1897.
7 Ewing 1978: 63.
8 Smith 2006.

CASE STUDY: FOCUS ON BEAUTY AND TWENTY-FIRST CENTURY WOMANHOOD

The famous idiom "beauty is in the eye of the beholder," suggests that perceptions of beauty are fully subjective, but sociologists have spent decades studying the ways in which beauty norms are actually specific to cultural and historical moments.[1] In fact, we learn and internalize definitions of beauty, as we do all social norms, in the process of social-ization; "beauty is an attribute of the social system and not simply an individual enterprise."[2] Within North American society, beauty norms have centered around bodily features that are more common within dominant racial and ethnic groups.[3] Flowing blonde hair, long legs, light (or sun-tanned) skin, blue eyes, a thin and tall (but not too tall) frame, and sizeable breasts are all components of idealized feminine beauty. Men's norms call for thick and straight (or wavy) light colored hair, a tall and thin but muscular frame, tanned skin, and meticulously groomed body hair. These norms are culturally specific; we can con-trast them with contemporary Japanese beauty norms, which prize narrow hips and bust, pale skin and a hairless body.[4] Beauty norms are also deeply classed, age-specific, and raced. For example, since beauty norms in the United States are based on idealized *white* fea-tures, Black individuals are, by definition, outside of the racialized beauty expectations for hair, even if they employ straighteners, hair extensions and hair bleaching techniques.[5] Because expectations for beauty work require a certain disposable income, social status is rein-forced by adherence to beauty norms; what is considered beautiful is an upper- to middle-class style.

Dominant gender paradigms don't just encourage body work, but demand it. While the social scripts for embodied beauty have changed across time and place, both the social rewards of normative beauty and the pervasion of efforts to achieve it are constant.[6] Dominant social norms for appearance give greater value to bodily characteristics that are normative and devalue bodily characteristics that deviate; society draws strong connections between bodies and the people that inhabit them, so this privileging and devaluing of different physical attributes is in turn applied to the individuals who possess those traits. And the unequal valuation of differing physical characteristics has real-world implications for individuals. For example, women who opt out of normative beauty practices experience social marginalization, decreased earnings, and less career mobility.[7]

We internalize beauty and body norms and ideals in the process of everyday life, and there are very real positive sanctions for doing so. In his research on bodies and consumer culture, Mike Featherstone finds that the "body projects" that individuals undertake to better resemble the dominant beauty ideals yield tangible rewards (which he discusses in Marxian terms as "exchange value"). Not only are normatively attractive individuals evaluated more positively by others (as more likeable, more competent, etc.) and more likely to possess a higher social status, but individuals evaluate their own worth in line with their physical self-evaluation. Normatively attractive individuals rate *themselves* as more confident, likeable, and successful than less attractive ones. This "appearance phenomenon" is significant; a number of studies have demonstrated higher performance on standardized tests, better health, and improved career trajectories for normatively attractive individuals.[8] It is no surprise, therefore, that individuals work to approximate the gendered, raced, classed, and aged beauty ideals of a society as best they can.[9]

Connections between beauty and femininity have a long tradition in Western culture as part of dominant paradigms for womanhood and are accordingly informed by and constitutive of sexism and gender inequality.[10] According to 2012 data from the American Society of Plastic Surgeons, ten times as many women utilize plastic surgery as do men: more than 12.5 million cosmetic procedures in the United States were performed on women, compared to 1.25 million procedures on men.[11] While the rates of invasive cosmetic procedures like liposuction have held relatively stable over the last few years, the rise in minimally invasive procedures such as fillers, chemical peels and Botox injections has been remarkable. This increase in the overall number of cosmetic procedures accompanies a significant statistical increase of women as recipients in proportion to men. Between 2000 and 2012, while the number of cosmetic procedures rose 98 percent overall (247 percent between 1997 and 2012), the use of procedures by women increased five times as fast as they did for men.[12] While both men and women are subject to bodily imperatives, the expectations and dividends of beauty are more substantial for women than men.

The deeply gendered aspect of "body projects" is not lost on plastic surgery consumers; in personal narratives collected by researcher Debra Gimlin, women stated that they engaged in body work as a conscious part of negotiating a gendered identity within the constraints of gender, class, and race norms. Gimlin found that plastic surgery was deployed by women to "make do" within a sexist and beauty-obsessed culture.[13] In other words, plastic surgery is being used to construct explicitly gendered bodies and identities, bodies and identities which are often hyper-normative. Were plastic surgeries simply the product of individual self and body concept, we would expect women to alter their bodies in a variety of ways, producing a range of gendered embodiments. Instead, cosmetic procedures are dramatically uniform in their production of normative femininities. For example, the two most common surgical cosmetic procedures for women are breast augmentation and liposuction, both of which are invasive methods that produce exaggerated physical characteristics in line with what North American society at large views as femininity: thinness and large breasted-ness. Further, these trends are not only deeply gendered but also racialized: 91 percent of individuals who employ cosmetic procedures are women and 70 percent are white.[14] Under the guiding hand of modernity's commodity capitalism, beauty (i.e. normative embodiment) has become something to be bought and sold.[15]

The beauty industry (comprising cosmetics, beauty treatments, hair care, dieting programs, etc.) is a multi-billion dollar industry; in the United States, more money is spent on beauty than on education or social services. The most common non-surgical cosmetic procedure in the world—accounting for more than *six million* treatments in 2012 in the United States—is Botox. Botox is the trade name for Botulinum

Toxin Type A, a muscle paralytic that is used to restrict muscle movement in isolated (usual facial) regions. The effect of the toxin is to temporarily reduce the appearance of wrinkles in an area of the face. The effects last three to six months and, at an average of $370 per treatment, Botox is one of the most profitable procedures for doctors involved in biomedical body modification.[16] According to the American Society of Plastic Surgeons, Botox accounted for 47 percent of non-surgical procedures and 42 percent of all procedures in the U.S. in 2012,[17] and 40 percent of non-surgical procedures and 25 percent of all procedures in Canada in 2011.[18] And Botox is ever increasingly biomedically and culturally significant, with a growth of 680 percent since 2000 and almost 5,000 percent since 1997.[19]

Advertised in magazines, discussed on news programs, and written into television entertainment, Botox has become a socially acceptable and, in many social circles, even expected part of middle- and upper-class beauty regimens. Like non-surgical cosmetic procedures more generally, it is also tied to dominant paradigms for gender, especially womanhood. While mature men are prized for their experience, dominant paradigms for gender locate women's worth in youthful, feminine embodiments, and these gendered characteristics shape the use of Botox. These gender paradigms are so successfully entrenched—regardless of their lack of scientific basis—that in the United States only 10 percent of individuals who used Botox in 2012 were men, and a shocking 15 percent of the women who sought out the procedure were under the age of 35! Lured by unproven speculation of Botox's prophylactic ability to prevent wrinkles before they appear, young women are increasingly integrating Botox into their lives as part of regular bodily maintenance.[20]

Sociologist Dana Berkowitz examines the role of Botox in U.S. society in her book, *The Rise of Botox: How the Anti-Aging Wonder Drug is Changing the Face of America*, and finds that women seek out Botox and make sense of their body work as necessary maintenance of the female body.[21] Berkowitz argues that Botox is part of larger social processes that are medicalizing aging and the body more broadly, particularly for women. Berkowitz highlights how aging itself is gendered (men are perceived to improve with age, like wine, while women spoil, like overripe fruit), and how anti-aging efforts like Botox draw on and reproduce gendered embodiment norms. Individual decisions about cosmetic body modification are always situated within social frameworks for understanding—social norms and scripts—and, as Berkowitz summarizes, "shaped by intersecting social, cultural, and economic forces and by hegemonic ideologies about whiteness, femininity, beauty, and aging."[22]

If we want to make sense of the gendered and racialized dynamics of Botox as well as its meaning and import in society, we need to focus on where dominant gender and race paradigms intersect with new technologies to construct social scripts. It is these scripts that encourage individual practices of embodiment that legitimate Botox as a way to meet expectations of white femininity in North America. And, in turn, these embodied selves act back on social scripts and ideologies of race and gender, normalizing particular new bodies and ways of being. Moreover, the process of employing cosmetic technologies requires individuals to "make sense" of their selves anew—to explain how their altered appearance better represents their "true self."[23] In the process of these accounts, individuals develop new embodied identities. Individuals employ this new technology within a social context (the dominant gender paradigm) that places immense value on normatively gendered, raced, and age-specific embodiments, and ultimately these individual practices normalize cosmetic body work and the bodies that they produce.

One of the effects of the normalization of body work in contemporary society has been a shift in cultural conceptions of cosmetic surgery from a maligned practice engaged in by the narcissistic celebrity or elite to an acceptable and even expected response to embodied "flaws" among everyday individuals. Research and data on Botox suggest that, for many women, engaging cosmetic technologies has become a regular part of "doing respectable femininity in the everyday" much like shaving or wearing high heels.[24] This new technology of the body has become so benign that it is, as soap opera star Lisa Rinna put it, "like changing the oil in your car."[25]

Researcher Suzanne Fraser has argued that cosmetic surgery affects dominant gender paradigms and social scripts such that all individuals are shaped by these biomedical technologies, not just those who avail themselves of them.[26] Women are aware of these contradictions and binds. For example, actress Julianne Moore recently spoke out in *Health Magazine* about the effects of technologically-enhanced bodies in Hollywood. She mused that there's "a new normal" because of the pervasiveness of cosmetic procedures (particularly in Hollywood) such that, "cosmetic surgery itself starts to look normal, and we lose track of what a real face is like."[27]

While cultural forces may well be oppressive, individuals often experience their own use of cosmetic technologies as empowering, validating, and agentic. Despite the fact that idealized beauty norms are unattainable, the majority of individuals that employ Botox (and cosmetic surgery in general) express satisfaction with their bodily manipulations.[28] The empowerment experienced by individuals who have availed themselves of beauty work may be the result of lessening social pressure created by increased conformity, or it may be the product of an increased sense of self-esteem. In either case, women who choose plastic surgery are not "'cultural dopes', tossed and battered by cultural forces beyond their understanding" or "passively submitting to the demands of beauty." Instead, as Debra Gimlin suggests, we have to understand individuals as, "savvy cultural negotiators," attempting to "make out" as best they can within a culture that limits their options.[29] Women are expected to use new technologies to produce normative bodies, just as they have been expected to shave or tan themselves, or don corsets as in ages past, and these modified bodies in turn become the new norm to which individuals are held accountable. Moreover, as these more transformative processes of body and identity work become normalized, the linkages between appearance and personal character are reinforced, completing the circuit between identity and belief, and fueling the fire that finds more value in normatively attractive bodies.[30] Contemporary bodies are canvasses upon which we, as individuals, enact our wills. There are many technological innovations that enable contemporary individuals to modify their physical bodies, but our choices of which technologies to employ are always shaped by, and made within, a larger social context rife with hegemonic ideologies and social structures. While our attention is often drawn to cutting edge technologies, body modification is not a new enterprise; individuals make sense of their own appearance within the context of beauty norms that value particular embodiments over others. Corsetry and tattooing have reshaped individual's bodies physically, while definitions of male and female, shifting social gender categories, and changes in clothing and clothing norms have reshaped bodies conceptually.

Technologies developed to directly and explicitly intervene in the body are being used to reshape the bodies and identities of individuals in line with twenty-first century beauty norms, but cosmetic biomedical interventions aren't the only way to change the shape of the body in line with gendered paradigms for beauty. In reality, the vast majority of body work engaged in by individuals is non-surgical and draws on both biomedical and information technologies ranging from fitness trackers to scientific systems of classification and expert knowledge. Many individuals are using new information technologies to engage in a dramatic reshaping of their own bodies. For example, the Internet can connect individuals engaged in solo body work to each other, allowing them to share information, technologies, and support.

One of the most highly publicized uses of information technology for body work in recent years has been pro-anorexia/pro-bulimia/pro-eating-disorder websites (known as pro-ana, pro-mia and pro-ED respectively).[31] While pro-ED websites are particularly active sites of body work, these spaces are only one piece of a larger eating disorder phenomenon in North America. Eating disorders are a significant and growing public health issue; researchers estimate that between 1 and 4 percent of adolescents and adults in the U.S. and Canada struggle with an eating disorder.[32] Deeply gendered (less than 10 percent of those with eating disorders are men), and often thought of as a phenomenon dominated by young white women, research demonstrates that different racial and ethnic groups experience eating disorders in distinct ways and are diagnosed differentially (e.g. women of color are less likely to be diagnosed).[33] If eating disorders were an individual phenomenon of psycho-medical pathology, we would see even distribution of cases across gender, age, and self-presentation categories. Instead, eating disorders are concentrated among particular populations, namely young *feminine* women. Research suggests that individuals who ascribe more strongly to normative femininity are more affected by eating disorders.[34] That is, the more an individual feels beholden to feminine womanhood, the more likely she is to engage in disordered eating to achieve—or exceed—these expectations. Social scripts for femininity normalize disordered eating practices such as binging, purging, and chronic dieting, making normative femininity a risk factor for eating disorders.

In everyday society, individuals with eating disorders are almost exclusively funneled through psycho-medical channels and are offered very few opportunities to find others with similar practices outside of the sphere of psychologists, recovery support groups, and in- and out-patient treatment programs. The impact of this is significant; individuals with eating disorders have been unable to build community or challenge dominant paradigms collectively because of highly structured psycho-medical control. Information technologies, however, have opened up the world of support groups and shared communities to individuals who were previously geographically or socially isolated. Access to information about eating disorders and a wide range of helplines, free services, and recovery-focused resources are more accessible than ever before online. Given the ubiquity of information technologies in the lives of contemporary young people, it is no surprise that individuals with eating disorders have turned to online spaces for information, support, and community. Online, individuals are more free to find like-minded individuals and create alternative communities that offer relief for those singled out as abnormal and pathologized as ill.

Simultaneous to the development of online recovery-focused resources, other online spaces have also emerged that accept or even promote eating disorders, including blogs, webpages, discussion boards, and social networking communities or groups. Individuals with eating disorders who experience marginalization within mainstream society have been able to find comrades online with whom to confide, collaborate, and organize. For the most part, these pro-ana, pro-mia and pro-ED online spaces are not recovery oriented, and instead frame anorexia, bulimia, and other eating disorders as personal choices or "lifestyles."[35]

In a 2007 survey of pro-ED websites, public health researchers found that the majority of these websites include weight-loss advice and support forums, as well as nutritional information, interactive calculators and food diaries. More than a third also supply information about eating disorders including risk factors, symptoms, and treatments, as well as information about recovery.[36] Most pro-ED sites are interactive and allow individuals to communicate with others one-on-one and/or in group forums. While most have a combination of anorexia and bulimia content as well as pro-recovery material, only a little more than half of these refer to eating disorders as a disease, and the rest frame it as a lifestyle choice. Almost two-thirds of sites have "tips and tricks" sections that provide information about how to restrict calories and lose weight, how to lessen the pangs of hunger, and how to conceal symptoms from family and healthcare providers.[37] Central to almost all pro-ED sites is a motivational component, texts and images called "thinspiration" or "thinspo," which serves as a motivator for continued weight loss.

"Thinspo," tips and tricks, interactive discussions, and support forums all work to redefine legitimate eating habits, give value and worth to hyper-thin embodiments, and create a community of support. Because pro-ED communities are focused on embodied practices, individuals work to make the body real online by posting pictures, sharing weigh-in statistics, and comparing bodily experiences, and individuals use these practices to help bridge the gap between the tangible body and online pro-ED spaces.[38]

Pro-ED online communities offer opportunities for people to find each other, develop a common language and set of symbols, provide and receive support, and craft what participants call a "pro-ana lifestyle."[39] Individuals undertake embodied identity work online, such as adopting an ana identity and losing weight, and engage in interactional practices which gain them recognition as authentic members of an eating disorder community. These processes are both constitutive of and rely on new information technologies, social scripts for gendered embodiment, and dominant paradigms for womanhood. In sociological terms, pro-ED online spaces are locations for body and identity work where new social scripts for embodiment (e.g. acceptable body size and eating habits) and identity (e.g. a positive anorexic self-concept versus a pathologized one) are learned, negotiated, and adopted. By asking for and offering support around bodily goals, accounting for daily successes and failures, and sharing experiences, individuals develop a shared sense of purpose and collectivity. In so doing they are able to cultivate non-normative gender scripts for embodiment on the individual and collective levels.

Pro-ED websites are places where hegemonic beauty norms and gender paradigms are translated into embodied practices in the lives of individuals. Indeed, pro-ED site content is focused on the need for women to control their bodies successfully in order to achieve perfection, themes that bear a striking similarity to more general social scripts for embodied womanhood in North America.[40] Gender paradigms for womanhood give value to women on the basis of their bodies and connect thinness with beauty, goodness, and femininity; these paradigms underlie the pro-ED embodied ideal and the individual body work undertaken in these communities. Hegemonic gender paradigms for women prize bodily self-control and flawless femininity, and these objectives are amplified in eating disorder scripts.

Pro-eating disorder online spaces have garnered quite a lot of media attention. Activists and intervention advocates have successfully argued that these sites warrant censorship because of their supposed potential for harm. As a result, most major Internet search engines and social networking tools have banned pro-ED content, and pro-ED online sites are quite transient as they are often shut down by hosting sites. For example, in 2001 YAHOO! and MSN agreed to shut down pro-ED websites at the request of national health associations, and were copied by a number of other Internet platforms.[41] More recently, in response to media attention and public outcry in 2012, major social networking sites including Tumblr, Instagram and Pinterest all removed and banned pro-ED blogs, pages, tags and searches. These sites have also inserted health warnings about eating disorders. For example, when you search for "thinspo" on Pinterest, you are directed to a statement that reads, "Eating disorders are not lifestyle choices, they are mental disorders that if left untreated can cause serious health problems or could even be life-threatening" and given contact information for the National Eating Disorders Association Helpline.

Research on pro-ana/pro-ED has been used to argue that these sites provide material support for eating disorders and therefore promote and prolong illness and increase individuals' negative body image.[42] And yet an increasing number of scholars are suggesting that the media attention on these websites (and accompanying hysteria) constitute a moral panic in which social anxieties about young women, the Internet, and body image are whipped into a frenzy around a tangentially related phenomenon.[43] If a moral panic is characterized by an out-of-proportion mobilization around a marginal group or practice, which masks broader social tensions or fears, then pro-ED sites fit the bill.

From fictional cases on television shows like *Boston Legal*, to episodes of *Oprah*, to extreme cases profiled in major newspapers like the *New York Times* and *Chicago Tribune*, media coverage of pro-ED sites has been sensationalized. There have been more than 350 articles on pro-ED sites since 2001, and much of the coverage has been fear-mongering and all of it has been in favor of limiting access to or removing these websites. Similarly, many academic studies assume that pro-ED sites are dangerous and proceed to make claims about the harm done by these websites despite weak empirical support.[44] Most objective research suggests, however, that pro-ED sites are a minor player in the eating disorder crisis. While about 12 percent of all young women and 6 percent of all boys report visiting pro-ED sites, participation in pro-ED sites has not been correlated with more severe illness.[45] In the largest study of pro-ED website users to date, a 2012 study by Rebecka Peebles and her co-authors concluded:

> Websites with pro-ED content may play both supportive and harmful roles for those struggling with disordered eating . . . [Individuals] seek support from a Web-based peer group, which poses both potential harms and opportunities for interventions within these online communities.[46]

Rather than supporting the panicked reaction common in media and academic writing on pro-ED sites, the researchers found that there is more complicated body and identity work going on than critics suggest.

While many website participants are finding support and developing new social scripts for embodiment on these sites, they may not be doing so in ways that lead to more self-harm.

Both the presence of pro-ED websites and the moral panic around them can be viewed as part of our broader culture's eating disorder crisis. The oversized response to young women's use of a new technology is reminiscent of the moral panic around dress reform and bicycle riding that emerged in the nineteenth century, the centerpiece of the previous case study on bloomers. In both instances, instead of focusing on the structural inequalities in society that continue to devalue women's lives and place women's worth on their bodies and appearances, media and power holders draw attention to the individual practices of women—pants wearing and pro-ED website creation and participation. This also draws attention away from the hegemonic control inherent in unattainable beauty norms. There is much to learn from looking in detail at *both* whether and how these websites are used by individuals to make and remake their embodied self, and what critics of these sites are worried about vis-à-vis gender and embodiment. If the nineteenth century moral panic was about women's role in society, then this twenty-first century panic is more likely about young women's bodily agency and ability to have a voice in knowledge creation about their experiences.

The pro-ED panic is a way to deflect attention away from the many ways hegemonic womanhood demands unhealthy practices among girls and women. Gendered ideals for women's embodiment, mainstream social scripts, and the media's use of hyper-thin (and photoshopped) models are linked to the high levels of disordered eating among girls and women in North America. However, by blaming this eating disorder crisis on new technologies and their use (e.g. pro-ED sites), instead, power holders are able to shift attention away from mainstream culture and hegemonic gender paradigms and leave these social structures (and the gender inequality they are part of) intact. Sensationalizing pro-ED sites obscures the many similarities between eating disorder behaviors and the normalized—even celebrated—body work of chronic dieting, calorie counting and exercise in which girls and women are compelled to engage. Indeed the ideology of pro-ED—that "nothing tastes as good as thin feels"—is a classic Weight Watchers Inc. slogan that captures the social norms of thinness, to which girls and women are held accountable.

Botox and pro-ED websites are parts of a broad continuum of body work undertaken by women in service of hegemonic beauty norms that evaluate women's worth on the basis of their appearance. While it is easy to single out either practice as the extreme behavior of sick individuals or as the outcomes of new dangerous technologies, a more robust analysis recognizes them as products of hegemonic social paradigms for womanhood and social scripts for beauty and body work to which individual women are held accountable. While it is easy to criticize individual women for falling into the beauty trap, we need to step back and see the cultural bind in which twenty-first century women find themselves. If they cannot or choose not to engage in these types of beautifying body work, they experience social stigma, discrimination and marginalization; if they do participate, they risk being viewed as powerless creatures swept asea by dangerous practices they should have been strong enough to resist. Bringing a sociological lens to these issues draws our attention to the ways in which new technologies are being marshaled to reinforce hegemonic gendered body and beauty norms, and encourage normative body work by individuals. These normative practices are not caused by new technologies, but are instead a product of dominant paradigms and social scripts and the power these structures exert on individuals.

Notes

1 Ortner and Whitehead 1981.
2 Miller 2006: 8.
3 Hall 1995.
4 Miller 2006. As Miller explores, these dominant beauty norms (like those in the U.S.) reflect middle-class, urban ideals. Moreover, dramatic changes in beauty norms and body work in the 1990s and 2000s in Japan have brought more diverse body and beauty subcultures to the fore.
5 Robinson-Moore 2008.
6 Davis 1995; Lakoff and Scherr 1984.
7 Berry 2007.
8 Etcoff 1999; Jackson, Hunter, and Hodge 1995; Patzer 1985.
9 Balsamo 1996; Featherstone 1991; Miller 2006.

10 Black and Sharma 2001.
11 ASPS has collected national level data on plastic surgery since 1992. For more information see: www.plasticsurgery.org/news-and-resources.
12 American Society of Plastic Surgeons 2013.
13 Gimlin 2002: 109.
14 American Society for Aesthetic Plastic Surgery 2013; American Society of Plastic Surgeons 2013.
15 Giddens 1991.
16 International Society of Aesthetic Plastic Surgery 2012.
17 American Society of Plastic Surgeons 2013.
18 International Society of Aesthetic Plastic Surgery 2012.
19 American Society for Aesthetic Plastic Surgery 2013; International Society of Aesthetic Plastic Surgery 2012.
20 International Society of Aesthetic Plastic Surgery 2012.
21 Berkowitz forthcoming.
22 Berkowitz forthcoming.
23 Gimlin 2000.
24 Raisborough 2007: 28.
25 Berkowitz forthcoming.
26 Fraser 2003.
27 Dunn 2011.
28 Gimlin 2000.
29 Gimlin 2000: 96.
30 Gimlin 2000.
31 I am using pro-ED as an umbrella term to encompass pro-ana, pro-mia and other pro-eating-disorder sites.
32 Government of Canada 2006; Hudson et al. 2007.
33 Becker et al. 2003; DeLeel et al. 2009; Harris and Kuba 1997; Shaw et al. 2004. For women of color, there are two counterbalanced forces at work: on one side, racial and ethnic cultural norms may insulate individuals from dominant body size paradigms; on the other, the farther an individual falls from the dominant racialized ideals of beauty, the more vulnerable they may be to disordered eating as they strive to meet unattainable expectations (Hall 1995).
34 Bordo 1993; Hall 1995; Osvold and Sodowsky 1993; Pritchard 2008; Warin 2009.
35 Wilson et al. 2006.
36 Borzekowski et al. 2010.
37 Harshbarger et al. 2008; Norris et al. 2006.
38 Boero and Pascoe 2012.
39 Boero and Pascoe 2012: 29.
40 Norris et al. 2006.
41 Reaves 2001.
42 Bardone-Cone and Cass 2007.
43 Boero and Pascoe 2012; Ferreday 2003.
44 E.g. Norris 2006.
45 Custers and van den Bulck 2009; Wilson et al. 2006.
46 Peebles et al. 2012.

2
INFORMATION TECHNOLOGIES AND GENDERED IDENTITY WORK

Scholars and cultural critics dispute the nature of our modern technologically saturated society. For some, there was a golden age before smartphones and websurfing, when individuals sat around the dinner table and spoke to each other. According to these critics, information technology has estranged us from each other: children from parents, partners from each other, friends from friends. They say information technologies have led us to *Bowl Alone* and turn our brains into *The Shallows* (titles of bestselling books on the dangers of a technological society). In her book *Alone, Together*, technology scholar Sherry Turkle asks the half rhetorical question, "does virtual intimacy degrade our experience of the other kind and, indeed, of all encounters, of any kind?"[1]

Contrary to this dystopian analysis, some cultural critics counter that new information technologies are allowing different but not lesser contact. These new technologies are allowing individuals to connect with others—colleagues, friends, and family—across geographic distance, during busy lives and within complex relationships. In January 2014, frequent *New York Times* contributor Mark Oppenheimer's op-ed piece titled "Technology is not Driving Us Apart After All" profiled the research of sociologist Keith Hampton. Hampton has taken on the dystopian claims that new information technologies are decimating public life, and argues instead that, rather than becoming more estranged, individuals are actually more likely to congregate in public spaces, and more likely to interact with others. To substantiate these claims, Hampton attempted to document the same public spaces where sociologist William Whyte shot video footage for his groundbreaking 1970s urban studies research of how individuals used urban public spaces. When recreating these video observations 40 years later, Hampton found the same or even more extended interactions between individuals in public spaces.[2]

These experts are engaging in the same debate you likely have around your family's dinner table, in the classroom, or at a coffee-fueled meet-up. We are, as a society, conflicted. There is no doubt that the Internet is a socially transformative force; what seems to be the issue here is the specific nature of that ongoing transformation. Rather than adopting either a utopian view of the Internet as a vector for progressive change in the classical liberal tradition, or a pessimistic one of it as the purveyor of crude and simplistic stereotypical cultural narratives, a sociological analysis turns us toward examining the complexities of these changes.

New research suggests that more than 98 percent of young adults aged 18–29 are online on a regular basis (compared to 95 percent of youth under 18, and 85 percent of all adults).[3] Young people are engaging in a wide variety of activities in cyberspace, from socializing to creating media to exploring new interests and communities.[4] For those young adults with adequate resources to expect reliable access to the Internet, it is increasingly common to participate in a range of social networking technologies such as Facebook, Instagram, and Snapchat, as well as in virtual spaces like those created by games such as World of Warcraft or the Wii Fit, or in virtual worlds such as There.com and Second Life. The most recent research estimates that 67 percent of young people participate regularly in social networking and/or virtual interactive spaces.[5]

CYBERSPACE

Originally used by science fiction writer William Gibson, cyberspace refers to the intangible, metaphorical "space" that networked computers construct through and for electronic communication. It is a shorthand way of describing computer-mediated contact between individuals who may or may not share a temporal or geographical location.[6]

Among all of those who spend time online, there has been increasing interest in experiencing one of the "massive multi-user virtual environments" (MMUVEs), otherwise known as virtual worlds. As of 2009, 4 percent of all adults and 8 percent of youth regularly spent time in a virtual world, and these rates are even across gender, race, and household income.[7] Second Life, as we examined in the Preview, is one of the oldest and most popular of these virtual worlds. More than one million members are active in Second Life each year (averaging 400,000 new visitors each month), and more than 3.2 billion dollars' worth of goods have been sold and bought in this MMUVE.[8] There have been write-ups in all the national papers and articles in many magazines, not to mention plugs by National Public Radio, Microsoft, Apple, and many other corporations encouraging you to visit them on their "island" in Second Life.[9] While the pace of growth for Second Life has slowed, the virtual world continues to attract and retain users ten years after its creation, which is an improbably long time in terms of information technologies.

MMUVEs are only one of many online places where people use a self-designed "avatar" to navigate new virtual environments; estimates in 2007 were that over 18 percent of individuals aged 18–30 had created an avatar (a two- or three-dimensional virtual self-depiction) in an online space, compared to 5 percent of older Internet users.[10] We now use graphic representations of ourselves in a wide range of online and networked venues including games, social networking sites, and in online work or school environments such as Sharepoint and Blackboard.[11]

Exploring Virtual Worlds

Entrance into Second Life can be illuminating, exhilarating, and troubling all at the same time. Upon signup, an individual selects an avatar and name, and then is placed on "Social Island," where they have an opportunity to get used to communicating and navigating with their avatar (see Figure 2.1). In early versions of Second Life, everyone entered the world with an identical Barbie-like avatar, which was then customized; more recently, new residents are offered a range of avatars— humanoid, vampiric, or vehicular—from which to build an online self. The first order of business for new residents is to personalize this virtual

FIGURE 2.1 Social Island, a new resident's starting point in Second Life.

self. Using a number of controls it is possible to select from different "skins," literally skins for your avatar, either purchased or selected from the Second Life library, adjust numerous bodily features, and construct a body to represent one's self. One can play with height, weight, skin color, gender, facial features, hairstyle, and clothing while seeking the perfect combination of who one *is*, who one *wants* to be, and how one wants *others* to see them. In my own experience, I loved creating an avatar that reflected "who I was," if not physically, then metaphorically. Figure 2.2 is what I came up with. It is a pretty accurate depiction of myself, only better: a little more conventionally attractive, smoother skin, a little less chubby, and definitely dressed more fashionably. It is not really surprising that someone might choose to make themselves a "little better" given the option, when it is easy, painless, and reversible.

When an avatar leaves "Social Island" to begin exploring Second Life's many public and private spaces, they encounter a world that ranges from hyper-realistic to fantastical. Standard modes of locomotion around the islands include walking, flying, and teleporting. I navigated around in a rudimentary way without particular direction, wandering around looking

FIGURE 2.2 Author's avatar in Second Life.

for other people. The public space is huge, and sparsely populated. I explored several public parks, chatted with some strangers, and then dropped by the Transgender Resource Center, selecting a virtual place similar to an offline location I might frequent to find "my people." As I made my way through this new world, I found that while people's avatars did reflect a certain fanciful diversity—faeries, animals, hybrids, and inanimate objects were personified alongside men, women, and visibly gender nonconforming avatars—this world was simultaneously homogenous. Almost everyone (that was humanoid) was thin, beautiful, well dressed, and had chosen features typical of North American societies' Anglo-European ideals, including skin tone, facial features and body structure. Why, when people were able to construct their own avatars in any way they chose, was the outcome gender, racial and body size homogeneity? Is this homogeneity intentional, produced (purposefully or unconsciously) by this virtual world structure or design? Or is it an unconscious product of those who participate in Second Life? If it is intentional, what does that suggest about how all encompassing, and deeply rooted discrimination is in our social world? And, if it is unintentional, what indication is this of how limited our ability is to think "outside the box"? After all, given the freedom to choose anything, I had followed social norms too. These questions rushed through my head as I looked around. At first glance, it seemed that most people did what I did by creating their ideal self. In the process, however, we created a world that reflected dominant social body norms and hegemonic gender, race, and class scripts. Given the chance to choose to be anything, people usually followed entrenched social scripts and produced socially desirable bodies and identities—and in the process collectively created a world that reproduced the inequalities present in offline society.

The Internet as New Technology

When Netscape Navigator and Internet Explorer were introduced to the public in 1996, Internet participation skyrocketed. Before these first easy-to-use web browsers were available, only a handful of computer scientists, college students, and government workers were able to use the Internet in a meaningful way.[12] In June of 1995, less than 15 percent of U.S. adults had "ever used a home, work or school computer and modem to connect to computer bulletin boards or information services."[13] By November 1997, two years later, almost 40 percent of U.S. adults were online; 15 years later, Internet use had reached 85 percent of all adults in the U.S., with comparable statistics for Canada.[14] Not only are most North Americans online in some way, but people are participating in increasingly interactive and user-driven websites and virtual communities. The shift toward user-generated content (ranging from online reviews to social networking sites to Wikipedia) is written into the structure of virtual spaces, something technology innovator Tim O'Reilly named an "architecture of participation."[15] This architecture of participation enhances the interactive and democratic nature of the Internet; anyone can (and many do) develop content and cultivate new community spaces online. Technological utopianism—the idea that technologies can move us toward a better society—continues to drive innovation online, from new crowd funding platforms to digital democracy sites like change.org.

Like other technological advances in the past, the Internet does not reach all members of society equally. In fact, sociologist Daniel Myers argues that not only is access to technology different across economic strata in society, but it widens the socioeconomic gap and social inequalities between those with access to information technologies and those without.[16] Business and social services are increasingly found online (from help wanted advertisements and job applications to governmental support and social service information). Accordingly, a lack of regular or private access to the Internet not only limits individuals' social networking and communication, but their job prospects and ability to tap into community resources as well.

Evaluating Information Technologies

Both lay and academic interest in cyberspace and digital culture has exploded over the past 15 years. The Internet's social impact has secured a place at the center of public discourse, and scholars from predictable fields such as media studies and communication, to a broader range including feminist studies, sociology, anthropology, and history have all examined the relationship between cyberspace, society, and individuals.[17] Whether hailed as liberating or condemned as destructive, most scholars and social critics agree that information technologies have saturated the lives of individuals in the industrialized Global North and in some Global South countries.[18] This has created what Ben Agger terms a "worldliness of self," the "ability to go anywhere/anytime, [individual's] saturation with popular culture, their penchant for travel, their tendency to change jobs, spouses, their bodies" in a postmodern world.[19] Early research on cyberspace examined the social construction of online reality and argued that individuals engage in online forums in ways that either reveal or betray their true, essential, embodied self.[20] More recent work has focused on the unique nature of online spaces and interactions.[21] Many of these perspectives on information technologies theorize online and offline worlds as distinct and inherently different from one another, what Nathan Jurgenson calls "digital dualism."[22]

Other scholars have focused on how and why behavioral norms and scripts sometimes differ online from those observed offline, while at other times they do not, suggesting that while online environments allow some escape from existing gender/race/class norms, individuals continue to rely on existing social scripts to ground online interaction in familiar dynamics.[23] More recently, scholars have rejected the online "ruse" versus offline "self" dichotomy, suggesting that individuals both reinforce and contest existing social scripts and identities online. The concept that online and offline spaces and practices are mutually constitutive and inexorably woven together captures more accurately what research on information technologies documents and what most of us experience on a day-to-day basis. Our offline lives shape online activities in terms of who we connect with on social networking sites, how we construct our avatars, and which communities we participate in. In turn, our online activities extend offline to shape our sense of self, embodiment, and social world.

Conceptualizing online and material worlds as intertwined—different but not wholly separate (what Jurgenson calls "augmented reality")—raises questions about what online spaces and practices bring to embodied identity work. In an effort to understand the different possibilities that information technologies introduce, scholars use the language of "affordances," specific activities, interactions, and ways of communicating allowed by a particular technology.[24]

AFFORDANCE

The properties of a medium or technology that make particular activities, ways of interacting, or experiences possible. Affordances are all the possible actions a particular technology allows.

For example, telephones afford voice-based communication and simultaneous one-on-one interaction, while the affordances of email include text-based communication, searchability, and permanence (we can search, save, and archive emails). The different properties of technologies affect how we use them as well as what their effect on us as individuals might be. As technologies scholar Evgeny Morozov summarized, "although networks have their own dynamics, much of what is viewed as intrinsic to the Internet may have more to do with how it is currently configured and used than with any of its fundamental properties."[25]

Some scholars suggest that information technologies share many of the same affordances as past mediums. Sociologist Dana Fisher asserts that the Internet makes the work of social change organizations and activists more efficient and cost-effective, just as older media did in the past, drawing parallels that liken email to the phone and websites to newspapers and magazines.[26] Other scholars suggest that information technologies have some affordances that make them particularly significant for embodied identity work (including in terms of gender). These include anonymity, the ability to "tell one's story," social and identity support from a real but invisible audience, and geographical flexibility, among others.[27] These affordances not only allow, but encourage a range of social psychological processes that underlie identity work.

Identity Work in Cyberspace

We all engage in activities as part of being—or becoming—a particular kind of person: an individual who identifies as an Asian American man, a good student, and a working-class union activist might tell a story about his Korean grandparents, choose particular frames for his glasses, or speak about worker's rights (instead of business profits) as a way to make real, for himself and others, the different parts of who he is. Individuals shape and reshape who they are through language, behavior, appearance, and affiliation, within particular contexts. The construction and reconstruction of identity in the midst of everyday life has been conceptualized as "identity work."

IDENTITY WORK

The "range of activities individuals engage in to create, present, and sustain personal identities."[28] For example, choosing clothes that make one look like the "studious student" one is, or selecting a Facebook profile picture that highlights one's ethnic identity.

Individuals do identity work as part of everyday interaction and, in the process, reinforce and contest established personal identities and social identity scripts. This doesn't make individuals fake or calculating; it is simply how we, as social creatures, establish who we are and how we change over time. Identity work is also done in a multitude of more purposeful ways, such as through self-help or therapeutic efforts, group-focused collective identity construction, or as part of significant life changes.

While identity work has always been part of human culture, the opportunity to engage in identity work online is new. Once thought of as a deeply embodied product of material interaction and self-development, new media scholars have suggested that identity work is also done fruitfully online.[29] Philosophers and empirical researchers have theorized that some features of computer-mediated communication make identity work more possible, and suggest that the affordances of new computer-mediated technologies create important sites of identity play and construction. For example, some media scholars assert that the Internet's affordance of text-based interaction is key because it allows people to construct identities without having to situate them within existing bodies. Additionally, the Internet affords a space in which one can interact with a multitude of anonymous others, offering a "public arena where people feel they can 'privately' engage in identity work."[30] Some scholars have argued that this anonymity is particularly important; one study of teens online found that the anonymity of the Internet turned attention inward and that this, combined with the narrative nature of online interaction made it an active site of identity construction.[31] Amy Bruckman theorizes that the Internet allows people to try out, emphasize, and experience new or different aspects of their self, and that the very structure and features of the Internet, as text-based and anonymous, make it an "identity workshop."[32]

IDENTITY WORKSHOP

A space, offline or virtual, that encourages the development of new or transformed identities by fostering identity exploration, play, and adoption.

Of course, we don't do identity work alone. The Internet encompasses a collection of "virtual communities" where individuals interact in collective publics, but do so without necessarily revealing their offline identities, thereby lowering risk of stigma, sanction, and violence.[33] Combined with its continuous availability and relative affordability, this makes the Internet an institutional context primed for identity exploration. As scholar Darryl Hill summarizes, "we come to know ourselves by seeing ourselves reflected back to us through information and communication technology in a way never available before."[34]

We must avoid idealizing online interaction, however, or viewing *all* identity play as significant and radical. Sometimes play is just play, and the creation of new and different identities online can be insignificant. This is similar to how not all drag performance is an assertion of transgender identity; the common practice of dressing in drag for Halloween is usually unrelated to a person's embodied gender. In the same way, not all gendered behavior online is reflective of a "real" or even desired offline gendered self. The diverse array of online identity assertions have a variety of relationships to offline embodied selves. It is the possibilities offered by computer-mediated communication that are so significant. The context-specific norms and social scripts within online communities matter in much the same way as they do in offline groups. Rules of authenticity are as different online as they are across different offline spaces, and the Internet can be a context that offers new opportunities to play with and sometimes adopt new identities. Blogger Chris Messina captured this sensibility best when he said, "[t]here is more potential today for individuals to change their destiny than there's been in ages."[35]

Bridging Online and Offline Identities

Theorist Sandy Stone reminds us that "virtual community originates in and must return to the physical."[36] Nobody lives entirely in cyberspace; people are always navigating between multiple worlds, bringing offline identities, experiences, and bodies to bear on online interactions, and vice versa.[37] While there is a gap between virtual and material selves, the two exist in a dialectical relationship, each shaping the other. Not only does our offline life shape how we construct our online selves, but our virtual selves in turn shape who we are in offline life.[38] Those of us who interact in both the material world and in cyberspace, then, have contemporary lives characterized by multiple individual selves that emerge and play out in different social spaces.[39] These multiple personas are not new to the Internet; individuals have always cultivated and experienced a variety of identities shaped by the social and interpersonal demands of a variety of situations.[40] The Internet is just a new space, among many already established ones, in which individuals construct their lives in multiple ways through narrative, or "story."[41]

Narrative Identity, Discourses-in-Practice and Discursive Practices

Social psychologists Holstein and Gubrium ground their theory of identity development in the idea that identities are not something people are born with, but rather are created through the process of narrating one's life within a social context. We tell stories about who we are, and in the process figure out how to understand our experiences and develop a sense of self-continuity, even as new experiences and events change our identities and selves. This practice is what Holstein and Gubrium call "narrative identity." In their prolific work, Holstein and Gubrium use this concept to investigate how individuals develop and make sense of identities throughout their lives.

NARRATIVE IDENTITY

A theory of how individuals create an ever-changing sense of self-identity in the process of telling the stories that make up their lives. As new experiences shape the stories people tell about who they are, they come to think of themselves in new ways, engaging in an ongoing cycle of self-identification.

Life is an ongoing process of creating and recreating stories of who we are. These stories are not dreamt out of nothing, though. As Holstein and Gubrium explain, individuals "artfully pick and choose from what is experientially available to articulate their lives and experiences."[42] An individual's available accounts are the resources from which they construct identities and selves in culturally legible ways. For example, in order for a person to "story" why they became a doctor, they are likely to describe a life-long interest in helping people, because as a society we hold that story in high esteem and discredit stories about profiteering or experiencing a divine calling (which are other possible explanations). And yet these stories, or scripts, are not stamps that mold uniform identities and selves out of once differing people. In fact, these scripts are rewritten, modified, defied, and reconstructed by individuals, communities, and whole societies in the process of self-identification, social change, and technological innovation.

If we, as individuals, story our identities into being, we do so using the resources at our disposal and within the particular social and institutional contexts we have available, including school, family, and virtual communities. We look to these communities to provide a set of legitimized scripts. When starting college, for example, entrance into this new institutional setting is often marked by a shift in young adults' self-identity. College is an identity workshop that encourages students' development with increased anonymity, distance from parents, exposure to new experiences and access to new communities. Participation in structures that specifically encourage new identity formation, such as picking a major or joining a fraternity or sorority, all encourage young people to redefine themselves. And as part of redefining ourselves, we draw on the multitude of experiences we have had in our life, what Holstein and Gubrium call "resources," and pick particular incidents to highlight. Consider your own experience; while you likely participated in hundreds of different activities in high school, you talk about some more than others, assigning them differing levels of importance in shaping who you are. And, what is important now is likely to have evolved from what was important to you during high school. Part of why you highlight some activities and interests and not others is because they help you define and validate who you are at this point in your life. As your identity changes, the choices of which stories to highlight change as well, and these stories are tailored to the social contexts in which you present them.

In my own life, I have been and become many things: a designer, a lesbian, a researcher, an actor, a drag king, a mother, a feminist. I learned how to narrate each of these new identities, telling the story to myself and to others of how I was born and became this particular self. I did this, as we all do, in order to be viewed as authentic in each of these identities. I mined the stories of my own life for those that would bring context to and substantiate each of these identities, choosing to tell of my artist-mother, my first childhood crush on a girl, my scholar-father, my involvement in theater, my life-long gender nonconformity, my nurturing nature, or my activist spirit. I learned how to talk about myself as these different selves in ways that resonated with various other similarly identified individuals, and through this process solidified the pieces that make up "who I am."

Storying Ourselves into Being

Holstein and Gubrium contend that people create the story of who they are by using the narratives valued in a particular community or context, what they call "discourses-in-practice."

DISCOURSES-IN-PRACTICE
The social scripts from which individuals construct a legible identity.

The experience of sharing one's story in a group, for example, affords practice at appropriate presentation in the context of that group, and at constructing a story that satisfies both the individual's need to substantiate their own experience and the group's need to relate to the narrative. These narratives are accepted as assertions of self through modes of storytelling, or "discursive practices."

DISCURSIVE PRACTICES
How the self is constructed through storytelling processes and procedures.

For example, in her study of domestic violence, Donileen Loseke found that when women in violent situations seek social support, they encounter specific domestic violence narratives. In the process of getting help they are asked to produce their own story of abuse in a way that aligns with these social scripts. While creating their personal narrative that may be shared, for example in a support group meeting, individuals work to fit their own complex array of experiences into the established patterns.[43] In the process of fitting their story into the expected form, their individual identity is shaped by the social scripts dominant in this social context, and shaped too by the personal experiences of the individual. In Loseke's example, the specific discourses-in-practice of how an individual should make sense of and respond to domestic violence included a narrative that moves from serious violence to taking responsibility and control to holding strong even though "it won't be easy." In her study, when individual stories did not fit into this pattern, into the accepted discourses-in-practice, they lacked resonance with the group. In these cases facilitators and other participants were not as supportive or sympathetic to new group members, or otherwise expressed doubts about the abuse or the organization's ability to help. Developing a legible identity in line with a group's discourses-in-practice was essential for individuals to be seen and welcomed into a group.

Alongside these discourses-in-practice, domestic violence support groups provided new members with particular discursive practices that helped individuals to learn and adopt the context-specific discourses. As Loseke summarized:

> The institutional technologies of narrative work in these places are subtle techniques such as asking questions, rephrasing stories, ignoring some aspects of women's stories and dramatizing other aspects. Women's stories in these groups are interactionally shaped in ways compatible with the discursive environment informed by the formula story of wife abuse.[44]

In the process of learning how to tell one's story and taking advantage of the opportunities to do so, individuals developed a new "battered woman" identity that was in line with the social scripts privileged within the groups. The resulting self-stories, built out of group social scripts, were not untrue: they reflected the experiences and self-understanding of each individual. They were, however, shaped to resonate with the discourses valued by both the individual and the group. In other words, people learned to tell their story in a particular way and this telling reshaped how they thought of themselves and how they were seen by others.

The process described by Loseke occurs in most, if not all, groups. While everyone has their own personal history, people use a group's discourses-in-practice (established social scripts) in order to produce authentic, legible stories. Ultimately, identity is produced in groups through "the constellation of procedures, conditions, and resources through which reality . . . is apprehended, understood, organized, and represented in the course of everyday life."[45] Discourses-in-practice and discursive practices are mechanisms by which identity work is done, and Holstein and Gubrium use these concepts to theorize how dominant paradigms and social scripts affect individual identity.[46]

Re-storying Ourselves into New Ways of Being

The process of re-storying one's life necessarily produces new identities that reflect the available social identity scripts of a particular time and place. But, it is not a rote stamping process, as social psychologist Douglas Mason-Schrock notes:

> In this process of sense-making through story, the master patterns are adapted, modified, and later passed on in slightly altered form. Variations multiply, and so does the number of possible selves. And as lives are fitted to stories, lives may be led differently and new stories thereby created.[47]

When we tell stories of who we are, we adapt them to our needs. This process transforms the discourses-in-practice that we draw on to construct our storied selves.

Holstein and Gubrium's theory of narrative identity explains how we use the storytelling norms and patterns of a group (discursive practices) to fit our own biographical details into existing narratives (discourses-in-practice). We can see these processes at work in Douglas Mason-Schrock's research on a support group for gender nonconforming individuals. In this study of how people storied their changing identities, Schrock found that individuals learned and practiced how to fit their own biographies into established narratives of authentic trans* selves within support groups. He summarized this process in the following way:

> Narratives were maintained and transferred to new members largely through *modeling*. In this process, first of all, those transsexuals who were adept at telling self-narratives did so voluntarily. In telling their stories, they gave the new members clues about the types of significant events to look for in their own biographies. If the newcomers listened closely, they could find the rhetorical tools that could be used, with some slight alterations, to signify their own differently gendered "true self."[48]

Group members shared tools for identity work, which helped new members to create authentic and acceptable trans* selves. This process does not simply stamp discourses-in-practice onto individual lives; people take cues for producing authentic identities from the available discourses, and mold them to their own lives and stories.

This storying does not make these identities artificial; this is the same process that we all go through in developing and refining our identities. While this collective identity construction process might seem inauthentic or suspect when we observe it in a gender nonconforming group, one must remember that we assign a benign naturalness to these very processes when they conform to hegemonic norms. The development of cisgender identities (e.g., growing up from boy to man) is normalized and therefore accepted as inevitable, natural, and biological. In contrast, we require explanation for non-normative genders, viewing their development with suspicion and critique.

While *everyone* engages in discursive practices and uses discourses-in-practice in the process of constructing and refining gender identities, these acts are rendered invisible when they match normative social scripts. It is possible, however, to tease out how gender paradigms lead to particular discourses-in-practice by engaging a sociological analysis. For example, in her study of middle-school sex education, Jessica Fields examined how young people are given a language and conceptual framework for making sense of their own embodied gender and sexuality through middle-school health and sex education classes.[49] In the process of teaching sexuality curriculum, teachers communicate to students the dominant discourses-in-practice for gender: what it means to be a man, what sexual attraction feels like in the body, what men and women desire, etc. These discourses normalize and naturalize particular experiences of puberty (heterosexual desire), gender development (girls becoming women), and gendered interaction (boys/men want sex, girls/women want love), while ignoring others. In the process of engaging in class discussion, self-reflective writing, and class activities, students practice and internalize these discourses (discursive practices). In other words, as an identity workshop, schools are active participants in gender identity work for students in the process of teaching class content. By and large, schools cultivate normative genders and sexualities, yet these social scripts for gender are so pervasive, so naturalized, that they disappear. It is only when we focus attention directly on these dynamics that they become visible. Perhaps twentieth century literary critic Marshall McLuhan, who philosophized about how technology would change society, said it best: "Fish don't know water exists till beached."[50]

The available scripts from which individuals construct a gendered self come from a variety of sources. In addition to group and community storytelling, other invested parties construct scripts as well. One consequence of regarding trans* as a pathologized set of identities is that the medical community has been allowed to appoint itself gatekeeper for psycho-medical treatment. For much of the last 75 years, in order for individuals to gain access to gender affirming services, they were required to produce a very particular narrative about their life history and future desires. Not surprisingly, this acceptable script reinforced hegemonic gender norms: that there are only two opposing genders, and that one's gender is innate. The necessity of learning and telling this particular "transsexual" narrative has reinforced its validity as a social script; the dominance of this discourse-in-practice is the product of processes of medicalization that have privileged one particular story and discouraged other narratives. Now, as shifting social paradigms and technological developments change the relationship between medicine and the trans* community, the available and legitimate identities that trans* people story into being will continue to transform as well.

Narrative Identity Online

Existing work on behavior and identity suggests that individuals strive for consistency between who they are and how they behave, and that behavioral changes affect individuals' sense of self and identity.[51] Individuals develop identities and a sense of self through interaction with others and through the support or sanction of associated behaviors.[52] It is not a far leap to think that interacting with others in virtual spaces or through avatars might affect our real-world selves. A number of scholars have explored identity work online and have found that when we tell different narratives about who we are in virtual spaces, and behave differently than we do offline, those changes in online self-representations (aka avatars) affect our offline behaviors and self-perceptions.[53] An affordance of virtual worlds is that individuals can develop an avatar that they see as an extension of themselves ("avatar identification") and use it to interact with others. Research suggests that in the process of using their avatar online, people transfer expectations or understanding of their avatar's behavior to their own offline behavior, thus creating a feedback loop between their online and offline selves. This remarkable dynamic is called the "Proteus effect" (named after the shape shifting Greek god). In one study, the researchers who pioneered this work found that individuals who watched their avatar running on a treadmill had higher levels of physical activity offline in the following 24 hours.[54] In other words, engaging in virtual activity online affected whether individuals engaged in physical activity offline.

In an effort to harness the possibilities of the Proteus effect, business, therapeutic, and healthcare industries are using MMUVEs to administer social, psychological, and physiological health interventions alongside or in place of non-virtual ones. For example, the national fitness company Club One created a virtual club in Second Life, out of which it experimented with a 12-week program to help individuals to lose weight and to lower their risk of diabetes. This virtual program was similar to the offline health intervention that Club One offered to members.[55] Second Life participants attended online classes on health and nutrition, and support groups all through their avatars. Often, during these activities their avatars would be shown working out (swimming, for example) or eating (at the Club One restaurant used to teach about nutrition). While offline individuals might be sitting on their couch at home, their avatar would be moving as if it were exercising or eating at a measured pace in Second Life. What preliminary research on this program found was that engaging in these activities through a virtual self actually helped participants to manifest these changes in their embodied lives and transform their embodied self-concepts. As one participant said: "If I didn't have an avatar I would not be moving around, feeling so good about my body. Watching my avatar has changed me. It has sparked a shift in my brain, helping me make healthier decisions naturally." Second Life participants lost more weight, made more lifestyle changes and improved their overall health compared to a face-to-face program with identical content; their virtual presence in Second Life appears to have been essential to these changes.

The Impact of Online Activity on the Self

Every day, millions of users interact with each other via graphical avatars in real-time online games, groups, and communities. These activities can change how individuals behave, and can even radically transform their embodied identities.[56] Computer-mediated communication has made intentional self-presentation and transformation accessible, quick, and impermanent, and this mutability is one of the key features of virtual interaction.[57] Affordances such as the feeling of being present in an online space through an avatar ("presence"), an architecture of participation, flexibility, and real-time interaction all enable and encourage new social norms and scripts for embodied selves, including new gendered self-concepts.

Consider one example of gender in online support groups. Men and women behave very differently in support groups. Women tend to seek and demonstrate friendship, emotionality, and support, while men share information, organize meetings with experts, and develop plans of action. These behaviors are in line with dominant gender norms for men and women. Sociologist Clive Seale researched behavior in online support group communities to find out whether the anonymity of the Internet changed these dynamics. Seale examined the stories of men and women who participated in online cancer support groups dominated by another gender (i.e. women in prostate support groups and men in breast cancer ones). What he found was that men in these groups began to behave in ways that ran counter to hegemonic masculinity's focus on emotional control and distance. Men experienced increased emotionality and tenderness after joining a support group, and many embraced these new behaviors as valuable deviations from traditional masculinity. The new behaviors were clearly meaningful for these men beyond fitting in online; men described how their "selves" changed in response to both their experiences of cancer and their participation in the online support group. Seale quotes one participant who wrote:

> I suppose it is a fact that some men find it hard to get [emotion] across as well as they should! Me, after all we went through, it has left me with some sort of feeling of opening up more and just saying whatever I feel. This thing has some strange side effects on emotions that I don't think you can read or learn about other than experience them personally.[58]

It is particularly interesting that these same gendered changes were *not* reported in studies of *offline* support groups for men partners of women with breast cancer. This identity shift toward a non-normative masculinity does not appear to happen in traditional offline forums.

Seale draws the conclusion that "individuals may be using the relative freedom of the Internet to enact forms of masculinity and femininity deviating from the stereotyped gendered norms."[59] For the men in Clive Seale's study, the Internet facilitated the creation and adoption of new gender identity scripts because of its unique affordances.

Individual and Collective Identity Development Online

The Internet is transformative for both individuals and society. Not only does the Internet function as a place to develop non-hegemonic gender identities, but social changes and new technologies are facilitating the development and disbursement of new gender scripts in society.[60]

The process of learning and publicly embodying a new gender identity—normative or nonconforming—is an identity change born of intentional narrative construction. What the Internet affords is not the ability to create false, disembodied identities, but rather a new institutional context and set of affordances that support identity work. The actual gender identity work that individuals do online is no different from the work previously done in therapists' offices, support groups, and subcultural communities; the differences lie in the number of individuals who can participate, the ease of access to new groups and communities online, and the ability to act freely because the anonymity of virtual communication mitigates stigma.

The increased communication among trans* people, a product of computer-mediated communication, has fostered the sharing and refining of discourses-in-practice and discursive practices. For example, on many public trans* blogs and social networking groups, the types of information that individuals share runs the gamut from tips for gaining access to psycho-medical treatment and gender affirming body modification to life histories in which individuals produce and police appropriate discourses-in-practice. This practice of sharing life histories is an opportunity for individuals to learn and deploy the discourses-in-practice required to construct a socially legible trans* self. It also offers the trans* community at large a place to refine, challenge, and change the discursive practices used to construct and delineate authentic trans* identities.

A number of studies about gender identity work online have found that, in online communities, participants "collectively foster solidarity and authenticity by creating and telling self-narratives . . . newcomers learn how to tell authenticating stories by modeling and be[ing] guided by seasoned group members."[61] Examining this phenomenon Darryl Hill collected life histories from members of the Toronto, Canada, transgender community and found that the majority of them thought the Internet played a crucial part in their gender identity development. One example of the type of experience that Hill recorded comes from Melissa:

> I got on the Internet, and the first thing I did, you know, was talk to anybody I could talk to about it [transgenderism] . . . I wanted to talk to anybody or anything I could, just to get some kind of rationale behind it, the vocabulary, do something with it . . . To build a story, to build a way to talk about it . . . it was something I could never do before.[62]

Melissa explicitly talks about looking for the vocabulary and available scripts to help her build her own story of trans* experience. Melissa described to Hill the active and intentional construction of new personal, and ultimately social, discursive practices and discourses-in-practice for gender identity construction. It's not that Melissa's gender came from this group, but instead that she was able to learn and adopt the narrative practices that made her gender legible and authentic within the group and society at large.

Information technologies have helped individuals to learn, practice, and adopt new gender identity scripts, to learn about whether and how they want to shape their body as authentic trans* individuals, and has offered new—and often more accepting—gender paradigms with which people can make sense of the world. In turn, the increased diversity of gender identities and bodies visible in society—online and offline—has fueled ongoing trans*-inclusive social and cultural changes, techno-logical developments, and the acceptance of gender nonconforming individuals and communities.

Collective Identity Work Online: Negotiating Social Scripts

The impact of developing and acquiring new social scripts for gender in online groups and communities goes beyond the basic elements of ease, anonymity, and collectivity. The Internet has enabled the trans* community to reframe the existing limited pathological narratives of trans* selfhood, and develop new or transformed gender scripts outside of medical and psychological control. In other words, this technology has provoked change in social norms and scripts as well as in indi-vidual identity. While the last 50 years of twentieth century gender nonconformity in North America were dominated by medical and psy-chological discourses, the last 15 years have seen successful resistance to pathologizing narratives. The Internet has allowed transgender people to challenge medical identity scripts and to answer back to power-holders who police transgender narratives and control access to hormones and to gender affirming surgery. Online, individuals can share personal narratives that counter dominant medicalized scripts, share information about doctors and treatments, and advocate for changes in medical and social rights. The result has been that online trans* communities have been able to broaden the available identity narratives for transgender people. It is not that transgender communities did not rebel before the Internet, but rather that the Internet has made the personal and collec-tive impact of these engagements exponentially greater.

Let us compare two protests, similar in most respects except that one was able to use the Internet to mobilize; the differences in the results are striking. In 1993 the American Psychiatric Association (APA), the gov-erning body that sets diagnostic and treatment standards for psychiatric practitioners, held its convention in San Francisco.[63] The APA meetings inspired protest from the trans* community over the inclusion of GID in the *Diagnostic and Statistical Manual of Mental Disorders* (DSM), the ref-erence that psychologists rely on to diagnose mental illness.[64] A number of trans* rights activists spoke with APA attendees inside the conference, while a direct-action group named Transgender Nation[65] took responsibility for organizing a vibrant protest outside that culminated in the arrest of several activists. The protesters' message was exceedingly clear; a spray-painted message on the side of the convention center put it succinctly: "APA go away, transgender liberation now."[66] This 1993 protest was modestly significant. Certainly for San Francisco-based trans* activists it was a moment of solidarity, empowerment, and community building, and the protest garnered limited media coverage.[67] That said, the direct impact of the protest was limited for both trans* communities and most trans* individuals; as far as change in the psychiatric community, the APA did not even issue a formal response.

Fifteen years later, in the spring of 2008, trans* activists sought to intervene in the appointment of Kenneth Zucker as chair of the APA's Sexual and Gender Identity Disorders (GID) working group. This group was to revise GID in the fifth edition of the DSM. Toronto-based clinician Zucker advocated for aggressively pursuing "cures" for gender nonconformity in childhood. Zucker's methods, lauded by anti-gay organizations,[68] included removing "wrong-gender" toys, forcing single-gender play, and encouraging self and peer policing of behavior, desire, presentation, and identity.[69]

The extent to which parents and children are encouraged to fight against any inkling of desire for "wrong gender" toys, colors, desires, and lives is striking. Beliefs such as pink being "naturally" a girls' color and more generally that gender norms need to remain rigidly dimorphic underlie this compulsive resistance. Perhaps the most menacing judgments fundamental to this approach are that being "normally" gendered is more important than self-concept or happiness, and that being gender nonconforming is inherently pathological. The mother of one of Zucker's patients, profiled in a 2010 NPR interview, reflected that her son Bradley, "really struggles with the color pink. He can't even really look at pink . . . He's like an addict. He's like, 'Mommy, don't take me there! Close my eyes! Cover my eyes! I can't see that stuff; it's all pink!'"[70] For Zucker, liking pink portends gender disaster for young boys, but Bradley's distress is the direct result of Zucker's reparative therapy. Zucker recommended treatment for Bradley on the basis of one criterion: that Bradley's desires were not in line with normative gender scripts.

Given Zucker's efforts to "cure" gender nonconformity in children, it is no surprise that people organized to oppose his leadership of the APA's Sexual and Gender Identity Disorders working group. As part of this opposition, online networks were quickly abuzz with discussions about how to challenge Zucker's appointment. Discussion groups debated different approaches and shared information about Zucker's practices. Individuals wrote and posted articles, essays, and reflections on their own blogs and in a diverse array of transgender and LGBT community online forums. Organizations with strong online presences jumped to write and circulate petitions targeted at the APA.[71] The largest petition generated more than 3,500 signatures in the first week, and almost 10,000 in a three-month period. A September 2013 Internet search for the petition turned up more than two million websites that discussed it, including the mainstream information clearinghouse Wikipedia. While activists and allies posted YouTube videos about Zucker and the petition, news outlets including NPR and the *New York Times* ran print stories.[72] LGBT organizations released press statements against Zucker's appointment, and non-transgender blogs and communities posted information about the petition. In other words, the response to Zucker's appointment began online and spread rapidly and meaningfully to a diverse set of communities, and this outcry was loud enough to elicit press releases and formal statements from the APA.[73]

While it is impossible to prove causality between these efforts and the final revisions to GID in the DSM-V, this mobilization certainly affected the debate. After several rounds of proposed changes and public comment the final revisions to GID in the DSM were released in May 2013: the changes are profound. Perhaps the most obvious alteration is a renaming—from Gender Identity Disorder to Gender Dysphoria (in childhood or adulthood). While the initial proposed changes to GID in childhood—the committee headed by Zucker—were modest, the final proposal includes substantial change for both children and adults.

Most significantly, gender nonconformity is not in and of itself cause for pathologization. Instead, Gender Dysphoria is only diagnosed in the presence of distress; it is not the gender nonconformity that warrants psycho-medical treatment, but the distress it may cause to a person trying to navigate life while embodying a nonconforming gender. Moreover, the proposed revisions make space for genders outside of binary cisgender formations. For example, the former criterion of "[r]epeatedly stated desire to be, or insistence that he or she is, the other sex,"[74] is to be revised to "a strong desire to be of the other gender (or some alternative gender different from one's assigned gender)."[75] Transgender activists and allies have clearly managed substantive influence within the DSM revision process. Indeed, the APA issued a press release about Gender Dysphoria in the DSM-V that directly addressed many issues raised by trans* communities and activists, including the need to de-stigmatize gender nonconformity, to maintain access to care and insurance coverage, and to separate out gender nonconformity from the diagnostic category of "Sexual Dysfunctions and Paraphilic Disorders." That same press release acknowledged the wider import of these changes, noting that the "DSM not only determines how mental disorders are defined and diagnosed, it also impacts how people see themselves and how we see each other."[76]

Comparisons of these two protests offer a clear example of how individuals use technologies to shape dominant ideologies and available social scripts for gendered bodies and identities. Transgender activists used online technologies, and the unique assets they provided, to influence the medicalization of gender nonconformity. Simultaneously, these new ideologies, disseminated through technology, influence the social context within which trans* movements and individuals advocate for rights and recognition. More people were able to learn about and participate in debate over GID and its presence in the DSM in 2008 than in 1993, in part because technologies were available that lessened the impact of geographical isolation, stigma, and medicalization. At the same time, trans*-positive social changes over the last 15 years—partly facilitated by technological advances—have created an environment more receptive to trans* issues, and community organizing. And all of this has expanded available cultural gender scripts for whom individuals can be and what gendered embodiments are seen as authentic.

One product of these cultural changes has been a shift in dominant gender paradigms. As trans* individuals have participated in more community organizing they have taken a more prominent place within LGBT organizing, have come out in greater numbers, and have more successfully advocated for social recognition and social and civil rights. Public access to information and familiarity with trans* lives and civil rights issues is greater than ever before. Outspoken trans* activists and cisgender allies have challenged transphobia in the workplace, in law, and in popular culture. The development of a national trans* movement and the ensuing publicity, advocacy, support, and validation that the movement created have changed the social context within which we all live. Cisgender individuals have also benefited from easier access to information regarding gender nonconformity.[77] Most college students now have a working knowledge of trans* lives and issues; many report developing this knowledge, at least in part, online. These changes have altered the landscape within which gender nonconforming individuals negotiate their lives and identities.

Reproducing and Rewriting Social Scripts

While new technologies have been central in trans* organizing and community building and have supported the development of new gender paradigms, new technologies are also being used to maintain and support normative gender paradigms and identities. Like the invisibility of normative gender identity work offline, much of this normalizing activity takes place in the process of everyday interaction online. Both cisgender and trans* individuals use online spaces to do identity work and social networking sites, web chat rooms and discussion boards are particularly suited for constructing and substantiating gender identities (see Case Study 5).[78] Many of these commonplace online interactions are sites of identity work in ways that reinforce hegemonic gender ideologies.[79]

In her study of "BlueSky," Lori Kendall found that men in social chat rooms actively worked to (re)produce hegemonic masculinity and assert positive masculine identities despite the emasculating effects of "nerdiness." For the self-described nerds Kendall studied, constructing a normative masculinity online was one way to counter the stigma of offline gender nonconformity. The way many nerds did this was by drawing on dominant discourses-in-practice for heterosexual masculinity: objectifying women, talking about sex and sexual prowess, and by displaying knowledge about typically masculine endeavors like sports and mechanics. The nerd's displays of hegemonic masculinity and the use of masculine interaction styles pervaded online social spaces, and the discourses-in-practice were deeply racialized and gendered. Kendall recounts one instance where several regulars used sexual prowess and the sexual objectification of women to establish themselves as men. She highlights this exchange:

> Mender says "did I mention the secretary babe smiled at me today"
> Roger Pollack says "WOO WOO"
> Jet says "cool Mender"
> Jet says "did you spike 'er"
> Mender says "no, sir, I did not spike 'er."

In this interaction, talking about women as babes, turning immediately to a sexual question and objectifying women in the process are all tactics used by Mender, Roger, and Jet to assert masculine identities. As Kendall concludes, "the ironic sexism of much BlueSky discourse maintains 'the order of gender domination' (Lyman 1998: 172), almost irrespective of other aspects of BlueSky men's activities and behaviors with and toward the women in their lives."[80] In Kendall's examples from "BlueSky," established gender scripts pair with dominant gender paradigms to shape how technologies are used and shape the identities cultivated through these computer-mediated communications.

While hegemonic masculinity was reproduced in "BlueSky," the creation of new counter-hegemonic scripts also takes place online, and these new scripts ultimately facilitate new counter-hegemonic identities. Online chatrooms and games can be a place where teenagers try on and adopt new gendered selves. One study of Canadian girls aged

13–15 found that girls use online chat rooms, role-playing games, and social networking and messaging to try on new femininities before enacting them in the rest of their life.[81] In their study of both gender conforming and gender nonconforming girls, Deirdre Kelly, Shauna Pomerantz, and Dawn Currie "found girls bending and switching gender to improvise nonconformist femininities and to learn to express parts of themselves, such as aggression and sexual desire, that they had been made to feel were taboo offline."[82] Girls described learning to take romantic initiative with boys, resist sexual harassment, and do non-normative femininity:

> Shale and her friend Rose used Internet chat rooms to challenge emphasized femininity and perform a rebellious femininity. They delighted in annoying girls with ultra-feminine online names like Sweet Flower Petal and dreamed of hacking onto "small Web sites with the Hello Kitty buttons and saying, 'You've been hit by Cookie the Bloody WhaHaHa'."[83]

While online spaces can be sexist alongside offline ones, many girls felt more empowered to try on new and non-normative identities online, and more able to speak back to sexual harassment and sexist behavior. And these online practices empowered them to carry these behaviors and identities offline.

It is clear that gender is being done—and undone—by people and groups in a variety of technologically mediated locations. Support groups, romance/dating websites, and a myriad of other sites of identity work are rife with individuals using information technologies to engage in gender identity and body work. Sometimes this engagement is intentional and transformative (as in trans* support groups) and sometimes it serves to reinforce existing gender identities (as in romance/dating sites) or assert positive reformulations of marginalized identities (as in girls' identity work online). Regardless of focus, online spaces are active and agentic sites of both personal identity development and social script elaboration and extension.

STRUCTURAL INEQUALITY

Unequal opportunities, rewards or sanctions set in motion on the basis of an individual's social status or group membership rather than through individual action or initiative. These unequal social benefits or consequences are the outcome of the everyday function of social institutions, as opposed to the prejudice of individuals.

Reproducing Inequality Online

Alongside the creation of new social scripts and identities, individuals continue to reproduce social inequalities that are written into established scripts for behavior, identity, and embodiment. The utopian suggestion that as people "moved online" they would cast off gender, race, class, or other embodied characteristics ignores the fact that biases such as racism, sexism, and "ableism" are not only individual prejudices but also structural inequalities.[84]

Assertions that prejudice disappears in cyberspace inadvertently naturalizes its occurrence in the physical world by suggesting that the inequalities that exist there are inevitable. The fact is, race, class, and gender hegemony are manifest both through intentional discrimination and through social structures that reproduce inequality and construct default assumptions about what is normal, good, and desirable.

The average height for both male and female avatars in Second Life is over 6 feet, and almost all bodies are underweight and white. Given the demographics of North America and the self-reported participation rates within gender, race, and age categories, this is far from an accurate reflection of the offline identities and bodies of participants. In early versions of Second Life it was almost impossible to create non-white avatars, and while the set of available choices has expanded greatly over the last few years, the domain is still set up in a way that reinforces hegemonic beliefs by representing white features and skin tones as normal and natural, and non-white features as atypical, outside of the norm, and perhaps undesirable or even proscriptive. Many "skins" are available only in light skin tones, and do not allow you to adjust facial features to reflect phenotypically non-white characteristics such as a broad nose, or lack of an epicanthic eyelid fold. This phenomenon of normalizing white qualities is not isolated within Second Life; research on other virtual worlds as well as more generalist online spaces suggests that the very structure of online spaces reproduce racial hierarchies. Designers create drop down menus, avatars and virtual worlds using their own learned racialized scripts for embodiment, ultimately reproducing racial divisions and inequities through the choices and options available to users.[85]

What does the limited availability to portray non-white identities reveal about how deeply racialized hegemonic norms are integrated into our identities and beliefs as individuals and as a society? If you can be anyone online, why would people independently but intentionally produce only a narrow range of hegemonically normative bodies? And when creating a world in which people are encouraged to expand their identities and horizons, why would designers limit the choices for nonconformity? When I asked Second Life participants these questions, most responded that if you could be anyone, why not be what everyone desires—why not be the ideal? At the most basic, this offers a clear example of how dominant gender and racial identity paradigms shape people's desires and the identity choices that they make.

There is another layer of significance, though; if the ideal—who we *should* want to be—is thin, white, tall, able-bodied, and normatively gendered, are we really leaving prejudice behind and charting new identity territory online? Lisa Nakamura, one of the foremost scholars of race and racism online, thinks not. Thinking about the geographies of virtual reality, she highlights that, even if online spaces aren't explicitly racialized, "when players choose blackness, whiteness, or brownness . . . users *voluntarily* create racialized space."[86] What Nakamura finds in her research is that in the process of constructing online avatars people are reproducing racialized inequalities. Ultimately, online forums provide spaces for both individual identity work and for the reproduction of social inequalities and hegemonic norms.[87]

It is not just individual choice that encourages online racial homogeneity, however. As is the case in the corporeal world, there are sanctions for deviating from the racialized norm in online spaces; one way individuals may be penalized is through harassment. For example, many people of color who participate in an MMUVE report experiences of overt racism that range from name calling and refusal to engage in conversation to acts of cyberviolence where avatars are attacked.[88] Similarly, many feminine avatars possessing non-normative characteristics such as portliness, small breasts, or short stature report misogynist interactions. In a recent study Paul Eastwick and Wendi Gardner examined interaction in the online virtual world There.com, and found that there was a statistically significant decrease in the willingness of participants to help dark-skinned avatars, "implying that reciprocity concerns took on greater importance when the requesting avatar was light-skinned." In other words, Eastwick and Gardner found that racially biased behavior is produced online in much the same way it is offline, and that "real-world racial biases, as they are inextricably intertwined with the rest of the human social mind, may also emerge in virtual environments."[89]

In addition to personal harassment, the very structures of most virtual worlds reinforce hegemonic beliefs. In fact, whiteness is so taken for granted that it is hard to know how many avatars of color there are in virtual worlds because race is not among the demographic characteristics that have been tracked (while, in contrast, age and gender are tracked). Similarly, there are few groups or community spaces for communities of color. In addition to reproducing hegemonic racism, most of the available skins and clothing fit poorly on fat or disabled bodies.[90] The inability to find skins, clothing, or even gestures that accommodate larger avatars reinforces the idea that normal equals thin and that no one should or would want to be fat. One scholar and Second Life participant, Marissa Ashkenaz, conducted an informal study in Second Life, asking eight people to spend one week as fat avatars and to keep a journal about their experiences.[91] What Ashkenaz found was that not only were individuals unable to find hair, skins, or clothing that fit their bodies, they had a hard time getting others to engage in social interactions and were often ignored. Some even experienced significant overt harassment from other participants. Like race, participants bring social scripts for normative body size and attractiveness into virtual worlds and scorn bodies that fall outside of these norms.

Lisa Nakamura calls the reproduction of stereotypes online "cybertyping" and suggests that existing inequalities are written into information technologies in a variety of ways. Not only do people practice prejudicial behavior online, the structures of online spaces themselves (like the lack of racial categories available in surveys) construct and reproduce racial difference and inequality. Most significantly, however, Nakamura highlights how the Internet can be used for "identity tourism" wherein people reduce race to skin color and take on highly stereotypical racialized characters. A popular one, for example, is the Japanese geisha.

IDENTITY TOURISM

Taking on racialized, gendered, classed, or national identities in cyberspace without recognizing the offline circumstances and disadvantages of these social statuses.[92]

Nakamura argues that just as offline tourists in "exotic" places see a sanitized view of "native" life, online identity tourists "use race and gender as amusing prostheses to be donned and shed without 'real-life' consequences."[93] This reduces race and other embodied social statuses to seemingly meaningless features devoid of real consequence, which in turn perpetuates social beliefs that racism, sexism, and other bigotries do not exist online.

One danger of the Internet, then, might be the ability to play at other identities without an awareness of the lived experiences and inequalities that are part of that offline identity. Even when white individuals report experiencing racism when in "blackface," the way they make sense of those experiences and their significance is shaped by privilege. James Wagner Au shared one woman's experience of identity tourism (wearing her friend's "black skin"). While the avatar, Erica, experienced repeated instances of overt racism, she was able to return to her "real" self and leave those epithets and the discrimination they attend behind. She felt that there were "better things to worry about" than this racism. Of course, there may be better things to worry about if your experience of race is one of play and exploration, and not one of lived experience and marginzalition.[94] By rendering race absent under the guise of color-blindness, the hegemony of whiteness is reinforced. While Second Life may be a place where some people can be anything, for people of color, the realities of structural and individual racism make the virtual world a difficult place to be an avatar of color.[95] Although online spaces can and do facilitate identity negotiation and transformation, they can also reproduce the inequalities and stereotypes that are written into existing identity paradigms and social scripts.

Navigating Gendered Identities and Bodies Online

How do we make sense, then, of the immense breadth of possibilities opened up by computer-mediated communication when juxtaposed against the simultaneous presence of narrow, limiting social scripts and racialized, cisgender ideologies that shape identity work online? Eastwick and Gardner end their article on racial bias in virtual interaction by quoting a participant at an offline reunion for members of There. com. This group member, reflecting on the significance of the community, stated: "It may be a virtual environment, but the interaction is real."[96] Much like gender, online interaction might not be real, but it is clearly real in its effects. These effects are shaped by social ideologies and identity scripts, sometimes mimicking and sometimes expanding those found offline.

While so much early Internet hype forecast that new online technologies would suddenly allow us to cast off the shackles of hegemonic gender, race, class, or sexuality and redefine ourselves in any way imaginable, this is not the case. Gender, race, and other embodied characteristics are more than personal identities; they are structural components imbedded in all interaction. They are the means through which individuals know who they are and with whom they are communicating, and as such they guide *all* communication. Instead of casting them off and becoming free floating entities, in the absence of their bodies people work even harder to substantiate themselves, and they often reconstruct normative identities in the process.[97]

While new technologies do shape bodies and identities, they do so within a social and historical context. Available scripts and identity paradigms mediate the production of new selves, and even when our physical bodies are not visible our experiences of them continue to house and provide authenticating resources for these identities. Our ability to use technologies to produce new identities, even when those identities are made available by new social scripts, is always filtered through our own experience. If, for example, our life experiences have produced a deep moral investment in the idea that gender is a natural expression of sex, then our awareness and acceptance of new gender scripts will likely be constrained. In contrast, if our biography has encouraged the interrogation of gender, perhaps because of our own gender nonconformity or exposure to people who question binary gender categories, we will likely be more receptive to expanded social scripts. It is still unclear, though, what the long-term effects of online social spaces will be on our offline gendered bodies and selves, and how we might create new ways of being that work outside of these normalizing forces.

In her groundbreaking essay about gender online, Jodi O'Brien takes up the question of whether and how online communication will complicate gender dichotomies. O'Brien asserts that because the gendered body is the means by which we make sense of social interaction it remains an organizing principle even in its absence. So while online communication may allow individuals to categorize themselves and others in the absence of physical cues, the Internet is not a space where the self and body cease to be mutually constitutive. Indeed, we do imagine an embodied self even when the body is not physically present.

Online identity work is both constrained by existing gender scripts, and generative of new ones. We must be recognizable to others if we hope to interact with them. As O'Brien elaborates:

> Even if it is possible for me to conceive and author characters that
> defy categorization along conventional lines, others cannot engage

in meaningful interaction with me ("meaningful" being defined here as mutually comprehensible and generative) unless they too know something about the "script" through which I am representing myself and/or characterizing the situation.[98]

Because we cannot proceed from introduction to interaction until we have been able to categorize the other person in a recognizable way, the ability to "be anything" online is limited by the ability to fit new selves into agreed upon social scripts.[99] O'Brien concludes:

> It is possible to mentally transgender or ungender oneself in one's own imagination. It is possible to enact and negotiate this re/ungendering through interactions with others. And it may be the case that this is easier to accomplish online. But this does not mean that an institutionalized gender binary—and its consequences—will necessarily cease to exist.[100]

Like other scholars mentioned in this chapter, O'Brien argues that new information technologies have the possibility to provide sites of counter-hegemonic identity work, but are not necessarily used to do so.

In the late 1990s, when O'Brien was writing this essay, online trans* communities were just coming together. The cautions she suggests in our approach to online communication are critical for making realistic sense of the radical gender potential—or lack thereof—in computer-mediated communication. That being said, the evolution of online communication over the last ten years suggests that there is a middle ground between utopian visions of a gender-free society, and O'Brien's "state of the 'net'" at the close of the twentieth century.

Online forums have significance in people's real lives; online community can mediate lack of support in the offline world, can provide tools to produce more legible gendered selves, and, over time, can change the offline cultural context within which we all live. The cumulative effect of all this may be the alteration and expansion of social gender scripts. Intentional identity work within gender-oriented communities was significant in the lives of the trans* individuals, in part because the expectation of individuals in these communities was that gender work was being done. Participants assumed that the gender of online compatriots was being intentionally negotiated and presented in ways that would transcend the online interactions and spill over into embodied lives. The way in which we use technology as well as the content we create within in it is shaped by dominant gender and racial ideologies. Although the Internet is not a utopian site of gender fluidity and play, it is a site where identity work can happen in meaningful ways, and where societal gender paradigms and scripts can be rewritten. The examination of online technologies in this chapter suggests that these forums are sites of new and transformed gender identity scripts, and that these scripts are changing individuals' gender identities.

Notes

1 Turkle 2011:12.
2 Oppenheimer 2014. He also found, not incidentally, dramatically more women in public spaces than in the 1970s.
3 Pew Internet and American Life Project Tracking surveys (March 2000–December 2012). Available at: www.pewinternet.org/Static-Pages/Trend-Data-(Adults).aspx and www.pewinternet.org/Static-Pages/Trend-Data-(Teens).aspx.
4 Ito et al. 2010.
5 Ibid.
6 Gibson 1982.
7 Lenhart et al. 2010.
8 Linden Research, Inc. 2009 and 2013.
9 In recent years there have been academic and popular press articles about the world of Second Life that cover nearly as much subject matter as the press deals with offline. Topics have included Second Life in relation to addiction, sex, teaching, business, team development, streaming sports events, law and copyright/intellectual property, lifelike clothing, harassment, ethical responsibility, Second Life libraries and librarians, cultural affinities (or lack thereof) for Second Life, medical and health education, and virtual consumption. Most recently numerous articles have focused on the fate of Second Life ten years in, and amid a rash of newer virtual spaces and technologies. And most of these highlight the significance of an online space that has held its own for a decade and which remains relevant. There is a book about the Second Life newspaper, the Second Life *Herald*, another on non-profit organizing in Second Life, and many articles have appeared in sources as diverse as *The Wall Street Journal*, *The Chronicle for Higher Education*, *Time* magazine, and *Phi Delta Kappans*, the magazine of the premier professional association for educators.
10 Pew Internet and American Life Project 2007.
11 Gartner Research 2007.
12 Stryker 2008: 146.

13 Madden 2006: 3.
14 All U.S. data is from Pew Internet and American Life Project. All surveys prior to March 2000 were conducted by the Pew Research Center for People and the Press. For Canadian statistics, see Middleton and Sorensen 2005.
15 O'Reilly 2003.
16 Myers 1994.
17 Cavanagh 2007; Earl and Kimport 2011; Hine 2000; Lin and Lundquist 2013; Orton-Johnson and Prior 2013; Shostak 1999; Smith and Kollock 1999.
18 Turkle 2011.
19 Agger 2008: 4.
20 Donath 1997; Jones 1995.
21 Carr 2011; Turkle 2011.
22 Jurgenson 2012.
23 Bruckman 1992; Kendall 2000; Kollock and Smith 1996; Mackinnon 1995, 1997 and 1998; Phillips 1996; Ray 2007.
24 Hutchby 2001.
25 Morozov 2013: 166.
26 Fisher 1998: 158–159.
27 boyd 2008.
28 Snow and Anderson 1987: 1,348.
29 Bruckman 1993; Burris and Hoplight 1996; Dickel 1995; Gergen 1991 and 2009; Hill 2005; Poster 1995; Turkle 1995 and 2011.
30 Broad and Joos 2004: 926.
31 Zhao 2005.
32 Bruckman 1992.
33 Fox and Roberts 1999; Rheingold 1993b.
34 Hill 2005: 28.
35 Frost 2006.
36 Stone 1991: 113.
37 Kendall 2000; Rheingold 1993a.
38 Turkle 2011.
39 Stone 1995; Turkle 1995.
40 Gergen 1991; Goffman 1959, 1963 and 1974; Holstein and Gubrium 2000.
41 Plummer 1995.
42 Holstein and Gubrium 2000: 103.
43 Loseke 2001.
44 Loseke 2001: 121.
45 Holstein and Gubrium 2000: 94.
46 Many more examples of this narrative process can be found in recent scholarship on coming out processes among children with LGBT parents (Joos and Broad 2007), narrative stories of midwives (Foley 2005), and construction of race and class identities (He and Phillion 2001).
47 Mason-Schrock 1996: 177.
48 Mason-Schrock 1996: 186–187.
49 Fields 2008.
50 McLuhan 1970: 191.
51 Devos and Banaji 2003; Eagly and Chaiken 1993 and 1998; Festinger 1957; Fiske and Taylor 1991; Harmon-Jones and Mills 1999.
52 Cooley 1902; Goffman 1959; Mead 1934; Snyder, Tanke, and Berscheid 1977.
53 Gottschalk 2010; Yee and Bailenson 2007; Yee, Bailenson, and Ducheneaut 2009.

54 Fox and Bailenson 2009.
55 Johnston, Massey, and DeVaneaux 2012.
56 Yee and Bailenson 2007: 25.
57 Turkle 1995.
58 Seale 2006: 355.
59 Seale 2006: 348.
60 Gauthier and Chaudoir 2004; Hill 2005; McKenna, Green, and Smith 2001; Shapiro 2004.
61 Schrock, Holden, and Reid 2004: 66.
62 Hill 2005: 44.
63 Stryker 2008.
64 Recall from the last chapter that the inclusion of Gender Identity Disorder (GID) in the DSM both marks it as a mental disorder and functions to police access to transgender treatment and surgery. Simultaneously some people see GD/GID's inclusion as evidence that gender nonconformity needs to be taken seriously and that it deserves medical treatment and intervention. The inclusion of Gender Dysphoria/Gender Identity Disorder in the DSM, then, has been both praised and condemned by individuals within and outside of the transgender community. For a longer discussion of this debate, see Bryant 2008.
65 Transgender Nation was founded in 1992 as a focus group of Queer Nation and primarily focused on transphobia within the gay and lesbian community. Its name pays homage to and grew out of the same direct-action political ideology of Queer Nation and ACT-UP (Green 2004; Stryker 2008).
66 Green 2004: 79–80; Stryker 2008: 135–136.
67 Green 2004: 79–80; Olszewski 1993.
68 Ex-gay groups such as the National Association for Research and Therapy of Homosexuality have used Zucker's work to assert that gender nonconformity can, even should, be treated in childhood because of its ties to homosexuality in adulthood. This practice reinforces heteronormative and gender reductionist ideologies, and relies on the idea that homosexuality and/or gender nonconformity is wrong and should be cured. This argument rests firmly on solid ground only if we understand and accept heterosexuality and the sex/gender binary to be exclusively natural, biological, and ahistorical. For a longer discussion see Bryant 2006.
69 Brown 2006.
70 Spiegel 2008a.
71 "Objection to DSM-V Committee Members on Gender Identity Disorders" 2008. The petition reflects both the strengths and weaknesses of online organizing, though. On the one hand it mobilized huge numbers of people and garnered significant attention beyond the transgender community. On the other hand, the petition included misleading and false information about Zucker and the APA. For example, the petition states that Zucker himself advocates for reparative therapies, which is incorrect.
72 Spiegel 2008b.
73 American Psychiatric Association 2008.
74 American Psychiatric Association 1994: 581.
75 American Psychiatric Association 2013: 452.
76 American Psychiatric Association 2013.
77 Cisgender refers to individuals whose birth gender matches their birth sex. Refer back to Chapter 1 for a more detailed definition.
78 Bruckman 1993; Herring 1996; Rodino 1997.
79 Cook and Stambaugh 1997; Herring 1999; Soukup 1999.

80 Kendall 2000: 264.
81 Kelly, Pomerantz, and Currie 2006.
82 Kelly et al. 2006: 22.
83 Kelly et al. 2006: 11.
84 As used in Garland-Thomson 2005: 1,557–1,587; Kendall 2000: 220.
85 Pace, Houssian, and McArthur 2009.
86 Nakamura 2008b: 73.
87 Boellstorff 2008; "What Is Second Life?" 2014; Nakamura 2008a.
88 Mohammed 2009; Sanchez 2010.
89 Eastwick and Gardner 2008: 12.
90 Au 2008.
91 Ashkenaz 2008.
92 Nakamura 2002: 14–15.
93 Nakamura 2002: 14.
94 Au 2006.
95 Boler 2007; Sanchez 2010.
96 Eastwick and Gardner 2008: 29.
97 Herring and Martinson 2004; O'Brien 1999.
98 O'Brien 1999: 85.
99 Langer 1989; O'Brien 1999.
100 O'Brien 1999: 99.

CASE STUDY: FOCUS ON TRANS* ORGANIZING

The past 50 years have seen a steady rise in the number of individuals who are coming out as trans*—both adults and children who are accessing services and demanding social recognition and rights. Trans* community organizing, however, came into its own only in the last 15 to 20 years, blossoming in the mid-1990s. Conventional thinking about social movements would suggest that this shift in trans* organizing was rooted in the gay and lesbian movement, changes within medical treatment of trans*, and the fruits of 50 years of individuals' isolated activism, community advocacy, and organizing. The history, as told by leading trans* activists is quite different, however. While foundations certainly were laid by older support groups, conferences and publications, according to movement leaders it was the Internet that was central, critical, and transformational in the growth of a national transgender movement. This explanation, while unconventional, is not really surprising; the Internet has become one of the primary ways many of us access new information or connect with new people, and many scholars and activists have argued that the growth of information technologies over the last 20 years has been particularly meaningful for marginalized populations.

Dr. Sandra Cole, a sexologist, 20-year activist, and founder of the University of Michigan Health System Comprehensive Gender Services Program, put it this way:

> The strongest impetus of the trans movement happened with the Internet. It's not exclusively responsible because individuals and some small pockets of advocacy in the U.S. already had a few clubs and social gatherings in an effort to help, but that was a very quiet and private, somewhat underground kind of outreach and activity . . . The information available through the Internet, and the publications that have been simultaneously produced, have done

an enormous amount to educate transgender people that they are not alone and isolated, not the only one . . . You can just see the expansion and spreading of information dramatically influencing the social presence of transgender individuals in our culture.[1]

There has been a huge upsurge in information clearinghouses, support services, and online community development sites within gay, lesbian, bisexual, and transgender communities since Internet participation began to grow exponentially in the mid-1990s.[2] A 2002 Internet search for "transgender" pulled up more than 800,000 websites, but the same search in 2014 pulled 4,740,000 websites, six times as many sites in the span of just 12 years. These virtual spaces provide information about bodily interventions (surgery and hormones), help to build a social movement focused on changing existing trans/gender paradigms, and facilitate organizing for social and civil rights for individuals regardless of cisgender or transgender status.

Of course, the Internet was not the start of transgender support groups, or even activism. The emergence of a public transsexual presence in North America began with Christine Jorgensen's 1952 public coming out. Jorgensen's sensationalized and high profile story of medical transition in Denmark after serving in the U.S. Armed Forces was covered as a medical and psychological oddity, but demand for transgender and transsexual treatment in North America grew after media coverage of her story.[3] The medical community struggled to make sense of and respond to requests for treatment by transsexuals, which led to the development of gender clinics across North America in universities such as Johns Hopkins, the University of Minnesota, Stanford, and UCLA, and at the Clarke Institute of Psychiatry (now the Center for Addiction and Mental Health) in Toronto, Ontario.[4] While these and other similar centers did bring transgender people together, their strictly enforced mandates for changing one's embodiment, which included disappearing into "normal" society and severing ties to any transgender community (known as going "stealth") worked to prevent community development and even inhibited the development of interpersonal relationships. As she told me about these practices, Dallas Denny, a longtime transgender activist and founder of one of the oldest trans-gender information clearinghouses, explained, "transsexuals weren't in contact with one another under the medical model, because of confi-dentiality issues. There were few if any transsexual support groups, and there was just one little magazine published by Phoebe Smith out of Atlanta called The Transsexual Voice."

After a series of efforts in the 1970s to discredit gender affirming surgeries (what was then called "sex reassignment surgery") and shut down "Gender Identity Disorder" clinics, the entire system of trans-sexual medical service providers crumbled. Not only was access to medical services shattered, but any social support networks built up around them—limited as they were—were destroyed as well. Over the next 15 years a variety of print magazines, information clearinghouses, and support groups developed to meet the needs of the mostly closeted trans* community in North America. These provided access to other-wise unavailable information about gender affirming surgery, and other medical, legal, and employment issues. Local support groups provided a space to talk with other trans* people and perhaps to embody one's chosen gender among them. The ability to present oneself as desired was invaluable, if only for those individuals lucky enough to live near a safe space, and even if it was just once a month. These were usually the only places transgender people were able to fully disclose their identities, and other support group members were often their only confederates.

While trans* people have been present in organizing and activism since the beginning of gay liberation in the 1970s, trans* people (and issues) were sidelined in the mainstreaming of the gay and lesbian movement. It is hard to imagine what it was like then, a time when, except for Christine Jorgensen's autobiography and scarce medical texts, there were no books about trans* lives available to the public, no television shows, magazine articles, or websites from which individuals could learn about or even observe gender nonconformity—and certainly no day-to-day exposure to role models living openly in the community at large. Before the Internet, the primary sources of information and education were a few periodicals, remote organizations, and local support groups—and often knowledge about the first two rested on involvement with the latter.

The Internet became the central site of transgender organizing and personal and community growth in the late 1990s. Websites, listserves, and early social networking platforms provided a mass of information, guidance, and virtual public space to individuals not embedded in offline trans* communities. It was through these new spaces trans* people could connect, share knowledge and social scripts, assert new gender identities, and advocate for civil and social rights. The work of information, education, and support moved online.

The Internet has revolutionized the transgender movement in fundamental, significant, and incredible ways. Information technologies aid in the dissemination of information and expand access to peer and clinical support groups. Online spaces and the anonymity they offer can mitigate stigma and geographic isolation, connecting people from small or unsafe communities, and those who are part of marginalized religious, racial, ethnic, gender, or sexual groups.[5] Online technologies, and the unique assets they provided, have allowed marginalized groups to speak back to power holders. The shift to computer-mediated knowledge acquisition is one of several aspects of the Internet that has benefited the trans* community; online we find information about puberty and body development, medical care and advocacy, psychological and social support, and about cisgender and transgender lives. This online access, and the fact that an online identity can preserve offline anonymity, has been useful for family members coming to terms with transgender relatives. Individuals and families can access information about their sister or brother, parent, child, or themselves at all hours, freely, and more robustly than ever before. Moreover, online support groups often allow individuals to resist gender scripts in new ways. For example, research has shown that fathers feel freer to seek emotional support and share their emotions in online moderated groups than in face-to-face ones.[6]

An unanticipated outcome of this access to information and support has also been to free up social support organizations to focus on services and advocacy instead of on mailing informational packets out to interested individuals. While support groups remain an important source of community and identity development, much of the introductory work that had been managed by these offline organizations is now done online, freeing more time for these groups to focus on personal and community development. Much like face-to-face groups, online groups offer individuals safe spaces for self and family work.

Many online support groups have emerged to complement offline meetings, or even take their place for geographically isolated individuals, those without childcare or transportation, or youth that lack supportive family. Similarly, individuals are able to find more racially and ethnically resonant groups online, and these groups often better reflect their needs and cultural perspectives. We see this in the rise of online communities for trans* people but also for new mothers, young widows, caretakers, and blended families among other marginalized groups. Nancy Nangeroni,[7] a longtime transgender activist, was clear about why the Internet was so important:

> The Internet allows anonymous communication and so it allows people otherwise closeted to talk about things that they might not, and to talk about them with a stranger. Many cross-dressers fear discovery, they fear they'd lose their families, their jobs, or, at the very least, be socially humiliated. They can set up an email account through Hotmail or someplace like that and have anonymous communication or enter chat rooms.

The Internet affords a connection between people who are still closeted and/or in unsafe situations who often need the most information, education, and support. As Sandra Cole highlighted, this is especially true for youth, who have even fewer resources available to them:

> Youth now have grown up with the Internet, they're children of the Internet. So if they had any ideas about themselves or were just snooping around on the Internet they will run into transgender and they are able through all kinds of sources to find some relevance of social definition out there that might apply to them.

Research shows that the ability to access resources in private does not act as motivation to remain closeted, but rather helps individuals who do not have access to a local LGBT community or organization expand their knowledge about issues, meet other LGBT people, and solidify a positive identity.[8] This in turn helps to build a support network and sense of community.

Beyond structural and social support, new information technologies shape individual trans* bodies and identities as well. Because the Internet can render geographical distance irrelevant, does not require simultaneous presence for communication, and is available all hours of the day, it is an invaluable resource for support, information distribution, and movement recruitment. A single activist can create a website, list-serve, or email list that connects a diverse array of individuals otherwise linked to each other solely by an informal and sparse social network, thereby fostering community and networking. Many examples of this type of community organizing exist today, such as the Remembering Our Dead website.[9] Created by Gwendolyn Anne Smith in 1999 in response to the murder of the transwoman Rita Hester in 1998, the website memorializes the murder of transgender individuals and has led to the development of an offline activist event, the Transgender Day of Remembrance. Since 2002 more than 80 cities around the world have held Transgender Day of Remembrance events; it would be difficult to develop and orchestrate this type of mass activism without online sites to connect individuals. As the Day of Remembrance suggests, the Internet assists in community development and networking in particularly salient ways for highly marginalized groups. Because outing oneself online does not carry the same risks, many more people are willing to inquire about and become active in the community and its informational and social networks. This type of organizing has contributed to a vibrant online and offline activist community.

Aided by information technologies, trans* communities have been able to respond to transphobic violence with publicity and advocacy, and spurring new legal protections. Furthermore, the publicity that trans* communities have been able to bring to trans* discrimination has led to more just outcomes. Certainly the levels of harassment and violence focused on trans* people, and particularly trans* women of color, remain horrifyingly high (see Case Study 6 for a longer discussion); however, such attacks are more likely to elicit responses at the local, state, and federal levels than ever before.

The Internet has given people new access to information, community, and social scripts for gender and this has shaped individuals' embodied identities, family support and acceptance. Sadie Crabtree, a union organizer and leading transgender youth activist, explained:

> The Internet opens doors for young people, for people in rural areas, and for people who are closeted. It gives them safe ways to connect with others, and even to do activist work . . . People have been able to communicate with each other for quite a while but while there's mail, that's not a way to find people and you don't just dial a random [telephone] number. I think the Internet has revolutionized the way that people who are privileged enough to own computers and have Internet connections, connect with one another. Transsexual people got organized through the Internet; transgender came into its own because of the Internet.

All told, with the rise of the Internet, access to trans*-focused information, social networks, and organizations developed, which brought the movement for transgender rights to a critical mass. Not only has this interconnectivity allowed a highly marginalized community to advocate for change, it has changed the nature of the community itself.

It is important to temper utopian notions of the Internet's usefulness, however; one must keep in mind that access to the community and support available on the Internet is mitigated by social class and race in North America.[10] While it is undeniable that the Internet has become a central arena for individual and community development, large segments of the population are left out, particularly homeless, poor, and non-English-speaking individuals. While the technology of the Internet creates a nurturing community for those with access to it, this technology also widens the gap between those with that privilege and those without.

Notes

1 Unless otherwise noted, quotes from activists come from interviews I conducted. For a more detailed discussion see Shapiro 2004.
2 Cooper, McLoughlin, and Campbell 2000; Smith and Kollock 1999.
3 Meyerowitz 2002.
4 The first of these gender clinics was the Johns Hopkins Gender Identity Clinic, established in November 1966, which provided the entire range of medical services to transsexual individuals including gender affirming surgery. The success of this center led to the development of numerous other university affiliated centers around the country in the 1960s and 1970s.
5 Rheingold 1993b.
6 Malik and Coulson 2008; Nicholas et al. 2004.
7 Nancy Nangeroni ran an award-winning weekly radio talk show for more than ten years called Gendertalk (www.gendertalk.com). The radio show covered a wide array of issues important to transgender communities and was broadcast online to a wide audience.
8 McKenna and Bargh 1998.
9 www.gender.org/remember.
10 Horrigan and Smith 2007; Xavier et al. 2005.

CASE STUDY: FOCUS ON SOCIAL NETWORKING AND THE SELF

On February 13, 2014, Facebook introduced a new array of gender choices from which users could choose to self-identify. Members of the trans* community have been calling for more gender possibilities for years, but perhaps no one expected to see the enormous range of 56 genders that Facebook made available; at its debut these choices included the following gender and sex markers:

Agender	Gender Questioning	Trans* Male
Androgyne	Gender Variant	Trans* Man
Androgynous	Genderqueer	Trans* Person
Bigender	Intersex	Trans* Woman
Cis	Male to Female	Transfeminine
Cis Female	MTF	Transgender
Cis Male	Neither	Transgender Woman
Cis Man	Neutrois	Transgender Female
Cis Woman	Non-binary	Transgender Male
Cisgender	Other	Transgender Man
Cisgender Female	Pangender	Transgender Person
Cisgender Male	Trans	Transmasculine
Cisgender Man	Trans Female	Transsexual
Cisgender Woman	Trans Male	Transsexual Female
Female to Male	Trans Man	Transsexual Male
FTM	Trans Person	Transsexual Man
Gender Fluid	Trans Woman	Transsexual Person
Gender	Trans*	Transsexual Woman
Nonconforming	Trans* Female	Two-spirit

These custom gender identities are diverse and recognize both gender and sex as socially constructed and malleable. Normative and non-normative alignment (cis/trans), presentation (androgynous/feminine/masculine), flexibility (questioning, queer and fluid identities), sex (male/female/intersex), and gender (man/woman/person/bigender) are included, allowing the ways to be gendered on the world's largest social network to skyrocket in an instant. Along with these new identities, Facebook also allowed individuals to specify whether they use masculine, feminine or gender neutral pronouns, offering "they" as the gender neutral option regardless of gender identity. This is similar to the offline practice of asking individuals to state their chosen pronoun in conversation.

For many cisgender individuals the change was meaningless, but executive director of the Transgender Law Center, Mason Davis, told the Associated Press that for a large number of trans* users, it allows "for people to be their authentic selves online."[1] As the Facebook Diversity Team announced:

> When you come to Facebook to connect with the people, causes, and organizations you care about, we want you to feel comfortable being your true, authentic self. An important part of this is the expression of gender, especially when it extends beyond the definitions of just "male" or "female." So today, we're proud to offer a new custom gender option to help you better express your own identity on Facebook.[2]

Facebook's assertion that this change will allow more people to express their "true, authentic" selves raises questions about the role of online social networking in gender identity construction, presentation, and substantiation, particularly given their centrality in contemporary online life. Does this overestimate the importance of social networking in people's lives? Or are sites like Facebook significant in how we shape our public and private gendered and embodied selves?

Social networking websites emerged in the early 2000s as online services that allowed individuals to create site-specific profiles, identify connections to other users, and view the profiles and connections of these individuals.[3] While early social networking sites (SNSs) were primarily focused around mapping ones connections to others (e.g. Friendster and MySpace), as these sites have evolved they have become more dynamic and interactive (e.g. Facebook and Instagram). Social networking sites are characterized by three components. First, individuals create profiles that describe who they are, their likes and dislikes, and core aspects of their identity. These profiles are vestiges of the dating websites that inspired early social networking platforms and are structured by the SNS platform and completed by individuals. Profiles include some kind of description, often along with personal characteristics, demographic information, personal preferences, and history. Individuals also upload pictures, music, and video to create a space reflecting their "selves." Second, individuals seek out and formalize connections with other users, also known as friending. These "friends" can be both strong ties (people individuals know and interact with on a regular basis) and weak ones (casual acquaintances, friends of friends, etc.), and even connections to strangers with similar interests. Finally, newer SNSs allow for dynamic networking and ongoing conversation through spaces for comments, synchronous interaction, and instant messaging.

Since Friendster went live in 2002 as a new model of the dating website, use of social networking sites has grown exponentially. While early SNS use was concentrated among young people, this genre has grown, shifting to a broader population. In 2006 only 20 percent of adult internet users had created an SNS profile while 55 percent of online teens had done so.[4] In contrast, by 2013, 73 percent of online adults and 81 percent of teens used social networking sites. Additionally, 42 percent of online adults use more than one SNS, with different platforms emerging as more popular among different demographic groups; for example Pinterest is most popular among women, Twitter and Instagram among young adults and people of color.[5]

Of social networking websites, Facebook is by far the most popular, with more than 1.28 billion active users as of March 2014.[6] Begun in February 2004 in the Harvard dorm room of Mark Zuckerberg, within one month of Facebook's creation more than half of the student population at Harvard had an account and by 2005 it had expanded to more than 800 high schools, colleges, and universities.[7] Among people that use only one SNS, 84 percent use Facebook.[8] In fact, it is the most visited website in the United States, accounting for more than 7 percent of all

United States internet traffic,[9] and it continues to grow at an astounding pace, particularly outside of North America. While Facebook was originally developed for college-aged adults, the fastest-growing group of users are adults over 34.[10] Of people online, 84 percent of those aged 18–29 are on Facebook, as are 79 percent of online 30–49 year-olds, 60 percent of those aged 50–64, and 45 percent of internet users over 65. Seventy-six percent of women use Facebook, and 66 percent of men; the racial distribution of users mirrors that of the U.S. as a whole.

The structure of Facebook has been refined over the last ten years, though the core components of profiles, formalized connections, and dynamic and synchronous interaction have remained the same. Facebook is structured around individual user profile pages that include personal information, likes and dislikes, and education, work, or family networks. Users can post information on personal pages, "friend" link to other users' profiles, and interact through both private chats and messaging and public communication of wall posts. A "news feed" allows individuals to track the activities and contributions of friends to the site and respond to announcements from the over 900 million groups, event and community pages on Facebook. Users can also buy and sell in the Marketplace, play interactive games with other users, and share photos (Facebook is still the most popular photo sharing site on the web). Because Facebook allows external websites to integrate easily with the SNS, the platform has become almost ubiquitous online; as of March 2013, more than ten million websites integrate with Facebook and more than 850 million people a month interact with Facebook in this way.[11]

In 2012 the average Facebook user had 130 friends, was connected to 80 community and event pages, and posted 90 pieces of content per month.[12] Most users report turning to Facebook to strengthen existing relationships, keep on top of friends' activities and life events, develop connections among casual acquaintances, minimize loneliness, and relieve boredom.[13] Average Internet users are less likely to report being lonely or socially isolated and, despite the pervasive dystopian rhetoric that the Internet is degrading social life and relationships, there is no evidence that there is a decline in social ties due to the use of information technologies. Forty percent of users are "friends" on Facebook with *all* their close offline friends.[14] SNS users are equally likely to know their neighbors and be engaged in neighborhood activities as those without an SNS profile, and are even more likely to be politically engaged.[15]

While personal webpages or blogs are produced by one person and can be only viewed by others, the interaction inherent in SNSs allow individuals to make visible their connections, and this display becomes part of the identity work that individuals undertake to substantiate their public selves and provide context for their presentation of self.[16] The collective act of constructing a profile produces a "digital body" upon which to base social norms and scripts.[17] As one social media scholar elaborates:

> The meanings produced on the profiles are not the accomplish-ment of individual performances, but instead are an effect of the cultural negotiations that take place within a network. Users can add meaning to each other's profiles by adding comments including text, images or video, transforming the shape of their networked "digital bodies."[18]

Social networking websites, like communities, support groups and virtual worlds, are active sites of embodied identity work. These online spaces, shaped by dominant ideologies, structure interaction through social norms and scripts, and encourage identity work on the part of individuals. Furthermore, individuals' identity work changes the land-scape of the social networking platform itself.

The identity work that takes place in Facebook is a collaborative endeavor; the contributions of others, in the form of wall posts, photo tags, likes and connections, shape how individuals present their self on the platform.[19] While one could, theoretically, develop a profile that bore little resemblance to one's offline life, it is unlikely that one's friends would provide role support for this inauthentic self-presentation. Not only would friends hold one accountable for these misrepresentations, but the content they provide in the form of pictures, accounts of shared activities, and comments would likely contradict these claims. Indeed, research has shown that user profiles are fairly accurate representations of offline selves.[20] While this is partly a product of the offline relationships that drive Facebook friendships, people want others to see themselves as they do, what social psychologists call "self-verification."[21] Just as Second Life allows for identity work through the construction and manipulation of an avatar, the Facebook profile allows individuals to construct a public self and refine this identity over time. The interactive nature of Facebook encourages many of the same processes that avatar presence does; we come to identify with our profile, and to internalize the interactions we have through it, and their significance for identity.

Sociologist danah boyd argues that the consequence of the collaborative nature of SNS platforms like Facebook is that they become "networked publics," spaces where people are "bound together through technological networks."[22] These networked publics are characterized by four attributes: their persistence (what you create continues to exist even when you're offline), searchability (you can be sought out, and can search for others), replicability (posts, pictures, and profile can be copied and pasted), and the presence of an invisible, interactive audience (profiles are public and can be accessed without our knowledge, by others). These characteristics are different from other social spaces, and they affect how people act and interact and, ultimately, how they construct, reconstruct, and substantiate their identities.

As a networked public, Facebook has its own norms and social scripts that guide behavior and self-presentation and which are learned through participation. We import some of these scripts from offline life, but SNSs have also developed norms and scripts particular to this type of networked public. For instance, because Facebook limits our ability to present different parts of our self to different social groups (what social psychologists call "audience segregation"), users learn informal rules like when to tag other people in pictures, and when to refrain.

Profile construction is also a learned activity and one that demands that individuals create and substantiate an embodied identity in the absence of physicality or a holistic presentation of self. Presentation of a public self, self-reflexivity (thinking about one's "self" as others might see one), collaborative identity construction, and ongoing identity work is done using the discourses-in-practice within our virtual communities. In her research on teens, for example, danah boyd notes, "[b]y looking at others' profiles, teens get a sense of what types of presentations are socially appropriate; others' profiles provide critical cues about what to present on their own profile."[23]

A lifetime of identity construction that leads us to speak (or write) in particular ways, or to draw on some examples and not others, comes with us into these networked publics, and shapes how we talk about ourselves and others. These tracers of socialization, the lingering after-effects of internalizing gendered social norms, scripts and practices, shape our online interactions and consequently bring the embodied self online. Amy Bruckman, a longtime scholar of virtual communities, has examined how our offline lives shape our online interactions. She and colleagues have studied both how individuals' online behavior is shaped by gender, race, age, and other personal characteristics, and how others "read" these characteristics in text-based interactions. In 2000, they designed an online, game-based experiment to test whether and how identity manifests in online spaces. More than 11,000 people participated in the experiment over a one-year period. Berman and Bruckman found that *how* individuals communicate tells an audience more about who they are than the actual content of discussions. Trying to explain how they knew an individual was a woman trying to pass as a man, one audience member in this experiment explained: "It's not what you said, it's how you said it!"[24] In that case, long, descriptive sentences used by the individual had made visible their gender socialization as a woman. What this research suggests is that when we move online, we bring with us our gendered (and other identity-based) ways of communicating and interacting.

Like narrative identity construction more generally, online profiles are a discursive practice that allow us to story ourselves into being. We do so using the discourses-in-practice learned through observing others' profiles. Because the body is not physically present in online spaces, individuals have to "write themselves into being," engaging in identity work in different ways in order to substantiate their gendered identities.[25] The unique norms and scripts for SNSs, the effects of socialization that we bring with us when we interact online, and the structure of Facebook that encourages some activities and inhibits others come together to produce particular kinds of gendered identity work. And the public nature of the SNS is critical for these processes; identity work requires the support of others and a networked public is primed to facilitate this kind of work. While profiles allow us to story ourselves into being, we don't have all possibilities at our disposal; we are bound by the gendered social possibilities of the platform as well as by the expectations of others who know us offline.

When Facebook expanded the gender choices with which people could identify, it radically transformed the gendered discourses-in-practice available for identity negotiation. For individuals, this meant that their profile could reflect their non-normative gendered self. Incorporating these non-normative genders into the architecture of the SNS granted them legitimacy and authenticity as gendered discourses. At a point in time when almost 10 percent of youth report a gender identity more diverse than the hegemonic binary—what researchers call "gender expansive" identities—Facebook's structural change has huge significance. Not only does this make available new discourses-in-practice, but these new discourses are available in a networked public primed for identity work.

Dominant ideologies shape the architecture and content of SNSs like Facebook, while characteristics of these networked publics enable particular types of interaction and constrain others. The social scripts that emerge guide individual behaviors and meaningful profile construction such that others will support and validate individual presentation. The use of pictures and video brings the body online visually, and status updates are able to make salient embodied practices and experiences. Interactive elements allow opportunities for self-reflexivity in profile and status updates, while allowing others to participate in identity work and provide social support for identity claims. All of these things make Facebook (and other SNSs) vibrant spaces where embodied identity work takes place, and the significance of this work is carried offline. While claims have been made that the Internet isolates individuals, degrades social life and networks, and allows individuals to hide behind

masks, research suggests that the opposite may well be true. For trans*
communities, the expansion of gender possibilities within the SNS signals a broader victory; trans* movements have long organized for the
right to gender self-determination and the cultural recognition afforded
by Facebook lends legitimacy to these calls.

Notes

1 Associated Press 2014.
2 "Facebook Diversity" 2014.
3 boyd and Ellison 2007.
4 Lenhart et al. 2007.
5 Ibid.
6 Facebook 2014.
7 Arrington 2005; Phillips 2007.
8 Duggan and Smith 2014.
9 Wilson, Gosling, and Graham 2012.
10 Fletcher 2010.
11 Facebook 2013; Ries 2010; Wilson et al. 2012.
12 Wilson et al. 2012.
13 Wilson et al. 2012.
14 Hampton, Lee, and Her 2011.
15 Hampton, Goulet, Rainie, and Purcell 2011.
16 Donath 2007; Donath and boyd 2004.
17 boyd and Heer 2006.
18 Van Doorn 2010: 585.
19 Van Doorn 2010.
20 Back et al. 2010; Gosling, Gaddis, and Vazire 2007; Waggoner, Smith, and Collins
   2009; Weisbuch, Ivcevic, and Ambady 2009.
21 Lampe, Ellison, and Steinfield 2006; Ross et al. 2009. For more on self-verification see
   Swann 1999.
22 boyd 2008: 125.
23 boyd 2008: 127.
24 Berman and Bruckman 2001: 84.
25 Sunden 2003.

3

NEW BIOMEDICAL TECHNOLOGIES, NEW SCRIPTS, NEW GENDERS

In 1939, soon after graduating from St. Anne's College at the University of Oxford, England, Lawrence Michael Dillon became the first transsexual man to undergo hormonal and physical procedures to bring his female body into alignment with his sense of himself as a man. Dillon came to a public masculine identity during his college years, although he had long looked and acted masculine and expressed desires to be a man. Even though Dillon knew himself to be a man, albeit one situated within a female body, he had no social support and no social scripts from which he could make sense of his situation. He was without any language to discuss gender nonconformity or transgenderism—indeed the word "transsexual" had yet to be coined—and there was certainly no discussion of any difference between sex and gender. Dillon experienced discrimination for years before his transition because of his gender presentation. He was unable to find anyone who would either support his gender identity or enable the physical changes he required to live as a man.

The contemporary experiences of many young trans* people stand in stark contrast to Michael Dillon's life story. A feature article in the *New York Times Magazine* on March 16, 2008, included a profile of Rey Grosz, a then 18-year-old white female-to-male transgender college student.[1] Rey reflected on growing up a masculine child, being mistaken for a boy, and coming out as transgender to himself at 14 and to his family at the age of 17. Rey's story has similarities to Michael Dillon's; both grew up masculine and developed a gender identity as a boy or man at a young age. However, while Michael Dillon negotiated his identity without a language for gender nonconformity, Rey not only gained language and learned social scripts to describe who he was from other trans* people, but he was also able to do so at a young age. Rey heard a transgender man speak at a Gay Straight Alliance meeting at his high school and immediately went home and ran a Google Internet search for the word "transgender." "The Internet is the best thing for trans people," Rey elaborated. "Living in the suburbs, online groups were an access point [for me]."[2] Unlike Michael Dillon, who had no access to information about trans* lives, Rey was able to find and use a wide array of information and support resources to validate, define, and negotiate his own masculine identity and female body. His ability to communicate with other trans* individuals, learn about affirmative psycho-medical care, and engage with others as a boy online, all helped Rey to redefine and assert who he was. In an illustration of the online identity work discussed in the last chapter, advances in communication technologies helped Rey to understand and define his gender identity; later developments in medical technology, the focus of this chapter, allowed Rey to reshape his body to reflect his gender identity.

The last chapter examined how information technologies facilitate identity work, which in turn produced new gendered identities and social scripts for individuals and society. To fully understand how new technologies are changing individuals, we will now look at how biomedical technologies are being employed in a similar manner to know and to construct gendered bodies in new and transformative ways, and how these enable—or sometimes inhibit—individuals' embodiment of new identities.

New Body Technologies

The approach taken in this book, and one that is increasingly used within studies of the body, is to make sense of the body as something that is in dynamic relationship to both society and personal identity.[3] Individuals are always acting in and through their body and always within a social and cultural context, even when in a virtual space. Bodily change can be the product of a variety of factors including chance (e.g., an accident might cause changes in one's mobility), social structures (such as the military), and intentional manipulation (weightlifting or cosmetic surgery, for example). While body work is transformative and often purposeful on the part of individuals, these changes, whether by chance, social structure, or individual agency, are always already shaped by social norms and historical context.[4] When an individual chooses to get a tattoo, they may do so for any of a variety of reasons: an effort to adorn their body, mark a significant event, or signal participation in a community or identity category. But this agentic choice is informed by and given meaning through gendered beliefs about tattoos and their significance, body and beauty scripts, and dominant social paradigms. Approaching the body as something shaped by both individual identity and social structures, and as actively shaping identity and social scripts in turn, allows a better understanding of how new technologies are dynamically engaged with gendered bodies.

Body modification has changed dramatically in the last 50 years, as has societal acceptance of bodily transformation practices such as plastic surgery, use of pharmaceuticals, weightlifting, tattooing, shaving, and hair dyeing. More so now than ever before, it is common practice for individuals to produce and refine their gendered bodies in ways that both reinforce and contest normative social scripts. This chapter draws on a sociological approach to map the intricate, multiple connections between embodied identities, technologies, and social gender paradigms, and examines how the ability to construct new bodies is changing who people think they are and can be. By looking at the exponential growth of weight-loss surgeries in recent years, the relationship between racialized beauty norms and plastic surgery, and trans* identities and gender affirming surgeries, we will explore the complex implications of biomedical intervention. As we have seen with other technologies, while biomedical technologies themselves are impartial, neither liberating nor regressive, they are developed along lines and deployed in ways that can produce both socially normative bodies and counter-hegemonic ones.

Technologies and the Body

Biomedical technology is just one part of the larger phenomenon of biotechnology. Biotechnology, which emerged in the 1970s, brings engineering and industrial theories to bear on natural systems.

> **BIOTECHNOLOGY**
>
> Any intentional manipulation of organic processes or organisms. The United Nations defines biotechnology as "any technological application that uses biological systems, living organisms, or derivatives thereof, to make or modify products or processes for specific use."[5]

The oldest forms of biotechnology—seed saving, pest management, and crop cultivation—mark the actual development of agriculture. Early experiments into immunization have been traced back to 200 BCE. Both technologically-informed farming and primitive medical efforts have shaped societies and individuals for thousands of years.[6] Biotechnological interventions have taken on new significance in the last three decades, however, with the exponential growth of biological technologies and the advent of patents for living organisms, which turned biotechnology into a profit-making enterprise.[7]

Biomedical technology, or technology directed at maintaining and/or transforming the human body is of particular relevance to our investigation of gendered body work. Biomedical technology has become the medium through which we know and intervene into our bodies.

> **BIOMEDICAL TECHNOLOGY**
>
> Technology directed at maintaining and/or transforming the human body. Biomedical technologies use a technological framework to understand and manipulate biological systems.

These technologies are increasingly diverse and include genetic testing and manipulation, body scans, pharmacology, surgery including microsurgery, imaging, cloning, synthetic drugs, hormones and vaccines, prosthetics, ingestible biometric computers, and implants, to name just a few. Moving beyond discovery as a motivation for scientific research, the profitability of biotechnology has led to the development of numerous attendant profit-generating industries, such as elective and cosmetic surgery, DNA mapping services, genetic engineering, and "medi-spa" companies. In 2012, U.S.-based for-profit biotechnology firms—excluding healthcare, that is—generated 63.7 billion dollars in revenue; these numbers have continued to grow exponentially.[8]

The extraordinary growth in the techniques of biomedical intervention and their increasing centrality in the lives of individuals are significant beyond individual-level body work; biotechnology is simultaneously shaped by social forces and a source of individual, institutional, and social change. While both scholars and lay people tend to treat the body and bodily functions as natural and inevitable, we observed in Chapter 1 that they are actually socially constructed.[9] Let us take the general concept of "illness," for example, which is generally regarded as a straightforward matter of biology. Illness is deeply social; who gets sick, how, and with what outcome is strongly correlated to social class, gender, and race. Working-class men and women are at much higher risk of illness than their middle-class compatriots are, and women are more likely to be disabled by seemingly ungendered illnesses such as arthritis and strokes, than men.[10] Simultaneously, social class and rates of diagnosis and treatment are positively correlated; as income increases, the likelihood someone will be diagnosed and treated for serious medical conditions also increases. Race is highly correlated to health outcomes as well; people of color are less likely to be diagnosed with or recover from serious illnesses like cancer.[11] In other words, illness is much more than a biological phenomenon. Gendered, racialized, and classed social scripts for sickness all affect how bodies are understood, diagnosed, and treated, ultimately producing different (and unequal) outcomes.

The Social Body

The body is always *both* an individual product and an entity shaped by its social and physical context. The process of analyzing and assigning meaning to our body and its sensory experiences is a learned one shaped by social beliefs, expectations, norms and values, and mediated by internal psychological processes.[12] Individuals use their bodies to actively meet their own needs and effect change in their environment. This embodied work, like all social endeavors, occurs within a particular social context, shaped by dominant paradigms and rooted in existing social scripts. Conceptualizing it as a social construct, many theorists have questioned the shifting meaning of the body in light of biomedical developments that allow heretofore impossible manipulations of the body.[13] Feminist scholars in particular have paid attention to how new biomedical interventions affect gendered bodies and identities on the individual and social level.[14] Although bodily manipulation has a long history, new scholarship suggests that the nature and pervasiveness of contemporary interventions calls into question core social beliefs about the body as unique, natural, and fixed.[15] That is, advances in biotechnology, spurred on by its growing profitability, are altering individual bodies as well as the bodily landscape of society.

Recently, some scholars have used the term *somatechnics* to describe human-body focused technologies and to distinguish them from agricultural and/or animal-focused biotechnologies.

SOMATECHNICS

Technologies of the human body. The Greek words "soma" meaning "body" and "techne" or "expression of a craft" are drawn together to convey an understanding that the body and technology are always and already interrelated and mutually constitutive. Technologies shape how we know, understand, and shape the body and the body is a product of historically and culturally specific technological practices.

The word "somatechnics" has been coined in an effort to express that the body is always known and shaped through the technologies of a particular society. Nikki Sullivan has focused on body modification such as tattooing to make sense of how technologies are both shaped by and an intentional engagement with social scripts for gendered bodies.[16] Other pioneers of this concept have done work in a similar vein, including Susan Stryker, who has explored the social and techno- logical history of transsexualism, and Samantha Murray, whose work focuses on fatness and the emergence of bariatric surgery.[17] Research by each of these scholars demonstrates that modern embodied identities are always already in dynamic relationship to technologies, and more specifically that biomedical technologies are used to construct, main- tain, and transform gendered bodies and identities.

The desire to transform the body is, in part, a response to the separa- tion of body and mind we explored in the Preview; individuals often assert that their bodily flaws are mismatched with their true identi- ties and mask the people they truly are.[18] For example, in her study of women's body work, Debra Gimlin found that women believed that an imperfect body bespoke an imperfect self.[19] Because we see the body as a reflection of an individual's inner character, we strive for alignment. The women Gimlin interviewed turned to a variety of bodily manipula- tions including hairstyling, plastic surgery, and exercise to address the gendered body and character flaws they identified. Bodily manipula- tion, then, can be an effort to create alignment or justify misalignment between appearance and character, between identity and body. Clothing can be selected to display class, personality, sexuality, and oppositional consciousness, as documented by Dick Hebdige in his groundbreaking research on punk sub-cultural aesthetics.[20] What these scholars found is that a great number of body modifications, whether superficial or invasive, are efforts by people to change their body structure to reflect a current or desired inner identity. But the relationship between the body and identity is multi-directional; research on body modification has also demonstrated how changes in the body spark identity shifts for individuals.

Technology and Body Work

It is now possible to alter the look of one's body through myriad, increasingly diverse somatechnologies: plastic surgery, steroids, growth hormones, hair dye, permanent makeup, hair transplants, sub-cultural body modification practices like tattoos and scarification, laser hair removal, machine-enhanced exercise regimens, and spa treatments—just to name a few. For individuals who want and have the means to engage in this body work, it is increasingly possible to transform the body in order to either manifest what was previously consigned to one's existing inner selfhood, or produce a body that corresponds to a sought after inner identity. This holds true for both normative and non-normative bodily changes; individuals can become more masculine men (for instance, through steroid use or testosterone shots), more feminine women (through breast augmentation and laser hair removal, as examples), as well as transverse gender norms to become more feminine men, masculine women, or differently gendered male, female, or trans* individuals. All of this work is *body work*. "Body work" refers to individual's efforts to shape the form or function of the body and to the technological and personal labor involved in those transformations.[21]

> **BODY WORK**
> The intentional manipulation of the body by an individual. This can include surface manipulation as well as more substantial interventions. The term has also been used to refer to the manipulation of an individual's body for pay, or the effect of work on the body.

The concept of body work highlights how social power relations governing gender, social class, race, religion, and sexuality manifest in and through the body.[22] Whether and how individuals engage in body work is shaped by social pressures, norms, and expectations specific to their location within the social matrices of power and privilege of their community. Moreover, individuals engage in body work as part of the dynamic relationship between body and identity, as both an impetus for and response to identity change. And they do so within biographical and societal contexts, using the technologies available to them. Accordingly, it is impossible to examine body work without situating it within a social context, informed by social paradigms and scripts.

Somatechnics and Social Norms

Social body norms have a direct effect on what individuals do to reshape their bodies. All of us engage in body work of various types daily, and it is no surprise that we do so for personal and social benefit. The case studies at the end of this chapter (on reproductive technologies and gender affirming treatment) share the same dynamics as the more routine body work that most individuals engage in every day: we do it because it matters. Substantial research has been done on body work, affirming that meeting or approximating hegemonic gender scripts leads to positive outcomes in individual lives, including increased work prestige, increased social status, higher income, and higher self-esteem.[23] For example, thin people tend to earn more and garner more occupational prestige than overweight people, and this dynamic is gendered in that the negative consequences are more severe for fat women than for fat men, who experience discrimination to a lesser degree.[24]

Both men and women are pressured to change their bodies, and are stigmatized if they do not conform to these demands. The development of weight-loss technologies may appear neutral on the surface, encompassing scientific research, surgical technique, and nutrition science, but in reality, everything from the emphasis on weight loss as an objective—as opposed to good health—to the acceptable biomedical techniques for accomplishing this rely on and reinforce contemporary body and gender paradigms. The dominant belief that the internal self is reflected in the body compels individuals to change their body to validate a positive self-concept and internal identity. Simultaneously, both social and medical support for biomedical weight-loss technologies reinforce body scripts that devalue fat bodies (often decreasing people's estimation of the worth of their own inner selves). Further, these dynamics are deeply gendered; fat male bodies are viewed as feminized while fat female bodies are de-feminized. Social forces are joined with contemporary advances in medical technology to form the foundation of a phenomenally profitable weight-loss industry, an industry that puts ever more pressure on individuals to conform to particular body size ideals.

A timely example of the dynamic relationship between somatechnics and social norms is bariatric (i.e. weight-loss) surgery. Even though versions of bariatric surgery have been used for more than 50 years, widespread access to this biomedical technology was limited until recent technological advances and marketing made it easier to access.[25] During the 11-year period from 1995 to 2006 bariatric surgery rates skyrocketed by 800 percent; in 2013, more than 179,000 surgeries were performed in the United States alone.[26] Individuals—mostly women— are using this set of biomedical technologies to reshape their bodies in dramatically increasing numbers.[27] Many individuals benefit from weight-loss surgery, which can reduce health problems, raise self-esteem, and facilitate alignment between body and identity. Like the other cases we have explored, however, the phenomenon begs more critical analysis. What makes bariatric surgery such an interesting case study is that the highly contentious debates about the surgery engage directly with contemporary body and gender paradigms and social scripts. These debates take place within both medical circles and larger society as they manifest in and through the bodies and identities of individuals.

The debate about "normal" bodies is, in fact, a debate over the dominant body paradigm, and it is taking place in part through debates about biomedical "treatments" for obesity. Dominant body paradigms posit the idea that fat bodies are inherently unhealthy, undesirable, and a sign of internal character failings.[28] These paradigms also conceptualize thinness as natural and universally achievable. Up for debate, however, is whether obesity is a product of lack of discipline and therefore treatable with biomedical technologies such as dieting and exercise, or whether fatness is disease and therefore a malady worthy of medical intervention and treatment.[29] Fat-positive activism over the last 20 years has challenged both the disciplinary and surgical approaches as well as social paradigms regarding body size more generally.[30] Groups like the National Association to Advance Fat Acceptance (NAAFA) and Health at Every Size take issue with dominant medical and social paradigms that link health to thinness and fat to disease. These organizations point toward historical and cultural variation in body size scripts, and stress that empirical research reveals a wide range of differences in health and body size; not all large bodies are unhealthy and not all thin bodies are healthy.[31] For many individuals whose bodies do not conform to normative body scripts, the presence of a counter-hegemonic paradigm supports their own positive social body and identity scripts.

In 2013, the scales tipped toward medicalized paradigms and biomedical "treatments" when the American Medical Association declared obesity a disease.[32] This specific framing shapes whether and how individuals experience and treat their bodies. For example, a biomedical paradigm will discount health-focused interventions that do not center on weight loss and focus, instead, on technologies such as weight-loss surgery, drugs like Alli, and the hunt for a "fat gene." A disease paradigm will also integrate weight loss into health insurance coverage, bolstering the profitability of bariatric surgery and other weight-loss industries. The construction of fatness as a disease is both bolstered by the increased use of bariatric surgery, and, simultaneously, further legitimizes the biomedical intervention.

While changes in social paradigms and scripts are ordinarily invisible, abstract social processes, they can be rendered visible through sociological analysis. In the case of weight-loss surgery, examining the discursive practices and discourses-in-practice embedded in the medical management of bariatric surgery makes visible the transformation of body paradigms and social scripts. Sociologist Patricia Drew spent several years studying the weight-loss surgery industry and found that bariatric advocates have legitimized this new biomedical intervention by first creating scripts for the ideal patient that draw on and reinforce hegemonic body paradigms and then requiring the adoption of these scripts in order to access bariatric surgery. To qualify as a bariatric candidate, individuals must adopt or, at the very least, pretend to adopt particular physiological, behavioral, and attitude scripts (much like transsexual scripts demanded in order to access gender affirming surgeries).

The bariatric surgery patients Drew interviewed all shared very similar stories about their bodies and how they came to consider weight-loss surgery. Of course, patients didn't make these particular stories up out of nothing; they encountered social scripts in promotional materials, at mandatory support group meetings, and in pre-surgery appointments with doctors and clinicians. Individual biographical components differed but most individuals incorporated into their own story the key narrative

elements of the dominant script: viewing themselves as sick, as empowered through the use of weight-loss surgery, and as responsible for their
body. Surgery candidates reinterpreted their own feelings and experiences to fit within the dominant discourse-in-practice—social scripts
that medicalized weight loss and legitimated weight-loss surgery—and
in the process participated in establishing new body scripts. Even when
individuals' own self-narrative did not contain the key elements of the
acceptable script, individuals in Drew's study described consciously and
strategically using the expected script to access surgery.[33] Drew concludes that these ideal patient scripts, or discourses-in-practice, learned
in part through mandatory support group meetings, which afforded
discursive practice, helped individuals to negotiate between larger
social body paradigms and individual embodied identity. Most patients
adopted the ideal patient scripts in part or in full and, in the process,
yielded to hegemonic body paradigms. Concomitantly, the social scripts
rooted in institutional ideologies shaped the bodies and identities of
participants. These ideal patient scripts, in turn, diffused into broader
culture and reshaped dominant body paradigms and scripts. Ultimately,
this new technology of bariatric surgery is transforming individual
bodies and identities. The application of the technology is simultaneously responding to and altering societal body paradigms, in this case,
paradigms of what constitutes a healthy body, and social scripts for
"normal" embodied identities.

There is more to the story, however. According to the U.S. Centers
for Disease Control, while women make up 59 percent of the obese
population in the United States they account for 85 percent of weight-
loss surgery patients.[34] If surgery was simply the product of obesity, then
men and women would be accessing surgery at rates equal to the ratio
of obesity in the general population. That is, statistically only 59 percent
of patients should be women. The dramatically higher rate of women
patients suggest that people use this new technology based on gendered
ideologies and gendered social scripts for ideal patients. In other words,
the technology is gendered and it produces gendered outcomes.

Patricia Drew's research with bariatric surgery patients and doctors
identified four intersecting gendered paradigms and scripts that lead

to the disproportionate use of weight-loss surgery by women. First, as many scholars have documented, North American societies' gendered body and beauty paradigms place higher body demands on women, and place more stringent sanctions on them for deviating from normative beauty standards.[35] Women are expected to go to greater lengths and exercise more discipline upon themselves and their bodies than men are.[36] Second, as Nelly Oudshoorn argued with regard to birth control (discussed in Case Study 6), because men's bodies are held as a normal baseline, women's bodies are seen as more in need of intercession, and as more legitimate targets for biomedical intervention. Women are also more likely to seek medical care in general—a fact which is, itself, a product of gendered body and health paradigms—and this holds true for weight-loss surgery. Third, weight-loss surgery requires participation in support groups, groups that our society views as largely the domain of women.[37] Finally, these gendered dynamics shape the social scripts disseminated by medical and media sources about weight-loss surgery. In her analysis of hundreds of brochures, advertisements, and websites about weight-loss surgery, Patricia Drew found that publicity materials pictured women much more often than men; in 21 issues of *Obesity Help*, only nine of the total 80 advertisements featured men as patients.[38] Drew concludes that not only do dominant ideologies shape the ideal patient scripts, but they also shape whether and how individuals use the new technologies. This, in turn, inspires change in both men's and women's bodies and identities, and reinforces the ideologies and scripts that produced these bodies and identities in the first place. As they use somatic technologies, individuals both reinforce and contest paradigms and scripts for femininity and masculinity.

Gendered Selves, Gendered Bodies

Anne Balsamo published a groundbreaking book in 1996, *Technologies of the Gendered Body*, which explored how body technologies in the late twentieth century were shaped by, and in turn reproduced, dominant gender paradigms and inequalities.[39] Examining primarily media and cultural products, Balsalmo analyzed technological interventions into the body, and concluded that these technologies were "ideologically shaped by the operation of gender interests, and consequently . . . serve to reinforce traditional gendered patterns of power and authority."[40] While people employ body technologies to improve the quality of their individual lives, these technologies are developed and used in tandem with hegemonic gender paradigms to reproduce gender inequality and maintain the status quo. In her analysis of body technologies and gender, Balsalmo asserts that technologies shape and are shaped by dominant gender paradigms and that these together reshape the gendered bodies and identities of individuals.

Biomedical Technologies and Gendered and Raced Bodies

Gendered biomedical technologies include a wide range of bodily interventions including hormone manipulation, non-surgical body work, and surgical body modification. These technologies can be used in both liberating and regressive ways; the technologies themselves do not have intrinsic goodness or badness. Contradictions often exist. Individuals often benefit personally from biomedical technologies like plastic and bariatric surgery, which can lead to increased self-worth and social approval but, simultaneously, the social scripts and paradigms these practices reinforce work to maintain social inequalities.

In one example, laser hair-removal treatments offer women a semi-permanent method of body work that, on a personal level, increases their ability to meet feminine beauty standards. However, on a societal level, this use of laser hair removal reshapes women's bodies in ways that reinforce and make "natural" contemporary gendered beauty scripts that define women's bodies as unmarred by body hair, and this in turn will place a stronger demand on women to conform to this ideal. Sociologists Samantha Kwan and Mary Nell Trautner summarize this process as it functions in society at large and conclude, "women's effortless authentic beauty is thus far from it. Beauty work is in large part this process of transforming the natural body to fit the cultural ideal, altogether while concealing the process and making it seem natural."[41]

The ability to produce socially valued bodies, i.e. bodies that possess the ideal skin color, facial features, and so forth, rests not only in the production of normative gender, but also requires race- and class-based privileges. And, as Balsamo pointed out, just as gender inequality affects somatechnics, racism affects the technologies that are developed and used. Often, body work falls in line with a narrow ideal characterized by features such as blonde flowing hair, a thin nose, almond-shaped eyes, large breasts, a small waist, and broad hips.[42] Women of color in North America face unattainable expectations because social scripts include very racialized beauty norms. As a society, North America prizes light skin, straight hair, and a list of features natural only in some white phenotypes. Similarly, body size is intertwined with social class; a well-toned body is often a mark of wealth: cheap food is more fattening and promotes poor health, and the time or means to cook nutritious meals and exercise regularly are often class-based privileges. Because of these inequalities, when women engage in body work, they do so within a system of racialized, gendered, and classed body norms that shape individual's ideas about what constitutes beauty, the body work they choose, and the meaning of their body work to others and in society at large.

The third case study, on beauty and twenty-first century norms, profiled the use of Botox. Use of cosmetic procedures (both surgical and non-surgical body work) has grown exponentially over the last 15 years, rising 247 percent between 1997 and 2012. This growth is not even across society: both cosmetic surgery and non-surgical cosmetic procedures have been predominantly a white women's practice. In 2012 more than 90 percent of cosmetic procedures were performed on women, and the proportion of women using cosmetic procedures compared to men is increasing with the popularity of minimally invasive procedures such as Botox. The racial composition of cosmetic surgery is changing as well.[43] Women of color are increasingly turning to cosmetic surgery; in 2012 white men and women made up 70 percent of patients, a significant decrease from 2000 when 86 percent of patients were white. In the United States between 2000 and 2013 there was a 526 percent increase in cosmetic surgery use by people of color, compared to an increase of 167 percent among white individuals, suggesting a trend among women of color toward using these technologies. The most common cosmetic surgery procedures for people of color are nose reshaping and eyelid surgery, which are procedures that alter racialized facial features, and breast augmentation, which creates a hyper-normative femininity.[44]

Regardless of individual intention, the use of cosmetic surgery can reinforce racialized gender beauty norms by reaffirming the hegemony of white body and beauty paradigms. Sociologist Eugenia Kaw examined these issues in her research on plastic surgery and race. In the early 1990s, Kaw interviewed Asian American women in San Francisco, asking why they used plastic surgery and what it meant to them. Women described plastic surgery as a way to better meet societal beauty scripts, and as Debra Gimlin found in her study of mostly white women, these Asian American women were conscious about what they were doing and how it mattered. One woman Kaw interviewed, Jane, commented:

> Especially if you go into business, whatever, you kind of have to have a Western facial type and you have to have like their features and stature—you know, be tall and stuff. In a way you can see it is an investment in your future.[45]

While the women Kaw spoke with were all vocal about their pride at being Asian, they also understood, as Jane summarized, that white features were viewed more positively in society. The plastic surgeons that Kaw interviewed expressed very similar views, while also revealing how racialized gender scripts not only shape individuals, but also whether and how technologies may be used. For instance, Kaw notes that doctors imply that white features are objectively more attractive, couching their racialized cosmetic procedures as efforts to help women achieve a look that is "naturally" more beautiful. One doctor stated, "90 percent of people look better with double eyelids. It makes the eye look more spiritually alive."[46]

This is not to say that all women of color use cosmetic surgery to achieve white features. Individual choices, however, exist within a racialized social context that produces particularly raced and gendered bodies concurrently. For the women in Kaw's study, experiences of body work were gendered and racialized in such a way that while plastic surgery was liberating on the individual level, it was detrimental on the societal level, reinforcing the social scripts for normatively gendered bodies and shaping even more ethnocentric beauty norms. Based on her interviews, Kaw suggests that social and ideological changes have coincided with the increased acceptance of plastic surgery in recent years to encourage surgical body work among Asian women. This body work, in turn, constrains available scripts for femininity by erasing racialized differences among women's bodies. We can extend the conclusions that Kaw draws to women of color more broadly to recognize how plastic surgery is "a means by which the women can attempt to permanently acquire not only a feminine look considered more attractive by society, but also a certain set of racial features considered more prestigious."[47] This raises serious questions about whether and how we as a society are producing increasingly normatively gendered bodies in the process and, more specifically, increasingly rigid racialized femininities.[48]

Although beauty scripts place a greater burden on women to meet bodily expectations, men are also subject to gendered scripts that propel them to enhance their masculinity through technological intervention. New biomedical techniques like injecting steroids or testosterone to boost muscle mass, or hair transplants to reverse balding, increase men's embodied masculinity and provide ways to help them meet hegemonic masculine norms. Recent revelations about the seemingly omnipresent use of steroids by male athletes are outcomes of scripts that declare that men's bodies are inadequate in their un-enhanced state. In 2013, after years of suspicion, Lance Armstrong admitted to his use of steroids but defended it by arguing that it was impossible to be competitive in cycling without doping because it was standard practice.[49] Similarly, the use of steroids in U.S. Major League Baseball has become so expected that revelations of use now do little to damage the careers of players like Alex "A-Rod" Rodriguez and Barry Bonds. The investigatory "Mitchell Report," submitted to the Commissioner of Major League Baseball, quotes National League Most Valuable Player Ken Caminiti as stating in 1992 that in his estimate, "at least half of Major League players were using anabolic steroids."[50] This widespread use of steroids and the subsequent bodily changes in cyclists and baseball players have shifted body scripts for athletes so much that un-enhanced bodies stand little chance of competing.

These technological interventions play a central role in reifying hyper-masculine bodies and naturalizing unattainable scripts, which may prove even more significant at a historical moment when men are increasingly subject to beauty and body norms. The increasing attention paid to men's bodies and the rising rates of eating disorders among boys suggest that boys and men are experiencing gendered body pressures at a new level. Men's magazines such as *GQ* have capitalized on the rise of the "metrosexual," a masculinity rooted in high levels of body work, to encourage and market body products to men. This body work encompasses not only pursuits of traditional male attributes by means such as working out and sculpting efforts, but also includes practices formerly confined to the pursuit of feminine ideals, such as shaving, waxing, dyeing, plucking, and renewed attention to clothing.[51]

Somatechnologies and Hyper-Normative Gender Scripts

Although photographic images are still commonly viewed as indisputable factual evidence, recent technological advancements in print and film now allow imperceptible alterations to print and video images. Because of the ability to alter media images to create smaller pores, bigger eyes, thinner legs, larger breasts, and more defined muscles, published and broadcast representations of idealized beauty have themselves become fictions. These alterations create idealized bodies that are more normatively "perfect" than is humanly possible. Manipulation of advertising images using computer programs such as Photoshop is ubiquitous, so much so that images *without* retouching have become news-worthy. Recent resistance to this manipulation on the part of some celebrities has made public how even thin and normatively beautiful actresses are subject to body-editing. For example, Keira Knightley, whose breasts were digitally enhanced in publicity for the 2004 movie *King Arthur*, refused similar manipulation for the 2008 movie *The Duchess*, and the ensuing tension between the actress and the movie studio was played out in the media. Similarly, Kate Winslet publicly critiqued the manipulated images of her legs in *GQ* magazine in 2003, an edit about which she was not consulted.[52] These and similar examples point to how no bodies—not even famous ones prized for their sex-appeal—meet the ideal without somatechnic manipulation.[53] Despite increased levels of body work, contemporary body ideals remain out of reach; computer manipulation of bodies in print and film media creates unreachable scripts for gendered bodies for both men and women, and these scripts have real consequences in the lives of individuals. The combination of new media and biomedical technologies is changing social body scripts and these, together, are impacting the gendered bodies and identities of individuals. Like with identity work, some transformations are unintended while others are purposeful efforts to transform the body.

Sociologist Jennifer Wesely focused on one group of women intentionally using biomedical technologies to construct hegemonically gendered and raced bodies. Wesely interviewed 20 women in the southwest of the United States to examine how women working in a strip club used body technologies to both construct profitable bodies, and to negotiate their own multiple identities (to demarcate their "true" self as separate from their "stripper" self). The women Wesely spoke with described engaging in a wide variety of often dangerous and painful technologies—plastic surgery, waxing, drugs, and diuretics—in order to produce the idealized femininity they felt was expected of them. Wesely found this gendered body work became a central focus of their lives. "As dancers, these women relied on their bodies in ways that necessitated their constant critique, attention, and maintenance, leading to more body technologies."[54] The pervasive use of these body technologies erased natural differences in bodies through implants, hair dye, tanning, and dieting, and reinforced hegemonic beauty scripts such that the ideal to which the women held themselves accountable was one that was biomedically constructed.

Predictably, the somatechnical changes the women manifested were not only gendered, but also raced; the women of color at the clubs Wesely studied spoke about how they had to look more sexy, and produce a more ideal femininity than white women to be seen as acceptable by both management and customers. This is very similar to what Eugenia Kaw found in her study of Asian American women and plastic surgery. A consequence of this body work, then, was the reproduction of racist beauty norms, and the re-entrenchment of phenotypically white bodies as the only ideal body type. The women Wesely spoke with felt compelled (financially and culturally) to engage in biomedical body work in order to produce an acceptably beautiful body and in so doing participated in a process that reinforced unrealistic hegemonic beauty standards. In the case of Wesely's study, the intentionally constructed nature of gendered bodies was rendered invisible and assumed to be natural because body work was ubiquitous at the strip club, and produced bodies that aligned with idealized femininities.

One particularly insightful part of Wesely's research is her investigation of how these bodily changes function in conversation with the multiple layers of identity that the dancers (and everyone else) construct and employ through body technologies. As Wesely explores, the women she studied were not dupes; they intentionally crafted their bodies because it made dancing more profitable. By the same token, however, these choices, which make sense within the world of strip clubs, set these women apart from mainstream society. The choices the strippers made about body work were both shaped and constrained by their context. Further, their choices have meaning and import beyond the personal level; the more the women shape their bodies to match an unrealistic feminine ideal, the more masked the constructed nature of femininity becomes, and the more normative, or, rather, hyper-normative the feminine body and identity scripts supported at the clubs become. The technologically enhanced bodies that the women who worked at the strip club constructed, shaped in line with the particular norms within that narrow context, are more feminine, more sexual, and more gendered than our broader society's normative scripts demand.

Through her ethnographic research, Wesely is able to document how the women experienced identity changes as the product of these technological interventions. The more technologies the women used to produce ideal bodies, the more wedded they became to their "stripper" identities. Even though the women often wanted to separate their "true identity" from their "dancer identity," body technologies such as breast enhancement, genital piercing, and hair dyeing would not allow them to leave the dancer-life behind. As one dancer commented: "In real life, when we're dressing in clothes ... if you've got huge tits you look awful during the day. They look good only in a G-string in a strip club."[55] Some body technologies used by the women met beauty scripts only in the strip club, but the women had to "wear" them all the time, which limited their ability to cast off a "stripper identity" at the end of the day. In light of this, these women purposefully engaged in other technological interventions in an effort to cordon off their "true" identities from their "stripper" identities, through wearing different clothing, by shaving, and through recreational drug use.

Along with altering their bodies, then, the women Wesely interviewed tried to walk the line between producing a marketable body and maintaining a body that was a meaningful reflection of their internal sense of self.[56] The women made choices about their bodies, but did so within a context that limited their options and as a result often were unable to embody their "inner selves." As Wesely concludes:

> Although body technologies have the potential to destabilize or challenge constructions of gendered bodies and related identity, this is even more difficult in a context that capitalizes on very limited constructions of the fantasy feminine body. Indeed, the women in the study felt tremendous pressure to conform to body constructions that revolve around extreme thinness, large breasts, and other features that conform to a "Barbie doll" image.[57]

The consequences of these choices, as Wesely suggests, are significant. A number of scholars have documented how women who embody hegemonic femininity earn more money for stripping, and the women Wesely talked with acknowledged that normative gender scripts alongside financial, peer, and managerial pressure, directly informed the changes they made in their bodies.[58]

On the personal level, this body work affected the identities of the women. They engaged in body work that was encouraged within the context of their occupation, and which was aimed at producing femininities in line with the dominant gender paradigms of the strip club.

In due course, this body work, in tandem with each individual's personal biography, shaped their identity. On an institutional level, the outcome of the biomedical construction of hyper-normative femininities by the women was an erasure of difference. By producing a very narrow set of femininities in line with hegemonic paradigms and gendered body scripts, the women naturalized a feminine body that was virtually unattainable without the use of body technologies, and in this process they erased the very real differences that had existed between each of their bodies.

A Sociological Perspective on the Meaning of Body Work

The technologies that are developed and used in a society are shaped by dominant paradigms and social scripts within a social context and filtered through personal history. Whether and how people manipulate their bodies using biomedical technology is different in distinct communities of a single nation, not to mention in different countries. These differences are based on different social scripts, paradigms of gender and embodiment, and available technologies within a particular micro (strip club) or macro (North American societies) context. While plastic surgery may be the dominant way to construct larger breasts within middle- and upper-class communities in North America, individuals without the same social and economic capital are more likely to use prosthetics, growth stimulants, or even the very dangerous injection of liquid silicone into breast tissue.[59] Men in different race, class, and sexual communities engage a diverse array of somatechnics to manage hair loss. Middle- or upper-class men often employ hair transplants (now the fifth most common cosmetic surgery procedure for men), while other men use less expensive over-the-counter hair-growth stimulants, such as the U.S. brand "Rogaine," wigs, toupees, or hairstyling techniques. Not only do rates of baldness vary by race, but also the forms of treatment utilized vary across race, class, and community.

Each of the examples discussed thus far emphasizes how biomedical technologies are in dynamic relationship to gender paradigms, scripts, bodies, and identities. Individuals deploy contemporary biotechnologies in order to shape both their physical self and their internal identity, but these endeavors are always already informed and constrained by context, as well as guided by reigning gender and race paradigms and scripts. Our analysis, therefore, must mediate between viewing new technologies as tools for personal agency, and the larger social implications of bodies produced by biomedical intervention.

Somatechnologies and New Gender Scripts

While each new biomedical technology may have the possibility of reifying gender scripts, it can also open up potential for new gendered bodies. Cisgender and trans* women can lift weights, play sports, and cut their hair; cisgender and trans* men can don makeup, wear high heels, and dance ballet. Multiple mundane technologies can be, and are, deployed to create new masculinities and femininities. Technologies can and do have multiple, contradictory personal and social implications. For instance, hair removal and surgical technologies are used simultaneously to create hyper-normative bodies and are used by members of the trans* community in order to shape public perception of their bodies so that this perception matches their gender identities.

The meaning of plastic surgery in the lives of individuals and in society is not inherent in the practices themselves; instead, social paradigms and scripts for gender and embodiment shape the meaning we give to biomedical interventions, and determine how available we make the technologies. Sociologist Elroi Windsor's sociological analysis of cisgender and transgender cosmetic surgery makes these processes visible.[60] Cosmetic surgery is unequally regulated; transgender individuals are required to obtain therapeutic permission to undertake cosmetic surgery, while cisgender individuals do not require approval before doing so. This is true even among procedures which are similar or even identical for cisgender and trans* individuals (e.g., breast augmentation).

Despite these different levels of social control, Windsor's research found incredible similarity between cisgender and transgender motivations before surgery and in outcomes post-surgery. Cisgender and transgender individuals all sought to "enhance the self through the body," hoping to look and feel better after surgery. And both cisgender and transgender individuals reported just such positive (and gendered) outcomes. Errol, a transgender man whom Windsor interviewed, who had undergone breast reduction, reflected, "I would have thought of myself as a man one way or the other, but I feel like a fuller man, if that makes sense . . . I feel less feminized with my chest gone."[61] Similarly Chrissy, a cisgender woman, reflected that her breast augmentation gave her, "the best feeling in the world. I *loved* it. I could not stop looking in the mirror. I was like, oh my God, this is what a woman looks like! I have boobs now!"[62] Cosmetic surgeries were used by both cisgender and transgender individuals to "articulate a gendered concept of the self."[63] While dominant paradigms discount the significance of plastic surgery for cisgender individuals, Windsor's findings suggest that, for the individuals in question, cosmetic surgery is more than just "cosmetic"—it is used to articulate a gendered self. Plastic surgery was important in how cisgender men and women constructed their gendered body and self-concept. Further, like cisgender individuals, the surgeries employed by transgender individuals help them articulate their gender, but do not fundamentally transform it; individuals' gender identity was supported but not changed through surgery. These findings run counter to dominant paradigms that normalize cisgender body modification as benign and pathologize transgender body modification as a last resort treatment for Gender Dysphoria.

Windsor concludes that both cisgender and transgender individuals,

> viewed surgery as helping them maintain a gender presentation that matched their inner gendered selves . . . They believed surgery would change their gendered appearances and aid their social gender identities. Both groups wanted to use surgery to affect a more desirable gender presentation that others could respond to more favorably, and neither group viewed the surgery itself as gender-changing.[64]

Cisgender surgeries and transgender surgeries share similar psychosocial significance for individuals, but we emphasize the significance of transgender surgeries and dismiss the significance of cisgender ones, which are in line with dominant gender paradigms and body work scripts. Despite pervasive similarities, surgeries for cisgender and transgender individuals are thought of very differently, not because of any significant differences in physical or psychological characteristics of the two populations, but instead because of (cis)gender paradigms and social scripts for normative embodiment. These paradigms and scripts lead psycho-medical institutions and society more generally to treat these surgeries with different criteria. Moreover, because we normalize cisgender surgeries and pathologize transgender ones, we ignore the diversity of experiences that exist among both groups.

The cases in this chapter suggest that, while we could make gendered, embodied selves in a multitude of ways, hegemonic body paradigms and gendered social scripts lay out a constrained set of gendered bodies that are intelligible to others and to ourselves. This "making sense" is a social and interactional process that takes place within particular social contexts and is shaped by personal history and socializing agents. When culturally inscribed somatechnologies change who we can be, social scripts adapt to new ways of being that reflect these new identities and bodies. As Victoria Pitts summarizes, "new practices for the body respond to, are shaped by, and are limited by the larger social and historical pressures that regulate bodies."[65]

The Complexities of Body Work

People transform their bodies using the technologies available in any given moment. This process is sometimes unintentional; working on computers for extended periods of time causes changes in eyesight and posture, being right or left handed will increase the size and musculature of the dominant arm. Transformations are sometimes incidental; sports create particularly gendered/muscled bodies, wearing high heels changes posture. Alongside these circumstantial changes, new technologies allow people to intervene directly and purposefully into the shape, function, and appearance of their bodies in transformative ways. The ability to manifest, in an embodied fashion, chosen identities and/or physiological features is significant, and these technologies are working hand-in-hand with existing body and gender paradigms and scripts to refashion people's lives. Returning to the comparison of Michael Dillon and Rey Grosz demonstrates how the dynamics of technologies and paradigms bear on the lives of individuals. These two men came of age in two very different historical moments, and the gender paradigms, scripts, and technologies of their day and the social contexts within which they were situated crafted radically different paths for each of them.

Michael Dillon came of age in the early 1930s, in England, at the same moment that author Radcliffe Hall was embroiled in an obscenity trial that catapulted language and knowledge of lesbianism and gender nonconformity into the public sphere. In Radcliffe Hall's *Well of Loneliness,* the gender and sexuality of the main character, Steven, are conflated such that Steven was understood as lesbian because of his gender nonconformity. This was one of the only places Dillon saw himself reflected in any way, and it was through this public debate that he learned about gender nonconformity. Radcliffe Hall's *Well of Loneliness* was about gender nonconformity that, culturally, could be understood only as homosexuality. Michael Dillon was told to make sense of his own gender nonconformity as homosexuality by the few people in whom he confided.

Michael Dillon struggled to make sense of his gender nonconformity, and spent years trying to situate himself within society. His quest for help, however, was thwarted, in part because there was no gender paradigm within which transgenderism could fit. When Dillon's search for medical help failed, he became a doctor in order to manifest socially his gender identity, and to support his own and others' bodily changes. He began taking testosterone in 1939 and endured more than 13 surgical gender affirming efforts (surgeries which were often failures). In 1944, just eight years after the publicized surgery undergone by Lili Elbe (who is credited with being the first male-to-female person to medically change her sex) and 11 years before Christine Jorgensen's public coming out after her surgery, Dillon became the first female-to-male (FTM) person on record to legally change his sex. He was finally able to bring his identity as a man into more alignment with his public role and body. Dillon wrote about what would eventually be termed transsexuality (including in his book *Self: A Study in Endocrinology and Ethics*), and struggled to make a life for himself. Dillon intentionally cultivated a heteronormative life, even taking on a misogynist persona as part of constructing his masculinity. After being publicly outed as transsexual in 1958, Dillon retreated to a life of monasticism in Tibet, and died in 1962 aged 47.[66]

Rey's life thus far has been very different from Michael Dillon's. After coming out to his family and starting college, Rey pursued hormone therapy and began to live his life as a man. Within a few months he began taking testosterone to produce masculine secondary sex characteristics like facial and body hair and a deeper voice. He also had gender affirming surgeries that created a more male body. In due order, Rey finished his undergraduate degree at Columbia.[67] Compared to Michael Dillon's long wait and multiple surgeries, Rey was able to engage in body-altering procedures with relative ease.

Rey's story is not yet fully written but already there is much more to tell about his path toward social masculinity than there was for Dillon, and a number of things are significant about Rey's experience. Rey is part of a growing population of young trans* individuals who have both the ability and social support to reshape their bodies, and his ability to manifest his chosen gender, in a bodily fashion, is remarkable. Compared to Michael Dillon's multi-year struggle to physically change his sex, Rey's ability to do so as soon as he turned 18 (at which point he no longer needed parental consent) marks a significant shift in accessibility, education, and legitimacy. Second, the respect and acumen with which journalist Alissa Quart constructed her magazine article that first profiled Rey and other young trans* individuals is heartening. In the span of 50 years, social scripts have expanded so significantly that they reflect a familiarity with the language and complexity of gender nonconformity. While Michael Dillon's few confidants could understand his gender nonconformity only as homosexuality, the *New York Times Magazine* article in which Rey Grosz was profiled freely used terms like transgender, transmale, and genderqueer, which were non-existent during Dillon's lifetime.

It is important not to romanticize transgender lives or choices without grounding them within the lived reality of transgender people, however.

Rey experienced significant levels of harassment and institutional resistance that caused him to move out of the dormitories at Barnard and even take a leave of absence from college. Because of discrimination and prejudice, rates of violence for transgender youth are significantly higher than for their cisgender peers, as are rates of poverty and homelessness.[68] The first national study of discrimination against transgender individuals, conducted by the National Center for Transgender Equality and National Gay and Lesbian Task Force, found that 63 percent of respondents to the national survey experienced significant discrimination (e.g. job loss, bullying, assault) and 23 percent experienced three or more significant discriminatory events. Among those who were transgender or gender nonconforming during K–12 education, 78 percent reported harassment, 35 percent survived physical assault and 12 percent sexual violence. Fifteen percent left K–12 or higher education because of harassment and violence.[69] These are shockingly high levels of violence. Researchers also found that lack of social support from family, peers, teachers, and school administrators led transgender youth to disproportionately high rates of suicidal thoughts, loneliness, and homelessness.[70] Fifty-one percent of youth who were harassed in school attempted suicide.[71] Moreover, class and race both affect outcomes for young people and adults, and trans* people of color experience more violence, higher rates of homelessness, and lower social status than their white peers do.[72]

All told, the life stories of Michael Dillon and Rey Grosz do reveal significant change in gender scripts over the past 50 years. These changes suggest that the possible ways of being in the world have expanded. While trans* has not yet been incorporated as normative into North American cultures, progress has been made. New technologies have been developed that range from the simple expansion of language to cutting-edge surgeries that allow and facilitate precise bodily changes. Dominant gender paradigms have shifted to include trans* embodiments as a possibility hand-in-hand with these technologies. Alternative gender scripts have proliferated, making it possible for individuals—including young people like Rey—to access information about trans* more readily and to construct more diverse gendered

identities and bodies than ever before. And, while there is still prejudice against trans* individuals, the difference between these two men's
life experiences reveal that changes in gender paradigms, scripts, technologies, and embodied selves are manifested in the everyday lives of
individuals.

As embodied gender continues to change, it may well fuel ongoing transformation of social scripts and paradigms, including a shift
in gender norms alongside more diversity of bodies. But, as established
in Chapter 1, technology is neither utopian nor regressive. Technologies are used in both non-normative ways that produce new bodies and
identities that support social change and spark an expansion in social
scripts, as well as in ways that reinforce expectations about gendered
bodies, inhibit social change, and provoke normative identity re-
entrenchment. Personal meaning making around one's body or identity
does not exist in a vacuum. Individuals' intentions are only part of the
impact of body work; historical context, social norms, and power relations all shape the reception, meaning, and import of new technologies,
bodies, and identities regardless of the desire or intention of individuals. Victoria Pitts, a scholar of the body, talks about body work as a
"project" and draws on theorist Elizabeth Grosz to elaborate that:

> No body projects limitlessly expand the range of possibilities for
> human subjectivity, nor do they "invent" the self as a matter of
> personal choice. Body projects may appear to be productions of
> the self, but they are historically located in time and place, and
> provide messages that "can be 'read' only within a social system of
> organization and meaning"
>
> (Grosz 1997: 239).[73]

This system of organization within which people are situated is bounded
by social statuses like gender, sexuality, race, and class which shape one's
ability to engage in body work and achieve socially valued embodied
identities. In other words, body work is always both a social and political
endeavor where individuals negotiate between social norms, power relations, and individual desires. The elements of this complex and dynamic

set of relations between identity, body, social scripts, dominant ideologies, and technologies are all part of how new embodied identities come to be. As is true of identity change, technologically-spurred body work is both liberating and regressive. This runs contrary to both utopian visions of body-agency wherein people can remake their embodied self as they wish, and disciplining narratives that suggest that individuals are rigidly constrained by a set of already available, static scripts for body and identity.

We are clearly living in a moment where gender paradigms, scripts, bodies, and identities are all being refined and renegotiated. New technologies are being deployed to re-entrench hegemonic masculinities and femininities and erase race and gender differences in bodies. Hormonal birth control places the burdens of sexual decisions on women and genital surgeries such as "hymenorrhaphy" (hymen reconstruction) reinforce the importance of virginity in women. Conversely, these same biomedical technologies such as testosterone and estrogen regimens and genital construction methods are allowing individuals to shape their bodies in new ways that create more diverse pairings of sex and gender, and these new embodied genders are revolutionary for individuals and for society.

We must recognize the social gender paradigms and scripts tied up with biomedical innovation and attune ourselves to whether and how these new technologies are disciplining, regulating, and transforming the gendered body in new ways. Are we on the brink of a new gender order? Somatechnic frontiers are certainly reshaping the body in previously unknown ways, and this process challenges gender norms and scripts to make space accordingly. The documented expansion of gender possibilities—for both transgender and cisgender individuals— certainly suggests that gender ideologies and scripts are being reworked. Just as information technologies do not move societies uni-directionally toward expanded identity possibilities, biomedical technologies are used in some ways that encourage the expansion of gender possibilities, while in others they help to resist this process. If, however, we take as true the dynamic and reciprocal relationships between technology, ideology, scripts, bodies, and identities, then gender will continue to transform itself alongside technological innovation.

Notes

1 Quart 2008.
2 Quart 2008: 34.
3 This is an approach rooted in pragmatism and built on the same theories we have used to understand the social self, including those of George Herbert Mead, William James, Charles Cooley, and Irving Goffman.
4 Pitts 2003; Shilling 2008.
5 United Nations 1992.
6 International Medical Congress 1913.
7 The defining U.S. Supreme Court case was Diamond versus Chakrabarty in 1980 (444 U.S. 1,028).
8 Ernst & Young 2013.
9 Armstrong 1983; Morgan and Scott 1993.
10 Link et al. 2008; Morgan and Scott 1993.
11 Johnson 2008.
12 Crawley, Foley, and Shehan 2007; Radley 1991; Watson 2000.
13 Archer 2000; Butler 1990 and 1993; Featherstone 1982; Turner 1984. For a longer discussion of this body of work, see Shilling 2007b: 8.
14 Franklin 2007; Grosz 1994.
15 For example, plastic surgery dates back to ancient Egypt. For an in-depth history of plastic surgery see Morgan and Scott 1993; Santoni-Rugiu and Sykes 2007.
16 Sullivan 2005 and 2006.
17 Stryker 2008; Murray 2008.
18 Gimlin 2002: 84.
19 Gimlin 2002.
20 Hebdige 1979.
21 Cregan 2006; Crossley 2001; Grimshaw 1999.
22 Gimlin 2002; Kang 2003; Wolkowitz 2006.
23 Kwan and Trautner 2009.
24 Conley and Glauber 2005; Hamermesh and Biddle 1994.
25 The first intestinal bypass was performed by A. J. Kremen in 1954.
26 American Society for Metabolic and Bariatric Surgery 2007 and 2013.
27 Murray 2008.
28 Not only do the legacies of Enlightenment thought draw connections between self and body (Pitts 2003; Sullivan 2006), but a number of scholars have documented how individuals in our society try to manifest their identities in their bodies (Goffman 1959; Schlenker 1980; Swann 1987). Individuals intentionally use identity cues to assert or confirm their self-identification, and when absent work to create them.
29 Murray 2008.
30 Gimlin 2002.
31 For example, traditional body norms in the West African nation of Mauritania prize fatness in women, just as Western norms have historically, because fatness is/was seen as a sign of wealth, social class, and health.
32 American Medical Association 2013.
33 Drew 2008b.
34 Drew 2008a.
35 Bartky 1988; Bordo 1993; Davis 1995.
36 McKinley 1999.
37 Krizek et al. 1999.

38 Drew 2008a. All issues of Obesity Help between July 2003 and January/February 2008 were coded.
39 Balsamo 1996.
40 Balsamo 1996:10.
41 Kwan and Trautner 2009: 59.
42 Gagné and McGaughey 2002.
43 American Society for Aesthetic Plastic Surgery 2013; American Society of Plastic Surgeons 2013a; International Society of Aesthetic Plastic Surgery 2012.
44 American Society of Plastic Surgeons 2013a.
45 Kaw 1993: 78.
46 Kaw 1993: 81.
47 Kaw 1993: 80.
48 Bordo 2003; Davis 1995.
49 Macur 2013.
50 Mitchell 2007: 60–61.
51 Coad 2008.
52 Albright 2007.
53 For a great example of how images are manipulated see the Dove Campaign video, Evolution. Available at: www.campaignforrealbeauty.com/home_films_evolution_v2.swf (Staav and Piper 2006).
54 Wesely 2003: 655.
55 Wesely 2003: 662.
56 Wesely 2003: 666.
57 Wesely 2003: 665.
58 Ronai and Ellis 1989; Sweet and Tewksbury 2000; Wood 2000.
59 Kulick 1998; Xavier et al. 2005.
60 Windsor 2011.
61 Windsor 2011: 122.
62 Windsor 2011: 124.
63 Windsor n.d.
64 Windsor 2011: 108.
65 Pitts 2003: 44.
66 Kennedy 2008.
67 Bentivoglio 2011.
68 Cisgender, as we discussed in Chapter 1, refers to a somatic state where one's birth gender (gender assigned at birth) matches one's birth sex (sex assigned at birth). Namaste 2006; Shilling 2008.
69 Grant et al. 2011: 33.
70 Pardo 2008; Pardo and Schantz 2008.
71 Grant et al. 2011: 45.
72 Xavier et al. 2005.
73 Pitts 2003: 34.

CASE STUDY: REPRODUCTION AND THE GENDER OF MEDICINE

Both the body and biomedicine are socially constructed, shaped by gender paradigms and given meaning through social scripts and interactional practices.[1] Because male bodies have been viewed as the baseline for normalcy, they have not been seen as warranting investigation, let alone intervention. Biomedical knowledge, and reproductive medicine more specifically, has both privileged masculinity and naturalized men's bodies,[2] whereas women have been more subject to medical experimentation, and their bodies are seen as more legitimate sites of medical intervention than men's.[3] For example, while changes in male's hormone levels (decreasing testosterone) are seen as a natural part of aging, changes in women's hormones are defined medically as menopause, an "estrogen-deficiency disease."[4] Scholars and feminists alike suggest that the placement of contraceptive and reproductive responsibility almost exclusively on women is also a product of this larger set of social beliefs that men's bodies are the normal, default, or unmarked category while women's bodies are in need of treatment.[5] These dominant paradigms are so subtly entrenched in our society that most people might not even think to question why there is no male birth control pill.

Since the advent of the female birth control pill in the 1960s, feminist scholars and activists have criticized pharmaceutical companies for not creating oral contraceptives for men. While 13 new contraceptives have been developed for women since World War II, there has not been a single new contraceptive developed for men in the last 100 years.[6] Nelly Oudshoorn, who has researched the development of a male pill, asserts that the lack of contraceptives for men reflects the scientific and medical bias that allows women's bodies to be designated as legitimate sites of medical intervention, particularly in terms of reproduction and sexual activity. This focus on women was matched until very recently by an equally prevalent absence of men's bodies in reproductive medicine.[7] For this to change, the very infrastructure of reproductive medicine—and the gendered social scripts for who a patient can be, that undergird it—needed to be expanded. As Oudshoorn documents, when the World Health Organization began to encourage research on male contraceptives in the 1970s, the scientific community was unequipped to heed the call. Scientists had to substantially reorganize family planning institutions, create new drug testing standards, clinics, and research specialties, and even develop new definitions of who could be categorized as a reproductive patient, before the research could move forward.[8] Indeed, until then, one of the prerequisites for being a reproductive patient was to be a woman. Even now, 40 years later, there is still no male oral contraceptive on the market.[9] For researchers to develop the new technologies necessary to create male contraceptives, a substantial shift in social gender paradigms and scripts is required. In other words, social scripts need to be expanded to allow the development of new technology.

These same gendered paradigms and scripts have shaped the study and treatment of infertility. Much research on infertility has been conducted, ranging in focus from biological components, to psychological impact, to social and interpersonal factors.[10] In it, individuals have shared the deeply personal, often emotional, and sometimes devastating experience of struggling to have a child. Infertility affects men and women in equal numbers, yet virtually all of this research has focused on women.

The inability of individuals to become pregnant or to impregnate is not a modern phenomenon, but before the middle of the twentieth century, infertility provoked a range of pseudo-scientific responses, folk remedies, and social arrangements such as informal surrogacy. Biomedical treatments began in the 1950s with hormonal treatments and now include a range of interventions, from hormonal stimulation to genetic screening and fertilization in a laboratory. The American Society for Reproductive Medicine (ASRM) defines infertility as: "a disease, defined by the failure to achieve a successful pregnancy after 12 months or more of regular unprotected intercourse," or "after 6 months for women over age 35 years."[11] Infertility can be caused by medical and physiological issues such as physical injury, hormone imbalance, chromosomal or physiological differences, and cancer. In addition, the ASRM's definitions of infertility assume heterosexual use of penile/ vaginal sex where both egg and sperm are available; in other words, the definition actually designates social conditions such as being part of a same-sex couple or being single as causes of "infertility" as well.[12] The modern, medical definition of infertility was intentionally debated and constructed by medical practitioners and reflects social norms and conditions. For example, infertility is defined as a "disease," as opposed to a "condition" or "disorder," specifically to ease insurance coverage, an issue in contemporary North American society. Infertility affects people of all social classes, races, and ethnicities, although access to treatment in the U.S. depends on financial resources.

Between 11 and 15 percent of heterosexual couples that include a cisgender male and a cisgender female of reproductive age (15–44) in the United States and Canada struggle to get pregnant and carry a child to term.[13] Male infertility and female infertility are each the cause of about 30 percent of all couples' infertility, 20 percent of infertility in couples is due to fertility challenges for both partners, and 20 percent is unexplained. The National Center for Health Statistics (NCHS) at the U.S. Centers for Disease Control began tracking male infertility only after 2000. Prior to that, only statistics for female infertility were collected. Despite the fact that male infertility has been proven to be equally likely as female infertility, most research on infertility still focuses on women, and most treatments still center on the female body.[14]

Gender paradigms shape the medicine of reproduction and infertility at all levels. Culturally, gender scripts shape the meaning of reproduction and infertility in society. For instance, anthropologist Emily Martin examined descriptions of reproduction and found that, in both medical and lay publications, descriptions of conception typically depict sperm that compete, race, hunt, and burrow, while eggs wait patiently to be inseminated. This is held as true even though a more accurate description of biological processes casts the egg as far more active and the sperm as more receptive.[15] In other words, knowledge about fertilization is gendered and is built on cultural gender scripts. Martin argues that not only does scientific knowledge-creation rely on hegemonic gender paradigms, the power of scientific metaphor maintains gender inequality by naturalizing it.

Just as scientific metaphor genders the behavior of cells involved in conception, dominant gender paradigms construct infertility as a women's problem, both somatically and socially. Women who are childless (whether by choice or infertility) violate core social scripts for womanhood and experience stigma accordingly. A 1988 study by Greil, Leitko, and Porter, for example, found that, no matter who had the physiological impairment, women felt responsible for and stigma from infertility. Infertility calls into question women's self-concept and gender identity and impacts their social role and identity.[16]

In an effort to better understand experiences of infertility, sociologist Liberty Barnes designed an ethnographic study that followed in the footsteps of the existing body of research on women who undergo infertility treatment. Instead of focusing on women, however, she turned her attention to the understudied experiences of *men* who sought treatment for infertility, and the support and medical institutions from which they sought help. When Barnes applied for the routine ethics approval process that all human-focused research projects must undergo, however, she was halted in her tracks. The oversight committee at her university (the Institutional Review Board, or IRB), as well as the IRBs at the hospitals where she wanted to collect data, and which employed the doctors and nurses working on men's infertility, all balked at her topic. Even though extensive research has been done on women and infertility internationally—and very similar research focused on female infertility had easily received IRB approval at her university a decade earlier—Barnes was told that there were serious concerns about her project.[17] The IRB felt that infertility was such a sensitive topic for men that they might be upset by participation in the study. The IRB demanded Barnes demonstrate her skills as an ethnographer to make sure she would treat the data collection "maturely" and respectfully, a request unheard of in other projects.[18]

Dominant paradigms and social scripts for infertility, masculinity, and biomedicine shape the analysis and treatment of male infertility. For Liberty Barnes, these gender paradigms shaped her ability to research men's experience of infertility, in large part because her project aimed to draw attention to problems in the male body which biomedical scripts work to conceal. The threat posed by Barnes' research was that it challenged dominant gender paradigms for men and social scripts for biomedicalization. While Barnes was ultimately able to do her research, she struggled for many months to gain IRB approval and had to change (and significantly complicate) her research methods in order to do so. After many written and phone consultations with the IRB committee it became clear that the central concern with Barnes' research was that her questions about infertility might challenge the masculinity of the men she planned on interviewing. Even though research on women's infertility included the potential to evoke these same negative emotions (sadness, failure, guilt, etc.) it is only when the research focused on men that these potential effects became a problem. In fact, elements of the research that Barnes saw as positive, elements that have been construed as positive in research with women, such as women having the opportunity to share their feelings—and for which men in Barnes study ultimately thanked her—were seen as a significant risk for men.

To gain IRB approval Barnes was required to tell men, several times, when they consented to participate in the study, that if the research provoked an emotional response she would stop the interview and make sure that they wanted to continue. In other words, gender paradigms for emotionality and the social scripts they generate—that men don't show emotion, for example—were inserted into the research design of Barnes' study on men's infertility. Warnings in the consent forms made clear to men that they *shouldn't* show emotion, since doing so was a risk of the research and one that might encourage them to terminate participation. The warning that Barnes was required to include in her consent form shaped the experiences of men who chose to participate, reminding them that showing emotion, even about something as difficult as infertility, was not masculine. Moreover, it reinforced the idea that infertility was something to be ashamed of. That is, the requirements that Barnes had to implement in order to gain IRB approval were both built on and reinforced hegemonic gender norms about men and men's bodies.

In this and other research on masculinity, some IRBs have prioritized validating men's feelings of masculinity over research methods or findings.[19] Liberty Barnes wrote about this experience with Christin Munsch, a scholar who faced similar hurdles in her study of men and gender inequalities. They suggest that IRBs are engaging in "emotional labor to protect individual men's masculinity, and require researchers to do the same."[20] Thinking about their experiences Barnes and Munsch conclude that while IRBs were created to protect marginalized populations, in practice they serve to protect the male research subject and their masculinity:

> [T]he IRB approval process relies heavily on cultural assumptions about men and masculinity, producing protocol modifications that idealize hegemonic masculinity. These modifications include mandatory scripts and procedures that socialize men and encourage gender "appropriate" behavior. Thus, IRBs serve as gendering institutions, reifying gender stereotypes and cultural assumptions about gender.[21]

Gender paradigms shape individual men and women at the same time as they structure research and treatment of infertility. Emerging scholarship on male infertility has found that the ability to impregnate is linked to normative manhood; male infertility challenges core aspects of masculinity including virility, power, and sexual prowess.[22] Men experience male infertility as an explicit threat to their masculinity and most men describe feeling stigmatized as unmasculine because of infertility.[23] Moreover, the intricacies of infertility treatment (producing a sperm sample on demand) can cause anxiety and gender panic for men. While social scripts conceive of men as always ready for sex, the realities of men's lived-experience is more complicated. When men are too embarrassed, nervous, or emotional to ejaculate for infertility treatments, their masculinity is again called into question. Moreover, different cultural prohibitions on masturbation exacerbate these feelings of emasculation.[24] Male infertility is also seen as a threat to masculinity culturally.[25] In newspaper coverage of male infertility (declining sperm counts, more precisely), Kenneth Gannona and colleagues found that mainstream media framed the issue of declining sperm counts as a crisis of masculinity. The language chosen in newspaper coverage to talk about the "fertility crisis" drew on stereotypically male activities for the metaphors used to describe the problem, and conflated fertility with masculinity.

Medical research and writing is also shaped by the cultural linkage between masculinity and fertility. Treatment protocols emphasize the importance of framing infertility as a "couple's problem" in part to lessen the stigma of male infertility. Efforts to shift attention away from inadequacies of the male body are coupled with the use of elaborate, often hyper-masculine metaphors by infertility doctors to mitigate the negative effects of pathologization for men. For example, in Liberty Barnes' research, one doctor described how he talks with men patients:

> The tests show [the] engine needs fuel. Fuel is hormones, LH and SH. I'm trying to figure out if your engine's running and your exhaust is blocked or whether your engine's not running and your exhaust is open ... I can fix exhaust, but it's hard to fix engines.[26]

This type of metaphor, using examples like planes, construction, or cars, explains the physiology of infertility in a way that helps men to maintain masculine power. As the doctor went on to explain to Barnes, "I think I come out with metaphors that [men] can relate to ... Then they'll understand and will be more empowered and less weak."[27] Just as the IRB was concerned that Barnes' research might disempower men by questioning their masculinity, medical treatment for male infertility concerns itself with maintaining the masculinity of men patients.

Ultimately, the social scripts for infertility provide men "with a limited range of linguistic resources from which to construct accounts both of what it is to be a man and of health-related issues and concerns."[28] In similar research on sperm, Lisa Jean Moore concludes, "[the] scientific discourses around semen emerge from an existing gender hierarchy, create new emergent ideal types of gender (in both popular and academic cultures), and in turn affect how gender is enacted."[29] That is, these broad social scripts and gender paradigms shape the dominant discourses of masculinity and infertility. In turn, these discourses guide knowledge production within social institutions and the beliefs and behaviors of individuals.

Institutionally, biomedical knowledge production links dominant gender paradigms with medical practices. Early medicine on infertility referred to the condition as "barrenness," immediately founding study on the assumption that infertility was universally a woman's problem. It is only with the advent of the microscope and the observation of sperm deficiencies that male infertility was even conceptualized.[30] Carrying forward these historical biases, the unit of treatment for male infertility is often the couple and not the individual so that the problem is shifted from the male body to the couple's bod*ies*.[31] This shift of the medical gaze away from the male body works to maintain the masculinity of infertile men, relying on existing gendered processes of medicalization to reinforce dominant gender norms and scripts.

The transfer of the burden of male infertility to women is accomplished most commonly by using the same treatment for male infertility as female infertility: in-vitro fertilization (IVF). IVF is the process whereby eggs extracted from female ovaries are fertilized by sperm in a petri dish and then after several days implanted into the uterus. IVF (or its offshoots) is the most common treatment for male infertility, although it is much more invasive for female bodies than male bodies. While the process requires cisgender men simply to produce sperm, usually through masturbation or sometimes through needle aspiration, cisgender women must undergo many weeks of hormone treatments and several surgical procedures. The logic of treating the female body for male infertility is only conceivable if social scripts position female bodies as legitimate sites of medical intervention, and if *male* infertility is seen as a *female* problem. That is, gendered (indeed, sexist) scripts for (in)fertility have shaped both the meaning and treatment of men's infertility such that treatments reflect and reinforce gender inequality.[32]

Instead of researching and developing treatments specific to male infertility, reproductive medicine has continued to use the existing, invasive procedures used for female infertility to treat male infertility.[33]

By displacing the discussion of male infertility onto IVF, medicine as an institution reconstructs male infertility as a "couple's" problem and places the burden of treatment success or failure on the woman's body's acceptance of IVF/implantation. All sperm become good sperm while women's bodies become responsible for accepting or rejecting the fertilized embryo. Drawing on her research on biomedicalization, sociologist Adele Clarke reflects, "it is difficult to conceive of a more sex and gender-constructing and maintaining discipline and set of practices and discourses than those of the reproductive sciences."[34]

As this case of infertility exemplifies, gendered practices are evident in how biomedical research and treatment is designed and undertaken, and what the outcomes are. By legitimating research and treatment in line with hegemonic beliefs and withholding support from procedures that challenges these paradigms, IRBs, and biomedicine more broadly, works to maintain gender and gender inequality. Further, institutional policies—whether IRBs or reproductive medicine—rely on and reinforce these gendered paradigms and the social scripts they generate. As Lisa Jean Moore summarizes: "While technological advancement has the potential for broadly expanding reproductive agency to a large variety of social groups, it is the tight control of this agency that is at the heart of the production and reproduction of an institutionalized gender power structure."[35]

Notes

1 Van der Ploeg 1995.
2 Martin 1987.
3 Ehrenreich and English 2005.
4 Fausto-Sterling 2000: 146–147.
5 Moscucci 1990; Oudshoorn 2000, 2003.
6 Oudshoorn 2003: 5.
7 Oudshoorn 1994.
8 Oudshoorn 2003.
9 While several new contraceptives are in clinical trial, they are some years away from release.
10 Becker 2000; Franklin 1997; Greil 1991.
11 American Society for Reproductive Medicine 2008.
12 Mamo 2007.
13 Bushnik et al. 2012; Chandra, Copen, and Stephen 2013.
14 Barnes 2014; Culley, Hudson, and Lohan 2013; Daniels 2006.

15 Martin 1991; Tomlinson 1995.
16 Becker 2000; Franklin 1997; Riessman 2000; Thompson 2005.
17 Thompson 2005.
18 Barnes and Munsch n.d.
19 Barnes and Munsch n.d.
20 Barnes and Munsch n.d.: 15.
21 Barnes and Munsch n.d.
22 Kampf 2013.
23 Edelmann, Humphrey, and Owens 1994; Mason 1993; Nachtigall, Becker, and Wozny 1992.
24 Inhorn 2007.
25 Gannona, Gloverb, and Abelc 2004.
26 Barnes 2014: 63.
27 Barnes 2014: 63.
28 Gannona et al. 2004: 1,174.
29 Moore 2002: 115.
30 Lorber 1989.
31 Van der Ploeg 1995.
32 Lorber 1989; Lorber and Bandlamudi 1993; Van der Ploeg 1995.
33 The earliest documented use of IVF for male infertility is 1984 (Cohen et al. 1985).
34 Clarke 1998: 22.
35 Moore 2002: 96.

CASE STUDY: SEX, GENDER, AND THEIR DIVERSITY

The construction of gender as binary and aligned with two binary sexes is a social endeavor that, while not universal, has dominated North American and European thought since the nineteenth century. This hegemonic paradigm asserts that male and female bodies are clearly, dimorphically distinguished by chromosomes (specifically XX for females and XY for males), internal and external biology (the presence of testes or ovaries, penis or vagina), as well as by naturally corresponding secondary sex characteristics (whether breasts or an adam's apple, and the appropriate presence or absence of body hair). In this idealized model all bodies clearly fit into one and only one of two possible sex categories, in which each individual's genetic information matches his or her genitals and those genitals are the visible key that decodes his or her sex and attendant gender.[1]

This two sex/two gender paradigm so strongly structures our social scripts and meaning-making that even scientists describe male biological attributes and processes as aggressive, violent, and strong and female biological functions as passive, soft, and receptive.[2] As biologist Anne Fausto-Sterling summarizes, "reading nature is a socio-cultural act."[3] The scripts for what "normal" bodies are and the dominant paradigm for sex and gender shape what we see when we look at the human body from a scientific or lay perspective. Researchers have increasingly documented, however, that this model is inadequate; it does not reflect the diversity of human (or animal) bodies and lives.[4] Reality is much more complex; though precise numbers do not exist, best estimates are that between 1 and 2 percent of infants are born intersex, that is, possessing atypical genetic and/or physiological sex characteristics.[5]

INTERSEX

An umbrella term for a range of bodily attributes in which an individual's chromosomes, genitalia, secondary sex characteristics, and/or hormones do not align with one binary sex category (male/female). These traits are also known as "disorders of sex development," nomenclature which has come to the fore in the last few years. For more information see www.accordalliance.org, the website of the Accord Alliance, a national non-profit focused on disseminating and enacting standards of care for disorders of sex development related services.[6]

Individuals with atypical sex markers have been treated differently in different historical eras. Throughout the twentieth century, when detected, individuals have been labeled as intersex and have most often undergone body modification at the insistence of medical professionals.

Many cases of atypical sex are undetected or unrecognized, however, until something precipitates closer inspection. For example, in 1996, eight individuals who had spent their whole lives classified, raised as, and identifying as cisgender women, failed the International Olympics Committee's chromosomal testing used to prevent men from competing as women.[7] This technologically "advanced" method of gender verification replaced the "primitive" method of genital inspections for women athletes in 1968. Instead of clarifying the "real" sex of athletes, however, this "advance" only muddied the waters. So much so, in fact, that the International Olympics Committee dropped genetic testing for sex in 2000. Instead it returned to a reliance on lived experience and presentation. In this case, instead of offering clarity into competitors' "true" sex, new technologies highlighted the very instability and constructed nature of sex and gender.

Human bodies are not as clearly distinct in terms of sex or gender as most people assume them to be. There are more physical and mental similarities between men and women than there are differences. Moreover, the continuum of bodily configurations that exist among individuals challenges the veracity of a bipolar model of sexed bodies. The variation in sex is viewed as disordered, however; until very recently, doctors—and the sciences that underlie their practice—have imposed a binary imperative on biological variation. Throughout the twentieth century, the constructed binary was so naturalized that the diversity of sexed bodies was literally not permitted to exist. Treatment of atypically sexed infants relied on the belief that gender was wholly social (and therefore malleable at least through the first two years) and that external genitals had to match gender category—that is, that both sex and gender had to be aligned in a particular, identical way.[8] The result was surgical intervention, wherein decisions about whether to make infants male or female had as much to do with social beliefs as any biological truth. Parents of intersex infants were pushed into surgical "correction" of their children's bodies, although these surgical interventions often served no purpose other than the construction of clear bodily distinction between male and female. Surgical and identity decisions were shaped by gendered beliefs. For instance, the idea that men need sexual satisfaction while women do not meant that infants were much more likely to be "made" female, in part because medical guidelines swayed surgeons away from selecting maleness unless the child would have a "large enough" penis, while "feminizing" surgeries often permanently destroyed sexual sensation for the girl child.[9] Meanwhile, our social investment in a binary sex system is so naturalized that parents would allow unnecessary alteration to their infants' bodies to make them fit this model, out of genuine concern for their wellbeing. This profound commitment to a sex/gender paradigm is a clear example of how dominant social paradigms for sex and gender inform technological intervention into and personal experiences of bodies.

Only in recent years has activism on the part of intersex individuals and advocacy groups changed the treatment of atypically sexed infants. The first edition of *Gender Circuits* profiled activist groups such as the Intersex Society of North America (ISNA). Driven by their own experiences of dishonesty on the part of parents and doctors, a life after surgeries that scarred their bodies and removed their ability to feel sexual pleasure, and gender identities mismatched to their surgically assigned sex, ISNA gave individuals a way to speak back to medical power holders about their treatment (and maltreatment). ISNA worked for many years to educate doctors and parents and to fight for new treatment protocols. Most significantly, activists argued that surgical or hormonal intervention into children's sex characteristics should be delayed until children had the chance to develop their own gendered sense of self and could participate in the decision-making. And ISNA and affiliated groups were quite successful; treatment protocols have changed, advocates are now available in many hospitals, and children and their families have access to more information than ever before. Because the landscape has shifted so significantly ISNA ended its tenure as an intersex activist organization in 2008 and has been replaced by Accord Alliance (www.accordalliance.org), which is focused on the health and wellbeing of individuals and families, and on building bridges between families and the medical community.

In 2005 an interdisciplinary conference of doctors, geneticists, advocates, and activists convened to develop more unified, consensus-based standards of care for the treatment of the wide range of conditions lumped under the umbrella of intersex. Mainly the result of long-standing activism on the part of intersex groups like the Intersex Society of North America, the standards of care that were articulated corrected many past ethical problems, calling for increased access to information and support, open communication with parents and children about diagnosis, procedures, and outcomes, delay of surgical intervention, and evidence-based decisions about gender assignment.[10] This conference did more than set forth new treatment protocols, however. The group also put forth a call to shift nomenclature from "intersex" to "disorders of sex development," or DSD for short. Advocates argued that the new terminology would be more parent-friendly, orient attention toward medical care and away from politicized identity, and be both precise and flexible.

Over the past five years this new language has come to dominate medical, psychological and advocacy discussions. Hailed by some because of its focus on biology as opposed to identity or social status, this shift has been criticized by others as an effort to turn a social problem into an individual disorder. Much as disability theory asserts that it is not the physical impairment that makes one disabled, but rather the lack of social accommodation and support, critics argue that the term "disorders of sex development" reifies atypical sex conditions, reducing them to medical disorders and obscuring the social forces at work.[11] While new treatment protocols were developed alongside the new term DSD, the term itself still implies a need for pathologization of those defined as such, and therefore there has been a recent push to shift nomenclature again to "differences in sex development."[12]

This debate over language is in large part a debate about the lack of place for atypically sexed bodies in society: Many sociologists have argued that the naming shift from intersex to DSD is an integral part of maintaining the naturalization of a binary cisgender male–man/female–woman construction.[13] As Sarah Topp asserts in a 2012 analysis of the nomenclature change, "the narrow view of language adopted by consensus participants and supporters has led to the adoption of a debilitating terminology that characterizes an entire group as disordered, defective, and in need of medical intervention."[14]

Both proponents and critics of the shift are engaged in an ongoing struggle over how to make sense of the variation in human bodies, which do not fit neatly into a binary sex model. Is this a medical disorder that can—even must—be corrected, or is it a valid and whole identity? The shift toward "disorders of sex development" is "a quiet revolution that has remade the meaning and import of bodies."[15] Certainly, atypically sexed bodies can be both in need of medical interventions and sources of identity and sense of self. What is at stake is which framing will dominate the social concept and ultimately social scripts for sexed bodies and gendered selves. As Topp concludes, "the decision to adopt disorders of sex development has threatened to pathologize an entire population and it did so without the group's consent."[16]

Even though evidence supports a more diverse conceptualization of sex, we as a society reinforce a two-sex system, revealing a lot about the power of sex and gender as a social institution. Our social order is based around two sexes: most marriage laws and norms assume only men and women; buildings are required to have single-sex male and female bathrooms and locker rooms but not private or unisex ones; schools and organizations divide individuals by male/female; and official forms offer only two distinct sex categories. The binary sex/gender paradigm works interactively with other social institutions to structure and direct our bodies and our identities. In this binary system, nonconforming bodies must be "disciplined"—as Foucault would say—into place by available technologies of power. Although this discipline does not work perfectly, these societal forces are so powerful that diverse bodies are forced to conform, at least on the surface. And if, as Jodi O'Brien posited, the gendered body is the means by which we make sense of social interaction, then most members of North American societies—naturalized into the concept of binary gender—assign one gender or the other to each person around them in an unconscious attempt to categorize the other person in a recognizable way, and create a foundation for meaningful interaction.[17] As a consequence, the social invisibility of DSD/intersex contributes to the naturalized belief in a binary sex/gender model.

As social context shifts and communities advocate for change, however, technologies can be used in new and non-normative ways. Nomenclature aside, groups like Accord Alliance have been strikingly successful in changing how DSD/intersex infants are treated at birth, counseling parents to leave them to develop their own gender identities and then decide whether to avail themselves of available technological interventions later in life. In many cases, DSD/intersex individuals are now choosing to leave their bodies as they are, and in the process are challenging norms for "naturally" sexed bodies.

Meanwhile, as we have explored throughout *Gender Circuits*, trans* individuals are also using new technologies to intentionally construct more diversely gendered and sexed bodies and have worked to reframe social scripts for gender nonconformity. In a similar set of debates over characterization through terminology, some trans* individuals bristle at the terms "Gender Dysphoria" and previously "Gender Identity Disorder," claiming that their gender—their internal sense of self—has never changed, that only their ability to manifest this self by having their body match it has.[18] As this debate plays out in media and press materials, in transgender activist and organizational statements, and among scholars and medical professionals, it is clear that this debate—like the debate over DSD/intersex—is really about sex and gender ideologies. The set of surgical procedures aimed at changing an individual's body to match a gender identity have traditionally been called sex-reassignment surgery (and before that sex-change surgery). In recent years, however, as the transgender movement has grown and activists have received more attention, this term has fallen into disfavor by many. Some activists argue that they are not changing their gender or sex, but rather correcting the alignment between their body and their internal sense of self. Many of these individuals have come to use the terminology "gender affirming surgery" (as we have in this book) to reflect these beliefs.

In response to changes in societal gender paradigms and scripts, brought on by transgender and DSD community/intersex activism, medical gatekeepers such as psychiatrists and surgeons are slowly relaxing medical barriers to breast and genital (re)construction surgery for trans* individuals. These changes are enabling individuals to make different choices about a range of bodily modifications. For example, an individual may choose to have breast augmentation or reduction, genital surgeries, or other feminizing or masculinizing surgeries, as well as use masculinizing or feminizing hormones, employ a combination of these biomedical interventions, or none of them. Rates of surgery, hormone use, and crossgender dress and bodily comportment vary dramatically across racial, economic, geographic, and sexual communities. Different types of body work dominate within different communities and in different historical eras. One of many reasons that transgender women and men with class privilege in North America are more able to gain recognition for their chosen identities than poor individuals is that the ability to deploy legitimized gender change scripts requires financial and social capital.

Some hormonal and surgical interventions are more common in contemporary North American society than others, in large part because the United States and Canada have bolstered the validity of some types of interventions—but not others—by requiring irreversible bodily changes in order to legally change one's gender status on official documents like driver's licenses, birth certificates, and bank records. As discussed in Chapter 1, while the requirements vary by state and province, those jurisdictions that do allow changes in legal status tend to require significant bodily transformations as opposed to less invasive ones like a change in personal identity or social role. Requirements for a legal change in one's gender status are slowly changing in response to activism on the part of trans* organizing, however. In June of 2013 the U.S. Social Security Administration announced changes to the requirements for gender change on a social security card, and several states have followed suit. While surgical intervention was required previously, new rules require only certification from a doctor of "appropriate clinical treatment."[19] This is certainly an improvement, making correct identification accessible for more individuals. It does not, of course, erase class barriers or de-medicalize transgender lives. New technologies and attendant new scripts for what gender individuals can be are challenging the paradigms that structure the dominant sex/gender system. If power is the ability to have one's own knowledge count as legitimate and true, then this debate reflects the growing power of trans* individuals and communities to set the terms of their own lives, in the face of hegemonic gender paradigms and the medical institutions empowered to maintain this system. In response to this increasing diversity of embodied genders it is likely we will see more shifts in hegemonic paradigms and scripts.

Debates over sex and gender identity reflect how language and associated explanations for atypically sexed bodies and gender nonconformity change alongside a broader range of gendered and sexed selves. Shifts in dominant gender and transgender paradigms have allowed for more diverse gender and sex scripts, and, in turn, individuals have advocated for visibility, support, and somatechnic interventions in line with these scripts. As examined in Chapter 1, medical gatekeeping was routinely used to police transgender body work by demanding that after gender affirming surgeries people live in line with hegemonic gender and sexuality scripts. Now, however, increasing numbers of endocrinologists and surgeons are willing to perform surgery or prescribe hormones even when individuals do not match heteronormative identity scripts, something that was rare only 15 years ago. Similarly, the new standards of care for disorders of sex development make substantial progress toward bodily integrity and agency for DSD/intersex individuals and shift attention away from the construction of normative bodies as an end unto itself. As legitimate discourses-in-practice expand, there is less pressure on individuals to normalize their bodies and their own narratives within prescribed boundaries; at the same time that possible narratives expand, the language of gender itself is broader and more readily accessible to individuals and groups.

These differences are also generational, which suggests that younger trans* individuals are constructing identities and coming out with very different gender paradigms, social scripts, and technologies at their disposal. Young trans* individuals are significantly more likely to claim a diversity of gender nonconforming identities.[20] As Rey, the young FTM who was profiled in Chapter 3, commented in a 2008 *New York Times Magazine* article:

> Some transmen want to be seen as men—they want to be accepted as born men . . . I want to be accepted as a transman—my brain is not gendered. There's this crazy binary that's built into all of life, that there are just two genders that are acceptable. I don't want to have to fit into that.[21]

Research has found that gender atypical behavior is quite common in children, and that recognition of persistent gender nonconformity in children has increased in the last ten years.[22] The increased visibility of gender nonconforming children, as well as the rise of affirming treatments and positive media coverage, has changed the social landscape for individuals in the United States.[23] This coincides with more knowledge about and interaction with trans* individuals within society at large.

There is a strong correlation between age and when individuals report meeting another trans* person for the first time (and presumably when they came to know about trans* and gained exposure to trans* identity and body scripts). In Beemyn and Rankin's National U.S. study, 76 percent of individuals under 22 years old had met another transgender individual by the age of 19, while only 32 percent of individuals between the ages of 23 and 32, and only 5 percent of people 63 years old and older had. That is, the lower the age-cohort a person is in, the more likely they are to have met a trans* person at a young age.

There is also a correlation between age and likelihood to embrace a trans* identity; in the same study, Beemyn and Rankin found that 27 percent of trans* individuals age 63 or older were totally closeted about their transgender status, while only 10 percent of individuals 22 or younger were, and only 9 percent of people age 23–32 were, with 34 percent of individuals age 23–32 describing themselves as out to all their friends (while only 17 percent of people 63 and over were).[24] These statistics alone do not imply any causality, but this data suggests that who people think they can be, and how able they are to manifest that identity in their body are changing significantly; these changes have everything to do with shifting gender paradigms and social identity and body scripts.[25]

Social change continues to be a slow process. Intersex and transgender social movements have brought sex and gender advocacy into the public sphere, and gender scholars across a variety of disciplines have documented the complexity of gender and the inadequacy of binary sex/gender systems. Hegemonic paradigms and scripts have not yet fully caught up and gender nonconformity remains pathologized. That said, even though transgender individuals face tremendous discrimination and prejudice, transgender youth are more visible and more accepted now than at any other time in modern Western history.[26] Similarly, children born with atypical sex characteristics are more likely to have a voice in decisions about their embodied sex than ever before. As individuals live in more diverse bodies and with more diverse identities, these paradigms will likely continue to loosen, and sex and gender scripts will likely expand. The biomedical technologies being used to produce embodied sex and gender differently will slowly shape public knowledge and discourse about sex, gender, and their diverse manifestations.

Notes

1 Kessler and McKenna 1978.
2 Allen 2007.

3 Fausto-Sterling 2000: 75.
4 Fausto-Sterling 2012.
5 Diamond 2007; Gurney 2007.
6 Preves 2003; Topp 2013.
7 Fausto-Sterling 2000.
8 For more discussion see: Topp 2013.
9 Allen 2007.
10 Lee et al. 2006.
11 Oliver 1996.
12 Davis 2011; Diamond and Beh 2008; Topp 2013.
13 Davis 2011; Feder 2009; Topp 2013.
14 Topp 2013: 191.
15 Hughes 2010: 161.
16 Topp 2013: 192.
17 Langer 1989; O'Brien 1999.
18 Bryant 2008; Waszkiewicz 2006.
19 Social Security Administration 2013.
20 Beemyn and Rankin 2011; Grant et al. 2011.
21 Quart 2008: 37.
22 Spack et al. 2012.
23 Meadow 2011.
24 Beemyn and Rankin 2011.
25 Grossman and D'Augelli 2006.
26 For more information about rates of violence see Beemyn and Rankin, 2011. More information can also be accessed through a related website: www.umass.edu/stonewall/translives.

REVIEW
SOCIOLOGICAL ANALYSES OF GENDER AND TECHNOLOGY

In the film *Kinky Boots*, Charlie Price adopts a new business plan of producing shoes for drag queens. He tries to ease the transition for the workers in his shoe factory with a proclamation: "The factory that started the century providing a range of footwear for men will go into the next century providing footwear for . . . a range of men."[1] Charlie's humorous comment is a strikingly simple way to explain his proposition, a proposition that reveals both ingenuity and a significant reframing. High-heeled shoes for drag queens are, at their most basic, a new technology for male bodies doing femininity. Steve Pateman, the real-life factory owner upon whom Charlie Price is based, did manufacture shoes for a broader range of men, women, and transgender individuals. By doing so, Pateman facilitated the embodiment of more diverse genders by creating shoes that allowed male-bodied femininities; that is, he developed a new technology and, in doing so, produced new gender possibilities. As *Gender Circuits* has explored, individual and social changes are the result of the interactive relationships between embodied identities, social scripts, technologies, and social paradigms. I return, then, to the question that I began this book with: how are new technologies reshaping gendered bodies and identities, and what does this mean for us as individuals and as a society?

The Impact of Contemporary Biomedical and Information Technologies

One of the first arguments introduced in this book was that technology is employed in the service of making meaning generally and doing gender more specifically. Moreover, technologies are shaped by the prevailing gender paradigms and scripts within a society. Consider, for example, a 1968 advertisement in which a woman in a spacesuit holds a bottle of the cleaning solution Lestoil (Figure 4.1). The advertisement copy reads, "Women of the future will make the moon a cleaner place to live."[2] Advertisers in 1968 could imagine living on the moon, but not without Earth's gender inequalities in household labor (nor, apparently, its cleaning products). While this lighthearted example minimizes the complex individual and social gendering processes discussed so far, it demonstrates how gendered social scripts manifest in society and work in concert with paradigms, technologies, and embodied individuals to shape and reshape the lives of individuals. Extending this to encompass a broader social context, we can see that our beliefs and social ideologies about gender shape how we interpret all aspects of the world around us and describe the realm of possibilities we can imagine for our lives and society. Social institutions, socializing agents and individual gender identifications all, in turn, shape the array of gendered bodies and identities rendered legible in a particular context.

Like the Lestoil advertisement, many of the examples analyzed in *Gender Circuits* have provided an opportunity to make sense of gender in a way that accounts for these social and individual forces. Our inquiry into new information technologies found that technologies are being deployed to simultaneously re-inscribe, resist, and rewrite social gender scripts. These gendered changes are meaningful in the lives of individuals as well as on institutional and societal levels. For instance, marginalized individuals use online community forums and discussion boards to discover and refine identities and to rewrite gendered body scripts. New biomedical technologies reshape gendered bodies in both normative and non-normative ways as well. Steroids and plastic surgery can be used to construct hyper-masculine men and hyper-feminine women, but they can also be deployed to manifest gendered bodies outside of the established strictures of masculine male men and feminine female women. New

Figure 4.1 1968 Lestoil advertisement.

technologies are neither regressive nor utopian. Rather, technologies are actively and purposefully deployed on individual and institutional levels, in the service of gender, body, and identity work. This is done within particular social contexts, and is shaped by attendant gender paradigms and scripts.

A Cyborg Society

In the mid-1980s, feminist philosopher Donna Haraway began to argue that we live in an increasingly "cyborg society," characterized by the hybridization of bodies and technologies that creates a blurred line between human and machine.[3] She contends that this hybridization is transforming the ways that gender, race, sexuality, and nation are written onto the body and integrated into the self on the individual level. In addition, this hybridization works at a societal level by influencing how categories of oppression and identity are located within relations of power. Haraway's theorizing foretold many of the contemporary issues that are taken up in this book.

Endeavoring to answer the question, "how is technology reshaping contemporary bodies and identities?" through the lens of gender, we have drawn similar conclusions as Haraway. Technologies are reshaping the most intimate aspects of individuals' bodies and selves and are doing so in conversation with gendered paradigms and scripts. People are using information and biomedical technologies to help to construct, define, and manifest new complex embodied identities; in the process, social scripts and gender paradigms are shifting. These changes in individual identities, social scripts, and paradigms are not producing an unbounded utopia, however. Technology has the potential to both facilitate progressive body and identity possibilities and re-entrench oppressive ones. Although technology is changing who we are as gendered individuals, the ways in which gender is changing are complex and variable.[4]

If we take a sociological approach and build our analysis on an understanding of gender as both socially constructed and real in its effects, we avoid both a utopian construction of technology as an egalitarian liberator, and a pessimistic one that casts technology as an oppressor, more efficiently reproducing racial and gender inequalities.[5] Instead, scholars must approach technology as a force of social change that has many affordances with the potential to both challenge and uphold the status quo. If core identities like gender and race are "floating signifiers"—systems of classification without true biological bases—then we must examine them "more like a language than a way in which we are biologically constituted."[6] We, as scholars, must approach identities as social projects around which institutional support is built or denied, including authentication from sources that may appear impartial, such as scientific theory. This book has endeavored to do just that by examining how technological change has challenged who people think they can be as gendered beings and how these transformed identities are manifested in the bodies of individuals and in society.

A Sociological Analysis of Technology and Gender

This book began with an examination of the relationship between the histories of gendered bodies and identities (both conforming and nonconforming) and technological innovation. While hegemonic ideology suggests that our gender flows directly from natural sex differences in the body, gender and sex are both, in fact, constructs. Social scripts shape how individuals portray and perceive gender, and work to create the constructed but seemingly natural gender/sex binaries. These "recipes for behavior"—these scripts—teach us how to make sense of our own and others' bodies and identities, and they teach us how to experience them as sexed (designated as male or female according to hegemonic scripts) as well as gendered (limited to man or woman according to hegemonic scripts). These gender scripts are not always proscriptive, nor are they stable over time. Because these scripts do not reflect the diversity of human experience, they are constantly contested, transformed, challenged, and re-entrenched by individuals, groups and institutions. Individuals continuously navigate the complex terrain of conformity and resistance, of hegemonic scripts, and of assertions of new ways of being in the world. Social institutions such as law and medicine exert power over the meaning, social status, and affiliated rights of different sex/gender configurations, while social movements (within and external to these institutions) endeavor to challenge and broaden the gender paradigms and social scripts of the day.

People of every era produce gender using the technologies available to them. As the mutual construction of gender and technology change over time, the criteria for appropriate and inappropriate gendered bodies and identities also change. The technologies available in a given historical moment work to develop particular subjectivities, and can be used to cultivate and validate some identities, prohibit others, and turn a blind eye to some. Simultaneously, changes in technologies alter what kinds of body work are available and required for different genders, and define which body codes are necessary to communicate a particular gender effectively. Gender is based on biological and physical processes, influenced by gendered scripts and norms, seen through the lenses of contemporary paradigms, policed by technologies of power, and finally defined and constructed by the individual, whose embodied gender will be enhanced and limited by available technologies.

What a Sociological Approach Illuminates

Bringing the five aspects of social life to which we have directed our attention—paradigms, scripts, technologies, bodies, and identities—to bear on the question of gender in this technological age sheds light on a number of important dynamics. Most significantly, it offers a way to analyze the nuanced and ever-changing relationships between aspects of individual and societal gender. The relationships between paradigms, scripts, technologies, bodies, and identities vary across time and place, and a sociological approach clarifies these relationships without eliding their differences, contradictions, or specificities. Moreover, a sociological analysis accounts for social context and individual difference, and highlights individual (personal experience), local (subculture, group, or community), and society-wide dynamics.

Each of the cases examined in this book offers evidence that new technologies are in dynamic relationship to societal paradigms and social scripts, and that these relationships result in the reshaping of gendered bodies and identities. In turn, gendered bodies and identities are affecting the development of technologies, social scripts, and gender paradigms within individual groups and communities, and in society as a whole. In other words, paradigms, scripts, technologies, bodies, and identities are intricately interconnected. A sociological analysis that accounts for this complexity allows us to make visible the hidden processes of socialization, and identity and body work. Through all of these processes, technology, paradigms, and scripts interact and transform our social and individual embodiments.

Rather than replacing existing empirical models and conceptual theories, our sociological approach extends these elaborations of gender, identity, body, and technology by accounting for a broad range of social forces simultaneously. Holstein and Gubrium's theory of narrative identity (as discussed in Chapter 2) helps to explain how social scripts are deployed and negotiated in the process of identity construction and reconstruction online. Bringing this theory of identity into conversation with a sociological analysis of technology allows us to recognize how technologies are opening up new arenas of identity work (as in blogging and social networking websites), and how new collective stories are being developed and deployed in new forums (including online discussion groups and interactive virtual worlds). Theories of technological innovation and bodily change are similarly clarified when analyzed sociologically. Embodied identities shape individual lives, as society at large assumes social status and personal values based on a person's appearance, and holds individuals responsible for doing the body work necessary for acceptable presentation. All technologies, however, can reify existing paradigms (for instance blepharoplasty and bariatric surgery), defy them (such as with gender affirming surgeries), or have the potential for both (as do hormone treatments and breast augmentation).

A sociological analysis enables us to decipher how social and individual change processes are intertwined. It reveals how gender paradigms and social scripts can vary across social contexts (as in drag troupes or strip clubs) and how these differences offer particular ranges of possibilities for gendered bodies and identities. Similarly, sociological analysis offers insight into how technological innovation is both shaped by dominant paradigms and is influential. Finally, a sociological analysis charts a path toward answering whether and how information and biomedical technologies can have real-life effects on bodies and identities.

New Areas of Inquiry

Using a sociological analysis to elaborate the social processes that underlie changes in gendered bodies and identities casts light on a number of key contemporary social changes. Simultaneously, it raises many new questions to be taken up in future scholarship. The analysis undertaken in this book highlights how social forces overlap and interact in social contexts to produce a wide array of lived experiences. While offering clarity regarding the interaction of social forces, it does not elaborate how individuals consciously or unconsciously navigate normative and non-normative social scripts—in fact, it raises provocative questions about how individuals make sense of the social scripts available to them, negotiate their personal relationship to these scripts, and assimilate available scripts into lived embodied identities. How do people actively negotiate between existing social scripts and new ones? How do they choose to accept, resist, or rewrite socially sanctioned discourses? And how do these choices impact social institutions? Future empirical research on these questions will be wonderfully illuminating.

Another area of inquiry for study is the mechanisms by which embodied identity and body changes take place, both on the individual and societal level. Some of the empirical studies and gender theories discussed in this book have offered insight into these mechanisms, but further research is needed. While this analysis allowed us to look under the hood, as it were, of embodied identity to make sense of how paradigms, scripts, and technologies interact with bodies and identities in the production of new embodied selves, it did not chart the particular processes by which this happens. Additionally, *Gender Circuits* raises new questions about how can we better understand the meaning and import of new body and identity forms. And with regard to hegemonic gender paradigms and scripts, there is much more to be explored when we tease apart and examine their re-entrenchment from their resistance and transformation. As research on this area of social change is elaborated, new analytical models and theoretical frameworks will emerge that will help to make better sense of these and similar changes.

What we have found to be true for gender using a sociological approach can also be used to make sense of other embodied identities and forces of social change. An analysis focused on race could elaborate how new technologies in the search for racial markers within the human genome are being used to revive and contest the biology of race. A focus on sexuality would enable us to look at how new technologies are reshaping the meaning and practice of sex and sexuality through the life-course. Analyses focused on sexual, racial, or class identity would illustrate the interactive relationships between new technologies affecting those identities and related paradigms, scripts, existing technologies, bodies, and identities. We might also anticipate that future research will explore the connections between gender and sexuality scripts in more detail and help scholars to map how the development and deployment of technology is implicated in these relationships.[7]

Making Sense of the Technologically Saturated World Around Us

The central questions taken up in this book are whether and how the development of new technologies is reshaping who people are as gendered individuals, and what the importance of these changes is. The many examples explored suggest that technological development is intimately tied up with changes in gendered bodies and identities. Scholars have argued that social change is marked by the challenges to established social body norms and these social changes often manifest in new identity schemas.[8] New technologies have created new sites of agency and social control, of power and inequality. And, as we have seen throughout this book, these technologies have gone hand in hand with changes in how people define themselves as individuals, and how much ability they have to make those subjectivities real and embodied.

We, as scholars, then, can make sense of body work as a significant phenomenon, one that is tied to larger social and cultural changes. The cases we have examined suggest that social changes have made room for more diverse bodies and identities. How, then, do we take the concepts and analyses developed throughout this text and use them to make sense of the world at large? A sociological analysis can help make better sense of public debate and discourse about embodied gender. Let us consider, for example, how these embodied changes are affecting dominant gender paradigms and social scripts in one final case study: the very public pregnancy of Thomas Beatie, a transgender man.

Case Study of Transgender Pregnancy and Thomas Beatie

Many transgender men have carried and birthed children; Thomas Beatie is not the first man to bear a child, nor will he be the last. He is, however, the first man in the United States to experience pregnancy in the public eye.[9] By turning our attention to this current site of social change and debate we can witness how bodies are being shaped by new technologies and how social scripts and gender paradigms are being challenged and changed in the process. The case of transgender pregnancy highlights how gendering happens in concert with social institutions and gender paradigms, as well as how these processes shape the lives and bodies of individuals.[10]

Because removal of reproductive organs is not always part of changing one's sex or gender, many male-to-female (MTF) individuals still have the biological capacity to impregnate and many female-to-male (FTM) people retain the ability to become pregnant. Although this usually requires temporary cessation of hormones, it does not necessarily halt, set back, or divert individuals' body or identity changes. Many transgender men and women report wanting children and express interest in using their own sperm or eggs (preserved before transition) were the technology to be made available.[11] Transgender individuals are caught in a particular bind in terms of pregnancy, however. The inability to become pregnant for trans* women, and the state of pregnancy for trans* men call into question the veracity of individuals' chosen genders.

While the desire for children is not restricted to women, the state of pregnancy is deeply gendered in our society; it is one of the primary ways that we differentiate women from men. For female-to-male transgender individuals who choose to bear children, therefore, their embodied identity rests on disengaging pregnancy from womanhood. In one of the only studies of trans* biological parents, Sam Dylan More interviewed nine German transgender men. He found that FTM individuals had to engage in significant identity and body work to mitigate the impact of societal pregnancy scripts that gendered them as women. One participant, Del, commented:

> I did not feel more feminine, but still the feminine image was imposed upon me externally . . . Sitting in the doc's office who

delivered me . . . was also humiliating in an (en)gendered way: that space was woman's space and fundamentally at the surface of my skin I didn't fit in.[12]

What Del highlights in his interview reinforces the scholarship explored throughout this book. Individuals are intentionally negotiating complex gendered body and identity scripts, and this holds particularly true for individuals whose gender identification and bodies stray from hegemonic norms.

While a number of transgender individuals have had children either before or after changing their sex and/or gender, this issue was catapulted into mainstream North American consciousness for the first time in 2008. Thomas Beatie, a transgender man, announced in an April 2008 issue of the gay and lesbian news magazine, *The Advocate*, that he was pregnant.[13] In his first-person account, Beatie shared his story of coming out as transgender and, a number of years later, deciding to have a child. His narrative focused on the discrimination and prejudice he and his wife, Nancy, had experienced thus far and asserted that what they chose to do was moral, natural, and logical. About his choice to bear children, Beatie acknowledged his wife's infertility but iterated, "wanting to have a biological child is neither a male nor female desire, but a human desire."[14] Moreover, he saw no conflict between his gender and his pregnancy. He wrote: "Despite the fact that my belly is growing with a new life inside me, I am stable and confident being the man that I am."[15] That is, for Thomas Beatie, like the men More studied, being a man and being pregnant were not mutually exclusive. In the process of navigating his gendered body through pregnancy he redefines what it means to be a man and perhaps even challenges the binary gender paradigm. He is embodying a new gendered identity and body that conflict with and challenge social scripts.

In the years since his first pregnancy Beatie has had two more children and has written about his pregnancies in the book, *Labor of Love: The Story of One Man's Extraordinary Pregnancy*. His story continues to be covered in mainstream media, including in a Discovery Channel documentary, on *The View*, and on *Good Morning America*. In 2012,

Beatie again made headlines when the state of Arizona refused him a divorce from Nancy, using his pregnancies as proof that he was "really" a woman.[16] This ruling offers a clear example of a social institution (law) using dominant paradigms to police gender. As of 2014 the case was in the midst of review by the Arizona Court of Appeals.

Making Sense of Transgender Pregnancy

Reactions to Beatie's very public pregnancy have been mixed, both within and outside of the transgender community. Within transgender communities Beatie's coming out, as it were, generated both praise and anger.[17] In a Salon.com article, Thomas Rogers spoke with leading transgender activists and scholars about Beatie. Some activists, like Mara Keisling, felt that Beatie's actions pushed what might be considered a more pressing transgender issue such as workplace protection and access to healthcare to the margins. Others expressed fears that this tabloid-style attention has put the validity of all transgender identities at risk and compromised the safety of individuals. In contrast, Jameson Green, a long-time transgender activist and author, felt that the attention generated by Beatie's disclosure would help to educate mainstream society about transgender lives.

In the mainstream media, stories have revealed attitudes that are as mixed as they are within the transgender community. A particularly transphobic television report involved MSNBC's Joe Scarborough repeatedly commenting that he was "going to be sick" when reporting the story. Notably, however, most news media have been positive and respectful; certainly the specials run by Oprah Winfrey and Barbara Walters displayed compassion and at least a superficial understanding of transgenderism, as did a cover story in *People Magazine*. All told, the media attention and public response was neither wholly progressive nor wholly regressive. While it is too soon to assess current public consensus about transgender pregnancy, or draw clear conclusions about the meaning and ultimate impact of Beatie's embodiment, we can make some cursory observations.

The most obvious effect of Beatie's news article was that it generated a new wave of public discussion about trans* lives, some of which was educational and some reactionary. The anonymous responses posted in online blogs were often lukewarm, and sometimes tended to hostility. Paisley Currah, a transgender-rights scholar summarized the range of public responses:

> Some bloggers felt that "she" was still a woman; others thought transitioning should mean Beatie had forfeited his right to give birth; still others (usually women) expressed annoyance at all the attention the first "pregnant man" was getting. A small proportion seemed to have no problem getting their mind around the idea.[18]

It is undeniable, however, that more people now know about trans* lives and possibilities, and it is very likely that more trans* individuals are thinking about pregnancy. In fact, we can see the changes in gender paradigms and social scripts for pregnancy that trans* activism has brought about in popular media coverage. For example, a January 2014 *New York Times* op-ed covered the issue of trans* pregnancy with incredible sensitivity and respect.[19] The author, a freelance journalist who writes about reproductive technologies, profiled the experiences of several trans* men who experienced discrimination when seeking help in becoming pregnant. Instead of focusing on the novelty of trans* pregnancy, the article examined new legal protections for trans* patients that bar discrimination.[20]

Research shows that these changes in consciousness matter in fundamental ways. For instance, Beatie's subsequent pregnancies generated much less uproar and attention. Similarly, other transgender celebrities such as Chaz Bono have received much warmer and trans*-knowledgeable receptions in media and public discourse. Indeed in June 2014 actress Laverne Cox was featured on the cover of *Time Magazine* and in an article titled, "The Transgender Tipping Point: America's Next Civil Rights Frontier."[21] While we could make sense of this shift in a multitude of ways, one possibility is that our social scripts for gender and for pregnancy are indeed changing. At the very least, the idea that a man can be pregnant is fathomable to more individuals than it was just a few years ago. As new gender scripts and paradigms are introduced in the public sphere, public discourse will likely produce *both* new possibilities for individuals and a societal retrenchment of hegemonic gender scripts. That is, the impact of transgender pregnancies and the debate that surrounds them are as complex as the matrices of forces at play in shaping their manifestation and meaning.

By situating Beatie's case within a sociological framework we can analyze how institutions participate in the production and enforcement of gender paradigms and scripts. For example, Beatie reported having difficulty finding doctors and hospitals willing to treat him.[22] The lack of institutional support or procedures for non-normative pregnancies is one way to control who is seen as a legitimate pregnant person, i.e. who is legitimated as a woman (or as a man). In fact, a number of European countries and several states in North America place sanctions on transgender individuals who bear children by limiting or revoking legal gender status changes.[23] There are a variety of structural constraints hindering treatment for pregnant men such as the lack of maternity spaces for men. There are also narrative constraints; the dearth of language for men who bear children limits the identities that can be storied into being. Gender ideologies and existing social scripts shape the range of possibilities for gendered bodies, identities, and practices. We can also imagine, however, the impact of changes to these paradigms and scripts; the more that scripts for pregnancy expand to include men, the less gendered pregnancy will become, and the more flexibility will emerge to define gendered bodies and selves.

Finally, examining the public experience of Thomas Beatie raises many questions about the "nature" of sex and gender in this time of increased technological intervention into the body. Shortly after Thomas Beatie's coming out, an editorial appeared in the science journal *Nature* that highlighted the shifting of body scripts. Responding to critiques that a pregnant man was "unnatural," the editors took up the question of sex and gender in a technological age. They wrote:

> When we consider this story [of Thomas Beatie] with the reasoning parts of our brains, exactly what was so "unnatural"? The longing to have a baby? That is a profoundly human desire,

whether the prospective parents are male, female or transgendered. Or is it that Beatie has acted on his certainty that he is a man who happened to be born without a Y chromosome? Biologists have found that gender-straddling and gender-switching behaviors are not at all uncommon in the "natural" world, either for humans or non-human animals.[24]

This editorial is an example of how scientific data are being deployed to challenge existing gender and sex paradigms in an explicit effort to expand the legitimate ways for individuals to be in the world. The editors of *Nature* continue by connecting these changes in gendered bodies and identities to technological development:

> True, modern biotechnology has considerably raised the stakes, and is allowing humans to manipulate their biological make-up to an ever-increasing degree. But it hasn't fundamentally changed the game. And its applications, however unsettling they may be to some people, are not, by definition, "unnatural."

This quote deploys new and transformed gender scripts for who can bear a child, and what it means to be a man, a woman, or even a parent. It also establishes the negotiation of a new gender paradigm rooted less in biological determinism and more in both social and technological logics.

The case of transgender pregnancy raises a whole host of new questions about gender on individual and institutional levels. If pregnancy is one of the key markers of womanhood in our society, what does it mean for pregnancy to be divorced from femaleness, and woman-ness? While Beatie's pregnancy raises new questions because it is outside of dominant paradigms, we can ask similar questions of naturalized—and therefore almost invisible—technological interventions. How does the use of fertility treatments to extend the reproductive lives of women past menopause raise many of the same questions about female embodiment and womanhood? Similarly, how are infertility treatments, testosterone therapies, hair transplants, penis enlargements, and steroid use changing the meaning and embodiment of maleness and manhood? And how will the ability to control futures more through in-vitro fertilization, genetic screening, and sex-selection challenge dominant gender paradigms and scripts for embodied gender? And what does it tell us about our social norms, that many of these questions are raised only when we are confronted by the case of a man's pregnancy?

All of the questions above center on the realities of gendered bodies and identities within a technologically saturated society. And these are questions that can only be answered with further empirical and theoretical inquiry across scientific and social scientific disciplines. For now, the analytical tools engaged in this book enable a robust understanding of the social forces that have produced these changes, and their significance on the individual and institutional levels.

Gender Circuits: Looking Forward

In closing, then, I return to the questions that began this book: how are new technologies changing who we are as gendered beings? And what does this suggest about where these changes are leading us as individuals and as a society? The many cases explored herein point toward dramatic changes in the gendered bodies and identities of twenty-first century individuals. New technologies are being engaged on individual and institutional levels to create, reinforce, and rewrite what it means to be men, women, and trans* individuals in our society. Contrary to post-modern claims that identities will cease to matter, our inquiry has revealed active negotiation and substantiation of gender identity on the part of individuals and a high social investment in particular identities on the institutional level. It is also clear that the body continues to play a central role in individual experience, even as technology enables more virtual possibilities. As Holstein and Gubrium remind us, "the body continues to be an omnipresent material mediator of who we are or hope to be."[25] The body plays a central role in our lives, acting as the canvas upon which we can display "who we are," and as the means by which we interact with the world around us.[26]

Sociological analysis can help us to make sense of the diverse social and individual changes that result from technological innovation, and of how these changes, in turn, spur further technological development. This approach offers a way to understand how social paradigms, scripts, technologies, bodies, and identities are in dynamic relationship to one another and how these mutually constitutive social and individual forces, together, are remaking gender. Yet, our understanding opens as many new doors of inquiry as it closes. While technology is impacting individuals in significant and transformative ways, it is neither a utopian field of unbounded possibility, nor does it flatly reproduce dominant scripts for identity. Rather, it offers both liberatory and regressive opportunities that respond to and enable a diverse array of changes. The possibilities are not infinite, but they are, as yet, tantalizingly open.

Notes

1 *Kinky Boots* 2005.
2 Lestoil 1968.
3 Haraway 1991.
4 Nakamura 2002.
5 Hall 1996.
6 Hall 1996.
7 See for example Ingraham's (1994) concept of "heterogender."
8 Shilling 2008.
9 Verlinden 2012.
10 More 1998.
11 De Sutter et al. 2002; Wierckx et al. 2012.
12 More 1998: 322.
13 Beatie 2008.
14 Beatie 2008: 24.
15 Beatie 2008: 24.
16 Transgender Law Center 2013.
17 Rogers 2008.
18 Currah 2008: 330.
19 Richards 2014.
20 The Affordable Care Act changed health insurance policy such that "transsexualism" is no longer defined as a pre-existing condition that can justify withholding insurance coverage. Until 2014 insurers were able to deny trans* individuals coverage for a wide range of medical treatments because of their gender identity.
21 Steinmetz 2014.
22 Beatie 2008.
23 More 1998: 320.
24 "Defining 'Natural:' Visceral Reactions to an Act Should Not Distract from the Real Ethical Issues" 2008.
25 Holstein and Gubrium 2000: 197.
26 Swann 1987.

REFERENCES

Adas, Michael. 1989. *Machines as the Measure of Men: Science, Technology and Ideologies of Western Dominance.* Ithaca, NY: Cornell University Press.

"Against Bloomers and Bicycles." 1897. *New York Times,* January 11, p. 1.

Agger, Ben. 2008. *The Virtual Self: A Contemporary Sociology.* Boston, MA: Blackwell Publishing.

Albright, Julie, M. 2007. "Impossible Bodies: TV Viewing Habits, Body Image, and Plastic Surgery Attitudes among College Students in Los Angeles and Buffalo, New York." *Configurations* 15(2): 103–123.

Alkalimat, Abdul, Doug Gills, and Kate Williams. 1995. *Job-Tech: The Technological Revolution and Its Impact on Society.* Chicago: Twenty-First Century Books.

Allen, Caitilyn. 2007. "It's a Boy! Gender Expectations Intrude on the Study of Sex Determination." *DNA and Cell Biology* 26(10): 699–705.

American Medical Association. 2013. "Press Release: AMA Adopts New Policies on Second Day of Voting at Annual Meeting." Retrieved May 6, 2014 (www.ama-assn.org/ama/pub/news/news/2013/2013-06-18-new-ama-policies-annual-meeting.page).

American Psychiatric Association. 1994. *Diagnostic and Statistical Manual of Mental Disorders.* 4th edn., Revised. Washington, DC: American Psychiatric Association.

American Psychiatric Association. 2008. "APA Statement on GID and the DSM 2008." May 9. Washington, DC: American Psychiatric Association.

American Psychiatric Association. 2013. "Gender Dysphoria: Fact Sheet." Retrieved February 8, 2014 (www.psychiatry.org/dsm5).

American Society for Aesthetic Plastic Surgery. 2013. "Statistics 2012." Retrieved January 7, 2014 (www.surgery.org/sites/default/files/ASAPS-2012-Stats.pdf).

American Society for Metabolic and Bariatric Surgery. 2007. "Fact Sheet on Metabolic & Bariatric Surgery." Retrieved October 30, 2009 (www.asbs.org/Newsite07/media/asmbs_fs_surgery.pdf).

American Society for Metabolic and Bariatric Surgery. 2013. "Estimate of Bariatric Surgery Numbers." Retrieved May 6, 2014 (asmbs.org/2014/03/estimate-of-bariatric-surgery-numbers/).

American Society for Reproductive Medicine. 2008. "Definitions of Infertility and Recurrent Pregnancy Loss." *Fertility and Sterility* 90:S60.

American Society of Plastic Surgeons. 2009. "2009 Report of the 2008 Statistics: National Clearinghouse of Plastic Surgery Statistics." Arlington Heights, IL: American Society of

Plastic Surgeons. Retrieved May 26, 2009 (www.plasticsurgery.org/Media/stats/2008-US-cosmetic-reconstructive-plastic-surgery-minimally-invasive-statistics.pdf).

American Society of Plastic Surgeons. 2013. "2012 Plastic Surgery Statistics Report: National Clearinghouse of Plastic Surgery Statistics." Retrieved January 9, 2014 (www.plasticsurgery.org/Documents/news-resources/statistics/2012-Plastic-Surgery-Statistics/full-plastic-surgery-statistics-report.pdf).

Anderson, D. Bryant and James W. Pennebaker. 1980. "Pain and Pleasure: Alternative Interpretations for Identical Stimulation." *European Journal of Social Psychology* 10(2): 207–212.

Archer, John. 1992. "Childhood Gender Roles: Social Context and Organisation." Pp. 31–62 in *Childhood Social Development: Contemporary Perspectives*, edited by Harry McGurk. East Sussex, England: Psychology Press.

Archer, Margaret S. 2000. *Being Human: The Problem of Agency*. Cambridge, England: Cambridge University Press.

Arikha, Noga. 2007. *Passions and Tempers: A History of the Humours*. New York, NY: Ecco Press.

Armstrong, David. 1983. *Political Anatomy of the Body: Medical Knowledge in Britain in the Twentieth Century*. Cambridge, England: Cambridge University Press.

Armstrong, Myrna L. and Kathleen Pace Murphy. 1997. "Tattooing: Another Adolescent Health Risk Behavior Warranting Health Education." *Applied Nursing Research* 10: 181–189.

Arrington, Michael. 2005. "85% of College Students Use Facebook." *TechCrunch* 7.

Ashkenaz, Marissa. 2008. "You Mean You Chose to be Fat?: Body Image in a Virtual World." Retrieved March 10, 2009 (http://marissaracecourse.com/2008/06/03/you-mean-you-chose-to-be-fat-body-image-in-a-virtual-world/).

Associated Press. 2014. "APNewsBreak: New Gender Options for Facebook Users" *The Washington Post*. Retrieved February 13, 2014 (www.washingtonpost.com/business/technology/apnewsbreak-new-gender-options-for-facebook-users/2014/02/13/661b9f f4-94d9-11e3-9e13-770265cf4962_story.html).

Au, Wagner James. 2006. "The Skin You're in." *New World Notes*. Retrieved January 21, 2010 (http://nwn.blogs.com/nwn/2006/02/the_skin_youre_.html).

Au, Wagner James. 2008. "Can A Female Avatar Be Too Thin?" *New World Notes*. Retrieved May 30, 2008 (http://nwn.blogs.com/nwn/2008/05/can-a-female-av.html).

Back, Mitja D., Juliane M. Stopfer, Simine Vazire, Sam Gaddis, Stefan C. Schmukle, Boris Egloff, and Samuel D. Gosling. 2010. "Facebook Profiles Reflect Actual Personality, Not Self-idealization." *Psychological Science* 21(3): 372–374.

Balsamo, Anne. 1996. *Technologies of the Gendered Body: Reading Cyborg Women*. Durham, NC: Duke University Press.

Bardone-Cone, Anna M. and Kamila M. Cass. 2007. "What Does Viewing a Pro-anorexia Website Do? An Experimental Examination of Website Exposure and Moderating Effects." *International Journal of Eating Disorders* 40(6): 537–548.

Barnes, Liberty Walther. 2014. *Conceiving Masculinity: Male Infertility, Medicine, and Identity*. Philadelphia, PA: Temple University Press.

Barnes, Liberty Walther and Christin L. Munsch. N.d. "The Paradoxical Privilege of Men and Masculinities in IRB Review." Unpublished manuscript.

Bartky, Sandra. 1988. "Foucault, Femininity and the Modernization of Patriarchal Power." Pp. 61–86 in *Feminism and Foucault: Reflections on Resistance*, edited by Irene Diamond and Lee Quinby. Boston, MA: Northeastern University Press.

Beatie, Thomas. 2008. "Labor of Love." *The Advocate*, April 8, p. 24.

Becker, Anne E., Debra L. Franko, Alexandra Speck, and David B. Herzog. 2003. "Ethnicity and Differential Access to Care for Eating Disorder Symptoms." *International Journal of Eating Disorders* 33(2): 205–212.

Becker, Gaylene. 2000. *The Elusive Embryo: How Women and Men Approach New Reproductive Technologies*. Berkeley, CA: University of California Press.

Becker, Howard. 1953. "Becoming a Marihuana User." *American Journal of Sociology* 59: 235–242.

Beemyn, Brett-Genny and Sue Rankin. 2011. *Understanding Transgender Lives*. New York, NY: Columbia University Press.

Bentivoglio, Katie. 2011. "Barnard Looks to Address Transgender, Gender Non-conforming Students." *Columbia Spectator*. Retrieved May 13, 2014 (www.columbia spectator.com/2011/04/07/barnard-looks-address-transgender-gender-non-conforming-students).

Berkowitz, Dana. Forthcoming. *The Rise of Botox: How the Anti-Aging Wonder-Drug is Changing the Face of America*. New York, NY: NYU Press.

Berman, Joshua and Amy S. Bruckman. 2001. "The Turing Game Exploring Identity in an Online Environment." *Convergence: The International Journal of Research into New Media Technologies* 7(3): 83–102.

Berry, Bonnie. 2007. *Beauty Bias: Discrimination and Social Power*. Westport, CT: Greenwood Publishing Group.

Bijker, Wiebe E. and John Law. 1992. *Shaping Technology/Building Society*. Cambridge, MA: MIT Press.

Black, Paula and Ursula Sharma. 2001. "Men are Real, Women are 'Made Up': Beauty Therapy and the Construction of Femininity." *The Sociological Review* 49(1): 100–116.

Blackwood, Evelyn and Saskia E. Wieringa. 1999. *Female Desires: Same-Sex Relations and Transgender Practices across Cultures*. New York, NY: Columbia University Press.

Blitz, Bernard and Albert J. Dinnerstein. 1971. "Role of Attentional Focus in Pain Perception: Manipulation of Response to Noxious Stimulation by Instructions." *Journal of Abnormal Psychology* 77(1): 42.

Blumer, Herbert. 1969. *Symbolic Interactionism: Perspective and Method*. Englewood Cliffs, NJ: Prentice-Hall.

Boellstorff, Tom. 2008. *Coming of Age in Second Life: An Anthropologist Explores the Virtually Human*. Princeton, NJ: Princeton University Press.

Boero, Natalie and C. J. Pascoe. 2012. "Pro-anorexia Communities and Online Interaction: Bringing the Pro-ana Body Online." *Body & Society* 18(2): 27–57.

Boler, Megan. 2007. "Hypes, Hopes and Actualities: New Digital Cartesianism and Bodies in Cyberspace." *New Media and Society* 9(1): 129–168.

Bordo, Susan. 1993. *Unbearable Weight: Feminism, Western Culture, and the Body*. Berkeley, CA: University of California Press.

Bordo, Susan. 2003. "The Empire of Images in Our World of Bodies." Pp. 105–114 in *Beyond Words: Reading and Writing in a Visual Age*, edited by John Ruszkiewicz, Daniel Anderson, and Christy Friend. Upper Saddle River, NJ: Pearson Education.

Borgmann, Albert. 2006. "Technology as a Cultural Force: For Alena and Griffin." *The Canadian Journal of Sociology* 31(3): 351–360.

Borzekowski, Dina L.G., Summer Schenk, Jenny L. Wilson, and Rebecka Peebles. 2010. "e-Ana and e-Mia: A Content Analysis of Pro-eating Disorder Web Sites." *American Journal of Public Health* 100(8): 1,526.

Bourdieu, Pierre. 1968. "Outline of a Sociological Theory of Art Perception." *International Social Science Journal* 20(4): 589–612.

boyd, danah. 2008. "Why Youth [heart] Social Network Sites: The Role of Networked Publics in Teenage Social Life." Pp. 119–142 in *Youth, Identity, and Digital Media*, edited by David Buckingham. Cambridge, MA: MIT Press.

boyd, danah and Nicole Ellison. 2007. "Social Network Sites: Definition, History and Scholarship." *Journal of Computer-mediated Communication* 13(1): 210–230.

boyd, danah and Jeffrey Heer. 2006. "Profiles as Conversation: Networked Identity Performance on Friendster." *System Sciences (HICSS), 2012 45th Hawaii International Conference* 3:59c.

Braithwaite, Ronald L., Torrance Stephens, Claire Sterk, and Kisha Braithwaite. 1999. "Risks Associated with Tattooing and Body Piercing." *Journal of Public Health Policy* 20: 459–470.

Brines, Julie. 1994. "Economic Dependency, Gender, and the Division of Labor at Home." *American Journal of Sociology* 100: 652–688.

Broad, Kendal L. and Kristin E. Joos. 2004. "Online Inquiry of Public Selves: Methodological Considerations." *Qualitative Inquiry* 10(6): 923–946.

Brower, Vicki. 2011. "Epigenetics: Unravelling the Cancer Code." *Nature* 471(7339): S12–S13.

Brown, Patricia Leigh. 2006. "Supporting Boys or Girls When the Line Isn't Clear." *New York Times*, December 2, pp. A1, A11.

Bruckman, Amy S. 1992. "Identity Workshop: Emergent Social and Psychological Phenomena in Text-Based Virtual Reality." Unpublished manuscript. Retrieved October 30, 2009 (www.cc.gatech.edu/~asb/papers/old-papers.html).

Bruckman, Amy S. 1993. "Gender Swapping on the Internet." Proceedings of INET 1993. Retrieved October 30, 2009 (www.cc.gatech.edu/~asb/papers/old-papers.html).

Bryant, Adam. 2007. "iSee Into the Future, Therefore iAm." *New York Times*, July 1.

Bryant, Karl. 2006. "Making Gender Identity Disorder of Childhood: Historical Lessons for Contemporary Debates." *Sexuality Research & Social Policy* 3(3): 23–39.

Bryant, Karl. 2008. "In Defense of Gay Children? 'Progay' Homophobia and the Production of Homonormativity." *Sexualities* 11(4): 455–475.

Bullough, Vern L. 1975. "Transgenderism in History." *Archives of Sexual Behavior* 4(5): 561–571.

Burris, Beverly and Andrea Hoplight. 1996. "Theoretical Perspectives on the Internet and CMC." Paper presented at the annual meetings of the American Sociology Association, August 17, New York.

Bushnik, Tracey, Jocelynn L. Cook, A. Albert Yuzpe, Suzanne Tough, and John Collins. 2012. "Estimating the Prevalence of Infertility in Canada." *Human Reproduction* 27(3): 738–746.

Buss, Arnold H. and Norman W. Portnoy. 1967. "Pain Tolerance and Group Identification." *Journal of Personality and Social Psychology* 6(1): 106.

Butler, Judith P. 1990. *Gender Trouble: Feminism and the Subversion of Identity*. New York, NY: Routledge.

Butler, Judith P. 1993. *Bodies That Matter: On the Discursive Limits of "Sex."* New York, NY: Routledge.

Cafri, Guy, J. Kevin Thompson, Lina Ricciardelli, Marita McCabe, Linda Smolak, and Charles Yesalis. 2005. "Pursuit of the Muscular Ideal: Physical and Psychological Consequences and Putative Risk Factors." *Clinical Psychology Review* 25(2): 215–239.

Carey, Nessa. 2012. *The Epigenetics Revolution: How Modern Biology is Rewriting Our Understanding of Genetics, Disease, and Inheritance*. New York, NY: Columbia University Press.

Carr, Coeli. 2006. "If the Shoe Fits, You're Lucky." *New York Times*, April 9, Section 9, p. 2.

Carr, Nicholas. 2011. *The Shallows: What the Internet is Doing to Our Brains*. New York, NY: WW Norton & Company.

Cavanagh, Allison. 2007. *Sociology in the Age of the Internet*. Maidenhead, England: McGraw-Hill International.

Chandra, Anjani, Casey E. Copen, and Elizabeth Hervey Stephen. 2013. "Infertility and Impaired Fecundity in the United States, 1982–2010: Data from the National Survey of Family Growth." *National Health Statistics Reports* 67: 1–18.

Charmaz, Kathy. 1994. "Identity Dilemmas of Chronically Ill Men." *The Sociological Quarterly* 35(2): 269–288.

Chicago Corset Company. 1881. "After Wearing Ball's Corsets Madame Adelina Patti Says . . ." Chicago, IL: Shober & Carqueville Lithograph Company.

Clarke, Adele. 1998. *Disciplining Reproduction: Modernity, American Life Sciences, and the Problems of Sex*. Berkeley, CA: University of California Press.

Coad, David. 2008. *The Metrosexual: Gender, Sexuality, and Sport*. New York, NY: SUNY Press.

Coe, Kathryn, Mary P. Harmon, Blair Verner, and Andrew Tonn. 1993. "Tattoos and Male Alliances." *Journal of Human Nature* 4(2): 199–204.

Cohen, Jaques, R. G. Edwards, C. B. Fehilly, S. Fishel, J. Hewitt, J. Purdy, G. Rowland, P. Steptoe, and J. Webster. 1985. "In Vitro Fertilization: A Treatment for Male Infertility." *Fertility and Sterility* 43(3): 422–432.

Collins, James and Richard Blot. 2003. *Literacy and Literacies: Texts, Power, and Identity*. New York, NY: Cambridge University Press.

Coltrane, Scott. 2004. "Household Labor and the Routine Production of Gender." Pp. 186–206 in *The Gendered Society Reader*, edited by Michael S. Kimmel. New York, NY: Oxford University Press.

Conley, Dalton and Rebecca Glauber. 2005. "Gender, Body Mass and Economic Status." NBER Working Paper No. W11343. Retrieved March 14, 2009 (http://ssrn.com/abstract=727123).

Connell, Raewyn W. 2009. *Gender*. Cambridge, MA: Polity Press.

Cook, Kimberly J. and Phoebe M. Stambaugh. 1997. "Tuna Memos and Pissing Contests: Doing Gender and Male Dominance on the Internet." Pp. 63–84 in *Everyday Sexism in the Third Millennium*, edited by Carol Rambo Ronai, Barbara A. Zsembik, and Joe R. Feagin. New York, NY: Routledge.

Cooley, Charles Horton. 1902. *Human Nature and the Social Order*. New York, NY: Charles Scribner's Sons.

Cooper, Al, Irene P. McLoughlin, and Kevin M. Campbell. 2000. "Sexuality in Cyberspace: Update for the 21st Century." *CyberPsychology & Behavior* 3(4): 521–536.

Copeland, Libby I. 1998. "At the Plate with Arms the Size of Pizzas: For One of the Hottest Hitters Ever, 19 is the Magic Number." *Los Angeles Time*s. Retrieved June 24, 2014 (http://articles.latimes.com/1998/sep/15/news/ls-22797).

Copes, John H. and Craig J. Forsyth. 1998. "The Tattoo: A Social Psychological Explanation." *International Review of Modern Sociology* 23: 83–89.

Cordaux, Richard and Mark Stoneking. 2003. "South Asia, the Andamanese and the Genetic Evidence for an 'Early' Human Dispersal Out of Africa." *American Journal of Human Genetics* 72(6): 1,586–1,590.

Cowan, Ruth Schwartz. 1997. *A Social History of American Technology*. New York, NY: Oxford University Press.

Crane, Diana. 2000. *Fashion and Its Social Agendas: Class, Gender and Identity in Clothing*. Chicago, IL: University of Chicago Press.

Crawley, Sara L., Lara J. Foley, and Constance L. Shehan. 2007. *Gendering Bodies*. Thousand Oaks, CA: Rowman & Littlefield Publishers.

Cregan, Kate. 2006. *The Sociology of the Body*. London, England: Sage.

Crossley, Nick. 2001. *The Social Body: Habit, Identity and Desire.* London, England: Sage.

Culley, Lorraine, Nicky Hudson, and Maria Lohan. 2013. "Where Are All the Men? The Marginalization of Men in Social Scientific Research on Infertility." *Reproductive Biomedicine Online* 27: 225–235.

Cumming, Helen. 1943. "War Booms the Tattooing Art." *New York Times,* September 19, p. 38.

Currah, Paisley 2008. "Expecting Bodies: The Pregnant Man and Transgender Exclusion from the Employment Non-Discrimination Act." *WSQ: Women's Studies Quarterly* 36(3–4): 330–336.

Custers, Kathleen and Jan van den Bulck. 2009. "Viewership of Pro-anorexia Websites in Seventh, Ninth and Eleventh Graders." *European Eating Disorders Review* 17(3): 214–219.

Daldry, Stephen (dir.). 2000. *Billy Elliot.* Universal Studios.

Daniels, Cynthia R. 2006. *Exposing Men: The Science and Politics of Male Reproduction.* New York, NY: Oxford University Press.

Davis, Georgiann. 2011. "'DSD is a Perfectly Fine Term': Reasserting Medical Authority through a Shift in Intersex Terminology." Pp. 155–182 in *Sociology of Diagnosis, issue of Advances in Medical Sociology,* Vol. 12, edited by P.J. McGann and David J. Hutson. Bingley, England: Emerald Group Publishing Limited.

Davis, Kathy. 1995. *Reshaping the Female Body: The Dilemma of Cosmetic Surgery.* New York, NY: Routledge.

De Beaumont, Charles d'Eon, Roland A. Champagne, Nina Claire Ekstein, and Gary Kates. 2001. *The Maiden of Tonnerre: The Vicissitudes of the Chevalier and the Chevalière d'Eon.* Baltimore, MD: Johns Hopkins University Press.

De Lauretis, Teresa. 1987. *Technologies of Gender: Essays on Theory, Film, and Fiction.* Bloomington, IN: Indiana University Press.

De Sutter, P., K. Kira, A. Verschoor, and A. Hotimsky. 2002. "The Desire to Have Children and the Preservation of Fertility in Transsexual Women: A Survey." *International Journal of Transgenderism* 6(3): 97–103.

"Defining 'Natural': Visceral Reactions to an Act Should Not Distract from the Real Ethical Issues. (Editorial)." 2008. *Nature* 452(7,188): 665–666.

DeGregory, Lane. 2007. "The Ripple Effect of Transformation." *St. Petersburg Times,* December 31, p. 1E. Retrieved August 11, 2008 (www.sptimes.com/2007/12/31/Life/Susan_Stanton_s_lonel.shtml).

DeGregory, Lane and Lorri Helfand. 2007. "His Second Self." *St. Petersburg Times,* March 11, p. 1A.

DeLamater, John and Michelle Hasday. 2007. "The Sociology of Sexuality." Pp. 254–265 in *21st Century Sociology: A Reference Handbook,* edited by Cliff Bryant and Dennis L. Peck. Thousand Oaks, CA: Sage.

DeLeel, Marissa L., Tammy L. Hughes, Jeffrey A. Miller, Alison Hipwell, and Lea A. Theodore. 2009. "Prevalence of Eating Disturbance and Body Image Dissatisfaction in Young Girls: An Examination of the Variance across Racial and Socioeconomic Groups." *Psychology in the Schools* 46(8): 767–775.

DeMello, Margo. 2000. *Bodies of Inscription: A Cultural History of the Modern Tattoo Community.* Durham, NC: Duke University Press.

Denzin, Norman K. 1987. *The Recovering Alcoholic.* Newbury Park, CA: Sage Publications.

Derry, T. K. and Trevor I. Williams. 1993. *A Short History of Technology: From the Earliest Times to A.D. 1900.* New York, NY: Dover Publications.

Devos, Thierry and Mahzarin R. Banaji. 2003. "Implicit Self and Identity." Pp. 153–175 in *Handbook of Self and Identity,* edited by Mark R. Leary and June Price Tangney. New York, NY: Guilford Press.

Diamond versus Chakrabarty. 1980. 444 U.S. 1,028.

Diamond, Milton. 2007. "'Is it a Boy or a Girl?': Intersex Children Reshape Medical Practice." *Science & Spirit* 18(4): 36–38.

Diamond, Milton and Hazel G. Beh. 2008. "Changes in Management of Children with Differences of Sex Development. *Nature Clinical Practice Endocrinology & Metabolism* 4: 4–5.

Dickel, M. H. 1995. "Bent Gender: Virtual Disruptions of Gender and Sexual Identity." *Electronic Journal of Communication* 5(4). Retrieved August 11, 2008 (www.cios.org/www/ejc/v5n495.htm).

"Divided Skirts." 1881. *New York Times*, October 31, p. 4.

Donath, Judith. 1997. *Inhabiting the Virtual City: The Design of Social Environments for Electronic Communities*. Boston, MA: MIT Press.

Donath, Judith. 2007. "Signals in Social Supernets." *Journal of Computer-mediated Communication* 13(1): 231–251.

Donath, Judith and danah boyd. 2004. "Public Displays of Connection." *BT Technology Journal* 22(4): 71–82.

Drew, Patricia. 2008a. "Surgically Altered Self: How Patients' Negotiations of Weight Loss Surgery Discourses Shape Self Conceptions." PhD dissertation, Department of Sociology, University of California, Santa Barbara.

Drew, Patricia. 2008b. "Weight Loss Surgery Patients' Negotiations of Medicine's Institutional Logic." Pp. 65–92 in *Research in the Sociology of Health Care*, Vol. 26, edited by Jennie Jacobs Kronenfeld. Bingley, England: Emerald Group Publishing.

Duggan, Maeve and Aaron Smith. 2014. "Social Media Update 2013." Pew Research Center. Retrieved June 16, 2014 (http://pewinternet.org/Reports/2013/Social-Media-Update.aspx).

Dunn, Jancee. 2011. "Julianne Moore Keeps it Light." *Health Magazine*. June 2. Retrieved January 15, 2014 (www.health.com/health/article/0,,20499604,00.html).

Dworkin, Shari and Lucia O'Sullivan. 2007. "'It's Less Work for Us and It Shows Us She Has Good Taste': Masculinity, Sexual Initiation, and Contemporary Sexual Scripts." Pp. 105–121 in *The Sexual Self: The Construction of Sexual Scripts*, edited by Michael Kimmel. Nashville, TN: Vanderbilt University Press.

Eagly, Alice H. and Shelly Chaiken. 1993. *The Psychology of Attitudes*. Fort Worth, TX: Harcourt Brace Jovanovich College Publishers.

Eagly, Alice H. and Shelly Chaiken. 1998. "Attitude Structure and Function." Pp. 269–322 in *Handbook of Social Psychology*, edited by Daniel Gilbert, Susan Friske, and Gardner Lindzey. New York, NY: McGraw-Hill.

Earl, Jennifer and Katrina Kimport. 2011. *Digitally Enabled Social Change: Activism in the Internet Age*. Cambridge, MA: The MIT Press.

Eastwick, Paul W. and Wendi L. Gardner. 2008. "Is It a Game? Evidence for Social Influence in the Virtual World." *Social Influence* 4(1): 18–32.

Edelmann, Robert J., Michael Humphrey, and David J. Owens. 1994. "The Meaning of Parenthood and Couples' Reactions to Male Infertility." *British Journal of Medical Psychology* 67: 291–299.

Ehrenreich, Barbara and Deirdre English. 2005. *For Her Own Good: Two Centuries of the Experts' Advice to Women*. Revised edn. New York, NY: Anchor Books.

Ellul, Jacques. 1964. *The Technological Society*, translated by John Wilkinson. New York, NY: Vintage Books.

English, Bella. 2011. "Led by the Child Who Simply Knew." *Boston Globe*. December 11. Retrieved December 12, 2013 (www.boston.com/lifestyle/family/articles/2011/12/11/led_by_the_child_who_simply_knew/).

Epstein, Julia and Kristina Straub. 1991. *Body Guards: The Cultural Politics of Gender Ambiguity*. New York, NY: Routledge.

Ernst & Young. 2013. "Beyond Borders: Matters of Evidence Biotechnology Industry Report 2013." Retrieved May 1, 2014 (http://www.ey.com/Publication/vwLUAssets/Beyond_borders/$FILE/Beyond_borders.pdf).

Etcoff, Nancy. 1999. *Survival of the Prettiest*. New York, NY: Doubleday.

Ewing, Elizabeth. 1978. *Dress and Undress: A History of Women's Underwear*. New York, NY: Drama Book Specialists.

Facebook. 2013. "Updates to Facebook Login." Retrieved July 1, 2014 (http://newsroom.fb.com/news/2013/08/updates-to-facebook-login/).

Facebook. 2014. "Facebook Reports First Quarter 2014 Results." Retrieved July 1, 2014 (http://files.shareholder.com/downloads/AMDA-NJ5DZ/3294889963x0x746640/f9ca7083-759b-40d1-8666-4cba02693b53/FB_News_2014_4_23_Financial_Releases.pdf).

"Facebook Diversity." 2014. Facebook. Retrieved July 1, 2014 (www.facebook.com/photo.php?fbid=567587973337709&set=a.196865713743272.42938.105225179573993&type=1&stream_ref=10).

Fausto-Sterling, Anne. 2000. *Sexing the Body: Gender Politics and the Construction of Sexuality*. New York, NY: Basic Books.

Fausto-Sterling, Anne. 2012. *Sex/Gender: Biology in a Social World*. New York, NY: Routledge.

Fausto-Sterling, Anne, Cynthia Garcia Coll, and Meaghan Lamarre. 2012. "Sexing the Baby: Part 2 Applying Dynamic Systems Theory to the Emergences of Sex-related Differences in Infants and Toddlers." *Social Science & Medicine* 74: 1,693–1,702.

Featherstone, Mike. 1982. "The Body in Consumer Culture." *Theory, Culture & Society* 1(2): 18–33.

Featherstone, Mike. 1991. "The Body in Consumer Culture." Pp. 170–196 in *The Body: Social Process and Cultural Theory*, edited by Mike Featherstone, Mike Hepworth, and Bryan S. Turner. London, England: Sage.

Featherstone, Mike and Roger Burrows. 1995. "Cultures of Technological Embodiment: An Introduction." *Body & Society* 1(3–4): 1–19.

Feder, Ellen K. 2009. "Normalizing Medicine: Between 'Intersexuals' and Individuals with 'Disorders of Sex Development'." *Health Care Anaylis* 17(2): 134–143.

Feinberg, Leslie. 1996. *Transgender Warriors: Making History from Joan of Arc to Dennis Rodman*. Boston, MA: Beacon Press.

Ferreday, Debra. 2003. "Unspeakable Bodies: Erasure, Embodiment and the Pro-Ana Community." *International Journal of Cultural Studies* 6(3): 277–295.

Festinger, Leon. 1957. *Theory of Cognitive Dissonance*. Evanston, IL: Row Peterson.

Fields, Jessica. 2008. *Risky lessons: Sex Education and Social Inequality*. New Brunswick, NJ: Rutgers University Press.

Fine, Gary Alan. 2001. *Gifted Tongues: High School Debate and Adolescent Culture*. Princeton, NJ: Princeton University Press.

Fisher, Dana R. 1998. "Rumoring Theory and the Internet: A Framework for Analyzing the Grass Roots." *Social Science Computer Review* 16(2): 158–168.

Fisher, Jill. 2002. "Tattooing the Body, Marking Culture." *Body & Society* 8(4): 91–107.

Fiske, Susan and Shelley Taylor. 1991. *Social Cognition*. 2nd edn. New York, NY: McGraw-Hill.

Fletcher, Dan. 2010. "How Facebook is Redefining Privacy." *Time*, May 20. Retrieved on September 5, 2014 (http://www.time.com/time/business/article/0,8599,1990582,00.html).

Foley, Laura. 2005. "Midwives, Marginality, and Public Identity Work." *Symbolic Interaction* 28(2): 183–203.

Foucault, Michel. 1965. *Madness and Civilization*. New York, NY: Pantheon Press.

Foucault, Michel. 1979. *Discipline and Punish: The Birth of the Prison*. New York, NY: Vintage.

Foucault, Michel. 1988. "Technologies of the Self." Pp. 16–49 in *Technologies of the Self: A Seminar with Michel Foucault*, edited by Luther H. Martin, Huck Gutman, and Patrick H. Hutton. London, England: Tavistock Publications.

Foucault, Michel. 1990. *The History of Sexuality: An Introduction*. New York, NY: Vintage Books.

Fox, Jesse and Jeremy N. Bailenson. 2009. "Virtual Self-modeling: The Effects of Vicarious Reinforcement and Identification on Exercise Behaviors." *Media Psychology* 12(1): 1–25.

Fox, Nick and Chris Roberts. 1999. "GPs in Cyberspace: The Sociology of a 'Virtual Community'." *The Sociological Review* 47(4): 643–671.

Franklin, Sarah. 1997. *Embodied Progress. A Cultural Account of Assisted Conception*. London, England: Routledge.

Franklin, Sarah. 2007. *Dolly Mixtures: The Remaking of Genealogy*. Durham, NC: Duke University Press.

Fraser, Suzanne. 2003. *Cosmetic Surgery, Gender and Culture*. New York, NY: Palgrave Macmillan.

Freedman, Estelle B. 1974. "The New Woman: Changing Views of Women in the 1920s." *The Journal of American History* 61(2): 372–393.

Frost, Dan. 2006. "Digital Utopia: A New Breed of Technologists Envisions a Democratic World Improved by the Internet." *San Francisco Chronicle*, November 5, Pp. F–1.

Futter, Ellen V. 2006. "Failing Science." *New York Times*, November 26, Section 14, p. 11.

Gagné, Patricia and Deanna McGaughey. 2002. "Designing Women: Cultural Hegemony and the Exercise of Power among Women Who Have Undergone Elective Mammoplasty." *Gender & Society* 16(6): 814–838.

Gamson, Joshua. 1998. *Freaks Talk Back: Tabloid Talk Shows and Sexual Nonconformity*. Chicago, IL: University of Chicago Press.

Gannona, Kenneth, Lesley Gloverb, and Paul Abelc. 2004. "Masculinity, Infertility, Stigma and Media Reports." *Social Science & Medicine* 59(6): 1,169–1,175.

Garland-Thomson, Rosemarie. 2005. "Feminist Disability Studies." *Signs: Journal of Women in Culture and Society* 30(2): 1,557–1,587.

Gartner Research. 2007. "Gartner Says 80 Percent of Active Internet Users Will Have a 'Second Life' in the Virtual World by the End of 2011." Retrieved June 13, 2014 (www.gartner.com/it/page.jsp?id=503861).

Gattey, Charles Neilson. 1968. *The Bloomer Girls*. New York, NY: Coward-McCann.

Gauthier, DeAnn and Nancy Chaudoir. 2004. "Tranny Boyz: Cyber Community Support in Negotiating Sex and Gender Mobility Among Female to Male Transsexuals." *Deviant Behavior* 25(4): 375–398.

Gergen, Kenneth. 1991. *The Saturated Self: Dilemmas of Identity in Contemporary Life*. New York, NY: Basic Books.

Gergen, Kenneth. 2009. *Relational Being: Beyond Self and Community*. New York, NY: Oxford University Press.

Gibson, John William. 1903. *Golden Thoughts on Chastity and Procreation: Including Heredity, Prenatal Influences, Etc., Etc*. Naperville, IL: J.L. Nichols & Co.

Gibson, William. 1982. "Burning Chrome." *OMNI* 4 (July): 72–82.

Giddens, Anthony. 1991. *Modernity and Self-identity: Self and Society in the Late Modern Age*. Stanford, CA: Stanford University Press.

Gill, Rosalind, Karen Henwood, and Carl McLean. 2005. "Body Projects and the Regulation of Normative Masculinity." *Body & Society* 11(1): 37–62.

Gimlin, Debra L. 2000. "Cosmetic Surgery: Beauty as Commodity." *Qualitative Sociology* 23(1): 77–98.

Gimlin, Debra L. 2002. *Body Work: Beauty and Self-Image in American Culture*. Berkeley, CA: University of California Press.

Gimlin, Debra L. 2007. "Discourses of Ageing and Narrative Resistance in a Commercial Slimming Group." *Ageing & Society* 27: 1–19.

Goering, Sara. 2003. "Conformity through Cosmetic Surgery: The Medical Erasure of Race and Disability." Pp. 172–188 in *Science and Other Cultures: Issues in Philosophies of Science and Technology*, edited by Robert Figueroa and Sandra G. Harding. New York, NY: Routledge.

Goffman, Erving. 1959. *The Presentation of Self in Everyday Life*. New York, NY: Doubleday.

Goffman, Erving. 1963. *Stigma: Notes on the Management of Spoiled Identity*. New York, NY: Simon & Schuster.

Goffman, Erving. 1974. *Frame Analysis: An Essay on the Organization of Experience*. Boston, MA: Northeastern University Press.

Gosling, Samuel D., Sam Gaddis, and Simine Vazire. 2007. "Personality Impressions Based on Facebook Profiles." *ICWSM* 7: 1–4.

Gottschalk, Simon. 2010. "The Presentation of Avatars in Second Life: Self and Interaction in Social Virtual Spaces." *Symbolic Interaction* 33(4): 501–525.

Govenar, Alan. 2000. "The Changing Image of Tattooing in American Culture, 1846–1966." Pp. 212–233 in *Written on the Body: The Tattoo in European and American History*, edited by Jane Caplan. Princeton, NJ: Princeton University Press.

Government of Canada. 2006. "The Human Face of Mental Health and Mental Illness in Canada 2006." Minister of Public Works and Government Services Canada, HP5–19/2006E.

Gramsci, Antonio. 1971. *Selections from the Prison Notebooks*. London, England: Lawrence and Wishart.

Grant, Jaime M., Lisa Mottet, Justin Edward Tanis, Jack Harrison, Jody Herman, and Mara Keisling. 2011. "Injustice at Every Turn: A Report of the National Transgender Discrimination Survey." National Center for Transgender Equality, February 3. Retrieved September 5, 2014 (www.thetaskforce.org/reports_and_research/ntds).

Green, Jamison. 2004. *Becoming a Visible Man*. Nashville, TN: Vanderbilt University Press.

Greil, Arthur L. 1991. *Not Yet Pregnant: Infertile Couples in Contemporary America*. New Brunswick, NJ: Rutgers University Press.

Grimshaw, Jean. 1999. "Working Out with Merleau-Ponty." Pp. 21–35 in *Women's Bodies: Discipline and Transgression*, edited by Jane Arthurs and Jean Grimshaw. London, England: Cassell.

Grossman, Arnold H. and Anthony R. D'Augelli. 2006. "Transgender Youth: Invisible and Vulnerable." *Journal of Homosexuality* 51(1): 111–128.

Grosz, Elizabeth. 1994. *Volatile Bodies: Toward a Corporeal Feminism*. Bloomington, IN: Indiana University Press.

Gurney, Karen. 2007. "Sex and the Surgeon's Knife: The Family Court's Dilemma . . . Informed Consent and the Specter of Iatrogenic Harm to Children with Intersex Characteristics." *American Journal of Law and Medicine* 33: 625.

Hacker, Sally. 1989. *Pleasure, Power and Technology: Some Tales of Gender, Engineering, and the Cooperative Workplace*. Boston, MA: Unwin Hyman.

Halberstam, Judith. 1991. "Automating Gender: Postmodern Feminism in the Age of the Smart Machine." *Feminist Studies* 17(3): 439–459.

Hall, Christine C. Iijima. 1995. "Asian Eyes: Body Image and Eating Disorders of Asian and Asian American Women." *Eating Disorders* 3(1): 8–19.

Hall, Stuart. 1996. "Race: The Floating Signifier." Lecture at Goldsmiths College.

Halnon, Karen Bettez and Saundra Cohen. 2006. "Muscles, Motorcycles and Tattoos: Gentrification in a New Frontier." *Journal of Consumer Culture* 6(1): 33–56.

Hamermesh, Daniel S. and Jeff E. Biddle. 1994. "Beauty and the Labor Market." *The American Economic Review* 84(5): 1,174–1,194.

Hampton, Keith N., Chul-joo Lee, and Eun Ja Her. 2011. "How New Media Affords Network Diversity: Direct and Mediated Access to Social Capital through Participation in Local Social Settings." *New Media & Society* 13(7): 1,031–1,049.

Hampton, Keith, Lauren Sessions Goulet, Lee Rainie, and Kristen Purcell. 2011. "Social Networking Sites and Our Lives." Pew Research Center. Retrieved June 16, 2014 (http://pewinternet.org/Reports/2011/Technology-and-social-networks.aspx).

Haraway, Donna. 1991. "A Cyborg Manifesto: Science, Technology, and Socialist-Feminism in the Late Twentieth Century," Pp. 149–181 in *Simians, Cyborgs and Women: The Reinvention of Nature*. New York, NY: Routledge.

Harmon-Jones, Eddie and Judson Mills. 1999. *Cognitive Dissonance: Progress on a Pivotal Theory in Social Psychology*. Washington, DC: American Psychological Association.

Harris, Diane J. and Sue A. Kuba. 1997. "Ethnocultural Identity and Eating Disorders in Women of Color." *Professional Psychology: Research and Practice* 28(4): 341–347.

Harshbarger, Jenni L., Carolyn R. Ahlers-Schmidt, Laura Mayans, David Mayans, and Joseph H. Hawkins. 2009. "Pro-anorexia Websites: What a Clinician Should Know." *International Journal of Eating Disorders* 42(4): 367–370.

Hausman, Bernice L. 1992. "Demanding Subjectivity: Transsexualism, Medicine, and the Technologies of Gender." *Journal of the History of Sexuality* 3: 270–302.

Hawkes, Daina, Charlene Y. Senn, and Chantal Thorn. 2004. "Factors That Influence Attitudes toward Women with Tattoos." *Sex Roles* 50(9/10): 593–604.

He, Ming Fang and JoAnne Phillion. 2001. "Trapped In-between: A Narrative Exploration of Race, Gender, and Class." *Race, Gender & Class* 8(1): 47–56.

Hebdige, Dick. 1979. *Subcultures: The Meaning of Style*. London, England: Methuen.

Heidegger, Martin. 1977. *The Question Concerning Technology*, translated by W. Lovitt. New York, NY: Harper & Row.

Herring, Susan C. 1996. "Gender and Democracy in Computer-Mediated Communication." Pp. 476–489 in *Computerization and Controversy: Value Conflicts and Social Choices*, edited by Rob Kling. San Diego, CA: Academic Press.

Herring, Susan C. 1999. "Posting in a Different Voice: Gender and Ethics in Computer-mediated Communication." Pp. 241–265 in *Computer Media and Communication: A Reader*, edited by Paul Mayer. New York, NY: Oxford University Press.

Herring, Susan C. and Anna Martinson. 2004. "Assessing Gender Authenticity in Computer-Mediated Language Use." *Journal of Language and Social Psychology* 23(4): 424–446.

Heyes, Cressida. 2003. "Feminist Solidarity after Queer Theory: The Case of Transgender." *Signs: Journal of Women in Culture and Society* 28(4): 1,093–1,120.

Hill, Darryl. 2005. "Coming to Terms: Using Technology to Know Identity." *Sexuality and Culture* 9: 24–52.

Hine, Christine M. 2000. *Virtual Ethnography*. Thousand Oaks, CA: Sage Publications.

Hochschild, Arlie. 1989. *The Second Shift*. New York, NY: Avon.

Holstein, James A. and Jaber F. Gubrium. 2000. *The Self We Live By: Narrative Identity in a Postmodern World*. New York, NY: Oxford University Press.

Horrigan, John B. and Aaron Smith. 2007. "Home Broadband Adoption 2007." Pew Internet and American Life Project. Retrieved September 5, 2014 (www.pewinternet.org/files/old-media//Files/Reports/2007/PIP_Broadband%202007.pdf.pdf).

Hudson, James I., Eva Hiripi, Harrison G. Pope Jr., and Ronald C. Kessler. 2007. "The Prevalence and Correlates of Eating Disorders in the National Comorbidity Survey Replication." *Biological Psychiatry* 61(3): 348–358.

Hughes, Ieuan A. 2010 "The Quiet Revolution." *Best Practice & Research Clinical Endocrinology & Metabolism* 24(2): 159–162.

Hughes, James. 2004. *Citizen Cyborg: Why Democratic Societies Must Respond to the Redesigned Human of the Future*. Boulder, CO: Westview Press.

Hutchby, Ian. 2001. "Technologies, Texts and Affordances." *Sociology* 35(2): 441–456.

Hyde, Janet Shibley. 2005. "The Gender Similarities Hypothesis." *American Psychologist* 60(6): 581.

Ingraham, Chrys. 1994. "The Heterosexual Imaginary: Feminist Sociology and Theories of Gender." *Sociological Theory* 12(2): 203–219.

Inhorn, Marcia C. 2007. "Masturbation, Semen Collection and Men's IVF Experiences: Anxieties in the Muslim World." *Body and Society* 13(3): 37.

International Medical Congress. 1913. *The History of Inoculation and Vaccination for the Prevention and Treatment of Disease: Lecture Memoranda*. London, England: Burroughs Wellcome.

International Society of Aesthetic Plastic Surgery. 2012. "ISAPS International Survey on Aesthetic/Cosmetic Procedures Performed in 2011." Retrieved January 7, 2014 (www.isaps.org/Media/Default/global-statistics/ISAPS-Results-Procedures-2011.pdf).

Irvine, Janice M. 1990. *Disorders of Desire: Sex and Gender in Modern American Sexology*. Philadelphia, PA: Temple University Press.

Ito, Mizuko, Sonja Baumer, Matteo Bittanti, danah boyd, Rachel Cody, Becky Herr-Stephenson, Heather A. Horst, Patricia G. Lange, Dilan Mahendran, Katynka Martinez, C.J. Pascoe, Dan Perkel, Laura Robinson, Christo Sims, and Lisa Tripp. 2010. *Hanging Out, Messing Around, and Geeking Out: Kids Living and Learning with New Media*. Cambridge, MA: MIT Press.

Jackson, Linda A., John E. Hunter, and Carole N. Hodge. 1995. "Physical Attractiveness and Intellectual Competence: A Meta-analytic Review." *Social Psychology Quarterly* 58(2): 108–122.

Jacobs, Jerry A. 1996. "Gender Inequality and Higher Education." *Annual Review of Sociology* 22: 153–185.

Janssen, Janine. 2005. "Tattoos in Prison: Men and their Pictures on the Edge of Society." Pp. 179–192 in *Spaces of Masculinities*, edited by Bettina van Hoven and Kathrin Hörschelmann. New York, NY: Routledge.

Jarrold, Julian (dir.). 2005. *Kinky Boots*. Miramax Films.

Jeffreys, Sheila. 2003. "FTM Transsexualism and the Destruction of Lesbians." Pp. 122–143 in *Unpacking Queer Politics: A Lesbian Feminist Perspective*, edited by Sheila Jeffreys. Cambridge, England: Polity Press.

Johnson, LaShaune. 2008. "Opening Remarks." Annual Audre Lorde Cancer Awareness Brunch and the Black Women and Breast Cancer Conference: Prevention, Disparities and Wellness, October 18, Simmons College, Boston, MA.

Johnston, Jeanne D., Anne P. Massey, and Celeste DeVaneaux. 2012. "Innovation in Weight Loss Intervention Programs: An Examination of a 3D Virtual World Approach." System Science (HICSS), 2012 45th Hawaii International Conference. 2,890–2,899.

Jones, Steven, ed. 1995. *CyberSociety: Computer-Mediated Communication and Community*. Thousand Oaks, CA: Sage Publications.

Joos, Kristin and Kendal Broad. 2007. "Coming Out of the Family Closet: Stories of Adult Women with LGBTQ Parent(s)." *Journal of Qualitative Sociology* 30(3): 275–295.

Jordan-Young, Rebecca M. 2010. *Brain Storm*. Cambridge, MA: Harvard University Press.

Jurgenson, Nathan. 2012. "When Atoms Meet Bits: Social Media, the Mobile Web and Augmented Revolution." *Future Internet* 4(1): 83–91.

Kampf, Antje. 2013. "Tales of Healthy Men: Male Reproductive Bodies in Biomedicine from 'Lebensborn' to Sperm Banks." *Health* 17: 20–36.

Kang, Miliann. 2003. "The Managed Hand: The Commercialization of Bodies and Emotions in Korean Immigrant-Owned Nail Salons." *Gender & Society* 17(6): 820–839.

Kang, Miliann and Katherine Jones. 2007. "Why do People Get Tattoos?" *Contexts* 6(1): 42–47.

Katz, Jonathan Ned. 1996. *The Invention of Heterosexuality*. New York, NY: Plume Press.

Kaw, Eugenia. 1993. "Medicalization of Racial Features: Asian American Women and Cosmetic Surgery." *Medical Anthropology Quarterly* 7(1): 74–89.

Kelly, Deirdre M., Shauna Pomerantz, and Dawn H. Currie. 2006. "'No Boundaries?' Girls' Interactive, Online Learning about Femininities." *Youth & Society* 38(1): 3–28.

Kendall, Lori. 2000. "'Oh No! I'm A Nerd!: Hegemonic Masculinity on an Online Forum." *Gender & Society* 14(2): 256–274.

Kendall, Lori. 2002. *Hanging Out in the Virtual Pub: Masculinities and Relationships Online*. Berkeley, CA: University of California Press.

Kennedy, Pagan. 2008. *The First Man Made Man*. New York, NY: Bloomsbury.

Kessler, Suzanne J. and Wendy McKenna. 1978. *Gender: An Ethnomethodological Approach*. Chicago, IL: University of Chicago Press.

Kimmel, Michael. 2005. *The Gender of Desire: Essays on Male Sexuality*. Albany, NY: SUNY Press.

Kimmel, Michael, ed. 2007. *The Sexual Self: The Construction of Sexual Scripts*. Nashville, TN: Vanderbilt University Press.

Kleinman, Daniel. 2005. *Science and Technology in Society: From Biotechnology to the Internet*. Malden, MA: Blackwell Publishing.

Kleinman, Daniel. 2008. *Science, Technology, and Democracy*. Albany, NY: SUNY Press.

Kling, Rob. 1996. "Hopes and Horrors: Technological Utopianism and Anti-Utopianism in Narratives of Computerization." Pp. 40–58 in *Computerization and Controversy: Values Conflicts and Social Choices*, edited by Rob Kling. San Diego, CA: Academic Press.

Koch, Jerome R., Alden E. Roberts, Myrna L. Armstrong, and Donna C. Owen. 2005. "College Students, Tattoos, and Sexual Activity." *Psychological Reports* 97: 887–890.

Kollock, Peter and Marc Smith. 1996. "Managing the Virtual Commons: Cooperation and Conflict in Computer Communities." Pp. 109–128 in *Computer-Mediated Communication: Linguistic, Social, and Cross-Cultural Perspectives*, edited by Susan Herring. Amsterdam, Netherlands: John Benjamins.

Kosut, Mary. 2000. "Tattoo Narratives: The Intersection of the Body, Self-Identity and Society." *Visual Studies* 15(1): 79–100.

Krizek, Claudette, Cleora Roberts, Robin Ragan, Jeffery J. Ferrara, and Beth Lord. 1999. "Gender and Cancer Support Group Participation." *Cancer Practice* 7(2): 86–92.

Kulick, Don. 1998. *Travesti: Sex, Gender, and Culture among Brazilian Transgendered Prostitutes*. Chicago, IL: University of Chicago Press.

Kwan, Samantha and Mary Nell Trautner. 2009. "Beauty Work: Individual and Institutional Rewards, the Reproduction of Gender, and Questions of Agency." *Sociology Compass* 3(1): 49–71.

Lakoff, Robin Tolmach and Raquel L. Scherr. 1984. *Face Value, the Politics of Beauty*. Boston, MA: Routledge & Kegan Paul.

Lamb, Warren and Elizabeth Watson. 1979. *Body Code: The Meaning in Movement*. London, England: Routledge.

Lampe, Cliff, Nicole Ellison, and Charles Steinfield. 2006. "A Face (book) in the Crowd: Social Searching vs. Social Browsing." Pp. 167–170 in *Proceedings of the 2006 20th Anniversary Conference on Computer Supported Cooperative Work*, ACM.

Langer, Ellen J. 1989. *Mindfulness*. Reading, MA: Addison-Wesley.

Laqueur, Thomas. 1990. *Making Sex: Body and Gender from the Greeks to Freud*. Cambridge, MA: Harvard University Press.

Laumann, Anne E. and Amy J. Derick. 2006. "Tattoos and Body Piercings in the United States: A National Data Set." *Journal of the American Academy of Dermatology* 55(3): 413–421.

Lee, Peter A., Christopher P. Houk, S. Faisal Ahmed, and Ieuan A. Hughes. 2006. "Consensus Statement on Management of Intersex Disorders." *Pediatrics* 118(2): e488–e500.

Lenhart, Amanda, Kristen Purcell, Aaron Smith, and Kathryn Zickuhr. 2010. *Social Media and Young Adults*. Pew Internet & American Life Project, 3.

Lenhart, Amanda, Mary Madden, Alexandra Rankin Macgill, and Aaron Smint. 2007. "Teens and Social Media: The Use of Social Media Gains a Greater Foothold in Teen Life as They Embrace the Conversational Nature of Interactive Online Media." Pew Research Center. Retrieved September 5, 2014 (http://www.pewinternet.org/files/old-media/Files/Reports/2007/PIP_Teens_Social_Media_Final.pdf.pdf).

Lestoil. 1968. "Advertisement." *Life Magazine* 64(14): 81.

Lin, Ken-Hou and Jennifer Lundquist. 2013. "Mate Selection in Cyberspace: The Intersection of Race, Gender, and Education." *American Journal of Sociology* 119(1): 183–215.

Linden Research, Inc. 2009. "1 Billion Hours, 1 Billion Dollars Served." Retrieved September 5, 2014 (http://lindenlab.com/releases/second-life-celebrates-10-year-anniversary).

Linden Research, Inc. 2013. "Second Life Celebrates 10-Year Anniversary." Retrieved January 23, 2014 (http://lindenlab.com/releases/second-life-celebrates-10-year-anniversary).

Link, Bruce G., Jo C. Phelan, Richard Miech, and Emily L. Westin. 2008. "The Resources that Matter: Fundamental Social Causes of Health Disparities and the Challenge of Intelligence." *Journal of Health and Social Behavior* 49(1): 72–91.

Lorber, Judith. 1989. "Choice, Gift, or Patriarchal Bargain? Women's Consent to In-vitro Fertilization in Male Infertility." *Hypatia* 4(3): 23–36.

Lorber, Judith. 1993. "Believing is Seeing: Biology as Ideology." *Gender & Society* 7(4): 568–581.

Lorber, Judith. 1996. *Paradoxes of Gender*. New Haven, CT: Yale University Press.

Lorber, Judith and Lakshmi Bandlamudi. 1993. "The Dynamics of Marital Bargaining in Male Infertility." *Gender & Society* 7(1): 32–49.

Loseke, Donileen R. 2001. "Lived Realities and Formula Stories of 'Battered Women'." Pp. 107–126 in *Institutional Selves*, edited by Jaber Gubrium and James Holstein. New York, NY: Oxford University Press.

Lyon, David. 1995. "The Roots of the Information Society Idea." Pp. 52–73 in *Information Technology and Society: A Reader*, edited by Nick Heap, Ray Thomas, Geoff Einon, Robin Mason and Hughie Mackay. London, England: Sage Publications.

Mackenzie, Donald and Judy Wajcman, eds. 1999. *The Social Shaping of Technology*. 2nd edn. Philadelphia, PA: Open University Press.

MacKinnon, Richard C. 1995. "Searching for the Leviathan in Usenet." Pp. 112–137 in *CyberSociety: Computer-Mediated Communication and Community*, edited by Steven Jones. Thousand Oaks, CA: Sage Publications.

MacKinnon, Richard C. 1997. "Punishing the Persona: Correctional Strategies for the Virtual Offender." Pp. 206–235 in *Virtual Culture: Identity and Communication in Cybersociety*, edited by Steven Jones. London, England: Sage Publications.

MacKinnon, Richard C. 1998. "The Social Construction of Rape in Virtual Reality." Pp. 147–172 in *Network and Netplay: Virtual Groups on the Internet*, edited by Fay Sudweeks, Margaret L. McLaughlin, and Sheizaf Rafaeli. Cambridge, MA: MIT Press.

Macur, Juliet. 2013. "Armstrong Admits Doping, and Says He Will Testify." *New York Times*. Retrieved June 13, 2014 (www.nytimes.com/2013/01/15/sports/cycling/lance-armstrong-admits-doping-and-says-he-will-testify-against-cycling-officials.html).

Madden, Mary. 2006. "Internet Penetration and Impact." Pew Internet and American Life Project. Retrieved September 5, 2014 (www.pewinternet.org/files/old-media//Files/Reports/2006/PIP_Internet_Impact.pdf.pdf).

Malik, Sumaira H. and Neil Coulson. 2008. "The Male Experience of Infertility: A Thematic Analysis of an Online Infertility Support Group Bulletin Board." *Journal of Reproductive and Infant Psychology* 26(1): 18–30.

Mamo, Laura. 2007. *Queering Reproduction: Achieving Pregnancy in the Age of Technoscience.* Durham, NC: Duke University Press.

Martin, Emily. 1987. *Woman in the Body: A Cultural Analysis of Reproduction.* Boston, MA: Beacon Press.

Martin, Emily. 1991. "The Egg and the Sperm: How Science Has Constructed a Romance Based on Stereotypical Male–Female Roles." *Signs* 16(3): 485–501.

Marx, Karl. 1977. *A Contribution to the Critique of Political Economy.* Moscow, Russia: Progress Publishers.

Mason, Mary-Claire. 1993. *Male Infertility—Men Talking.* London, England: Routledge.

Mason-Schrock, Douglas. 1996. "Transsexuals' Narrative Construction of the 'True Self'." *Social Psychology Quarterly* 59(3): 176–192.

"Maxim's 2007 Hot 100." N.d. Maxim.com. Retrieved April 14, 2008 (www.maxim.com/hot-100/2007-hot-100).

McGinn, Robert E. 1991. *Science, Technology and Society.* Englewood Cliffs, NJ: Prentice-Hall.

McGlen, Nancy and Karen O'Connor. 1998. *Women, Politics, and American Society.* Englewood Cliffs, NJ: Prentice-Hall.

McGovern, Art and Edwin Goewey. 1926. "Babe Ruth Brought Back by Physical Culture." *Physical Culture* 38–39: 107–111.

McKenna, Katelyn Y.A. and John A. Bargh. 1998. "Coming Out in the Age of the Internet: Identity De-Marginalization from Virtual Group Participation." *Journal of Personality and Social Psychology* 75(3): 681–694.

McKenna, Katelyn Y. A., Amie S. Green, and Pamela K. Smith. 2001. "Demarginalizing the Sexual Self." *The Journal of Sex Research* 38: 302–311.

McKinley, Nita Mary. 1999. "Women and Objectified Body Consciousness: Mothers' and Daughters' Body Experience in Cultural, Developmental, and Familial Context." *Developmental Psychology* 35: 760–769.

McLuhan, Marshall. 1970. *Culture is Our Business.* New York, NY: McGraw-Hill.

McLuhan, Marshall. 1994. *Understanding Media: The Extensions of Man.* Cambridge, MA: MIT Press.

Mead, George Herbert. 1934. *Mind, Self and Society from the Standpoint of a Social Behaviorist,* edited by Charles W. Morris. Chicago, IL: University of Chicago Press.

Meadow, Tey. 2011. "'Deep Down Where the Music Plays': How Parents Account for Childhood Gender Variance." *Sexualities* 14(6): 725–747.

Messner, Michael A. 2000. "Barbie Girls vs. Sea Monsters: Children Constructing Gender." *Gender & Society* 14: 765–784.

Meyerowitz, Joanne. 2002. *How Sex Changed: The History of Transsexuality in America.* Cambridge, MA: Harvard University Press.

Middleton, Catherine A. and Christine Sorensen. 2005. "How Connected are Canadians? Inequalities in Canadian Households' Internet Access." *Canadian Journal of Communication* 30(4): 463–483.

Miller, Laura. 2006. *Beauty Up: Exploring Contemporary Japanese Body Aesthetics.* Berkeley, CA: University of California Press.

Mitchell, George J. 2007. "Report to the Commissioner of Baseball of an Independent Investigation into the Illegal Use of Steroids and Other Performance Enhancing Substances by Players in Major League Baseball." New York, NY: Office of the Commissioner of Baseball. Retrieved March 8, 2009 (http://files.mlb.com/mitchrpt.pdf).

Mohammed, Methal. 2009. "Cultural Identity in Virtual Reality (VR): A Case Study of a Muslim Woman with Hijab in Second Life (SL)." *Journal of Virtual Worlds Research* 2(2).

Moore, Lisa Jean. 2002. "Extracting Men from Semen: Masculinity in Scientific Representations of Sperm." *Social Text* 20(4): 91–119.

More, Sam Dylan. 1998. "The Pregnant Man—An Oxymoron?" *Journal of Gender Studies* 7(3): 319–328.

Morgan, David and Sue Scott. 1993. "Bodies in a Social Landscape." Pp. 1–21 in *Body Matters*, edited by David Morgan and Sue Scott. New York, NY: Routledge.

Morley, David and Kevin Robins. 1995. *Spaces of Identity: Global Media, Electronic Landscapes and Cultural Boundaries*. New York, NY: Routledge.

Morozov, Evgeny. 2013. *To Save Everything, Click Here: The Folly of Technological Solutionism*. New York, NY: Public Affairs.

Moscucci, Ornella. 1990. *The Science of Woman: Gynaecology and Gender in England, 1800–1929*. Cambridge, England: Cambridge University Press.

Muñoz, Vic. 2009. "Gender Sovereignty." Paper presented at TransRhetorics Conference at Cornell University, Ithaca, NY. March 6–8.

Murray, Samantha. 2008. *The 'Fat' Female Body*. New York, NY: Palgrave Macmillan.

Myers, Daniel J. 1994. "Communication Technology and Social Movements: Contributions of Computer Networks to Activism." *Social Science Computer Review* 12(2): 250–260.

Nachtigall, Robert D., Gay Becker, and Mark Wozny. 1992. "The Effects of Gender-specific Diagnosis on Men's and Women's Response to Infertility." *Fertility and Sterility* 57: 113–121.

Nakamura, Lisa. 2002. *Cybertypes: Race, Ethnicity, and Identity on the Internet*. New York, NY: Routledge.

Nakamura, Lisa. 2008a. *Digitizing Race: Visual Cultures of the Internet*. Vol. 23. Minnesota, MN: University of Minnesota Press.

Nakamura, Lisa. 2008b. "Neoliberal Space and Race in Virtual Worlds." *The Velvet Light Trap* 62: 72–73.

Namaste, Viviane K. 2006. "Genderbashing: Sexuality, Gender, and the Regulation of Public Space." Pp. 584–600 in *The Transgender Studies Reader*, edited by Susan Stryker and Stephen Whittle. London, England: CRC Press.

Nicholas, D.B., T. McNeill, G. Montgomery, C. Stapleford, and M. McClure. 2004. "Communication Features in an Online Group for Fathers of Children with Spina Bifida: Considerations for Group Development among Men." *Social Work with Groups* 26(2): 65–80.

Norris, Mark L., Katherine M. Boydell, Leora Pinhas, and Debra K. Katzman. 2006. "Ana and the Internet: A Review of Pro-anorexia Websites." *International Journal of Eating Disorders* 39(6): 443–447.

Nosek, Brian A. and Jeffrey J. Hansen. 2008. "The Associations in our Heads Belong to us: Searching for Attitudes and Knowledge in Implicit Evaluation." *Cognition & Emotion* 22(4): 553–594.

"Objection to DSM-V Committee Members on Gender Identity Disorders." 2008. The Petition Site. Retrieved September 10, 2008 (www.thepetitionsite.com/2/objection-to-dsm-v-committee-members-on-gender-identity-disorders).

O'Brien, Jodi. 1999. "Writing in the Body: Gender (Re)Production in Online Interaction." Pp. 76–104 in *Communities in Cyberspace*, edited by Marc A. Smith and Peter Kollock. London, England: Routledge.

O'Brien, Jodi. 2005. *The Production of Reality: Essays and Readings in Social Interaction*. 4th edn. Newbury Park, CA: Pine Forge Press.

Oliver, Mike. 1996. "Defining Impairment and Disability: Issues at Stake." Pp. 39–54 in *Exploring the Divide: Illness and Disability*. Leeds, England: Disability Press.

Olszewski, Lori. 1993. "Transsexuals Protest at Psychiatry Meeting." *San Francisco Chronicle*, May 24, A13.

Oppenheimer, Mark. 2014. "Technology is Not Driving us Apart After All." *New York Times Magazine*, January 17. Retrieved June 17, 2014 (www.nytimes.com/2014/01/19/magazine/technology-is-not-driving-us-apart-after-all.html?_r=0).

O'Reilly, Tim. 2003. "The Architecture of Participation." O'Reilly Media. Retrieved April 24, 2014 (http://oreilly.com/pub/wlg/3017).

Orenstein, Peggy. 1995. *Schoolgirls: Young Women, Self-Esteem, and the Confidence Gap*. Garden City, NY: Anchor.

Ortner, Sherry and Harriet Whitehead. 1981. *Sexual Meanings: The Cultural Construction of Gender and Sexuality*. Cambridge, England: Cambridge University Press.

Orton-Johnson, Kate and Nick Prior, eds. 2013. *Digital Sociology: Critical Perspectives*. London, England: Palgrave Macmillan.

Osvold, Lise Leigh and Gargi Roysircar Sodowsky. 1993. "Eating Disorders of White American, Racial and Ethnic Minority American, and International Women." *Journal of Multicultural Education* 21(3): 143–154.

Oudshoorn, Nelly. 1994. *Beyond the Natural Body: An Archaeology of Sex Hormones*. New York, NY: Routledge.

Oudshoorn, Nelly. 2000. "Imagined Men: Representations of Masculinities in Discourses on Male Contraceptive Technology." Pp. 123–145 in *Bodies of Technology: Women's Involvement with Reproductive Medicine*, edited by Ann Rudinow Saetnan, Nelly Oudshoorn, and Marta Kirejczyk. Columbus, OH: Ohio State University Press.

Oudshoorn, Nelly. 2003. *The Male Pill: A Biography of a Technology in the Making*. Durham, NC: Duke University Press.

Pääbo, Svante. 2003. "The Mosaic that is Our Genome." *Nature* 421: 409–412.

Pace, Tyler, Aaron Houssian, and Victoria McArthur. 2009. "Are Socially Exclusive Values Embedded in the Avatar Creation Interfaces of MMORPGs?" *Journal of Information, Communication and Ethics in Society* 7(2/3): 192–210.

Padavic, Irene and Barbara Reskin. 2002. *Women and Men at Work*. Thousand Oaks, CA: Pine Forge Press.

Padawer, Ruth. 2012. "What's So Bad about a Boy Who Wants to Wear a Dress?" *The New York Times*. Retrieved December 12, 2013 (www.nytimes.com/2012/08/12/magazine/whats-so-bad-about-a-boy-who-wants-to-wear-a-dress.html?_r=0).

Pardo, Seth T. 2008. "Growing Up Transgender: Research and Theory." *ACT for (Trans) Youth, Part 1*. New York, NY: Cornell University. Retrieved June 8, 2009 (www.actforyouth.net/documents/GrowingUpTransPt1_March08.pdf).

Pardo, Seth T. and Karen Schantz. 2008. "Growing Up Transgender: Safety and Resilience." *ACT for (Trans) Youth, Part 2*. New York, NY: Cornell University. Retrieved June 8, 2009 (www.actforyouth.net/documents/Trans2_final.pdf).

Park, Katharine. 2006. *Secrets of Women: Gender, Generation, and the Origins of Human Dissection*. New York, NY: Zone Books.

Park, Katharine and Robert Nye. 1991. "Destiny is Anatomy." *The New Republic* February 18: 53–57.

Patzer, Gordon L. 1985. *The Physical Attractiveness Phenomena*. New York: Plenum Press.

Peebles, Rebecka, Jenny L. Wilson, Iris F. Litt, Kristina K. Hardy, James D. Lock, Julia R. Mann, and D.L. Borzekowski. 2012. "Disordered Eating in a Digital Age: Eating Behaviors, Health, and Quality of Life in Users of Websites with Pro-Eating Disorder Content." *Journal of Medical Internet Research* 14(5): e148.

Pew Internet and American Life Project. 2007. "February–March 2007 Tracking SPSS Dataset." Washington, DC: Pew Research Center. Retrieved September 5, 2014 (www.pewinternet.org/datasets/february-march-2007-tracking).

Pew Research Center for People and the Press. 2007. "How Young People View Their Lives, Futures and Politics: A Portrait of 'Generation Next'." Washington, DC: Pew Research Center. Retrieved September 5, 2014 (www.people-press.org/files/legacy-pdf/300.pdf).

Pew Research Center. 2010. "Millennials: Confident. Connected. Open to Change." February 24. Retrieved December 12, 2013 (http://pewresearch.org/millennials/).

Pfäfflin, Friedemann. 1997. "Sex Reassignment, Harry Benjamin, and Some European Roots." *International Journal of Transgenderism* 1(2). Retrieved September 5, 2014 (www.iiav.nl/ezines/web/ijt/97-03/numbers/symposion/ijtc0202.htm).

Phelan, Michael and Scott Hunt. 1998. "Prison Gang Members' Tattoos as Identity Work: The Visual Communication of Moral Careers." *Symbolic Interaction* 21(3): 277–298.

Phillips, David J. 1996. "Defending the Boundaries: Identifying and Countering Threats in a Usenet Newsgroup." *The Information Society* 12(1): 39–62.

Phillips, Sarah. 2007. "A Brief History of Facebook." *The Guardian* 25.

Pitts, Victoria. 2003. *In the Flesh: The Cultural Politics of Body Modification*. New York, NY: Palgrave Macmillan.

Plummer, Kenneth. 1995. *Telling Sexual Stories: Power, Change and Social Worlds*. London, England: Routledge.

Poster, Mark. 1995. *The Second Media Age*. Cambridge, England: Polity Press.

Preves, Sharon E. 2003. *Intersex and Identity: The Contested Self*. New Brunswick, NJ: Rutgers University Press.

Pritchard, Mary. 2008. "Disordered Eating in Undergraduates: Does Gender Role Orientation Influence Men and Women the Same Way?" *Sex Roles* 59(3/4): 282–289.

"Professor Assigns Students to 'E-Fast'." 2007. Tell Me More. National Public Radio. July 30. Retrieved August 1, 2008 (www.npr.org/templates/story/story.php?storyId=12346287).

Quart, Alissa. 2008. "When Girls Will Be Boys." *New York Times Magazine*, March 16, pp. 32–37.

Radley, Alan. 1991. *The Body and Social Psychology*. New York, NY: Springer.

Raisborough, Jayne. 2007. "Contexts of Choice: The Risky Business of Elective Cosmetic Surgery." Pp. 19–35 in *Risks, Identities and the Everyday,* edited by Julie Scott-Jones and Jayne Raisborough. Aldershot, UK: Ashgate.

Ray, Audacia. *Naked on the Internet: Hookups, Downloads, and Cashing in on Internet Sexploration*. Emeryville, CA: Seal Press.

Reagan, Charles E. 1996. *Paul Ricoeur: His Life and His Work*. Chicago, IL: University of Chicago Press.

Reaves Jessica. 2001. "Anorexia Goes High Tech." *Time Magazine*. July 31. Retrieved November 15, 2013 (www.time.com/time/health/article/0,8599,169660,00.html).

Reis, Elizabeth. 2004. "Teaching Transgender History, Identity, and Politics." *Radical History Review* 88: 166–177.

Reskin, Barbara F. and Patricia Roos. 1991. *Job Queues, Gender Queues: Explaining Women's Inroads into Male Occupations*. Philadelphia, PA: Temple University Press.

Rheingold, Howard. 1993a. "A Slice of Life in My Virtual Community." Pp. 57–82 in *Global Networks: Computers and International Communication*, edited by Linda M. Harasim. Cambridge, MA: MIT Press.

Rheingold, Howard. 1993b. *The Virtual Community: Homesteading on the Electronic Frontier*. Reading, MA: Addison-Wesley.

Richards, Sarah Elizabeth. 2014. "The Next Frontier in Fertility Treatment." *New York Times*, January 13, 2014, p. A21.

Ricoeur, Paul. 1991. *From Text to Action. Essays in Hermeneutics*, translated by Kathleen Blamey and John B. Thompson. Evanston, IL: Northwestern University Press.

Ridgeway, Cecilia L. and Kristan Glasgow Erickson. 2000. "Creating and Spreading Status Beliefs." *American Journal of Sociology* 106(3): 579–615.

Ries, Tonia. 2010. "250 Million People Engage with Facebook on External Sites Monthly." Retrieved February 13, 2014 (http://therealtimereport.com/2010/12/11/250-million-people-engage-with-facebook-on-external-sites-monthly/).

Riessman, Catherine Kohler. 2000. "Stigma and Everyday Resistance Practices: Childless Women in South India." *Gender and Society* 14 (1): 111–135.

Ritzer, George. 1993. *The McDonaldization of Society*. Thousand Oaks, CA: Pine Forge Press.

Robinson-Moore, Cynthia. 2008. "Beauty Standards Reflect Eurocentric Paradigms—So What? Skin Color, Identity, and Black Female Beauty." *Journal of Race & Policy* 4(1): 66–85.

Rodino, Michelle. 1997. "Breaking Out of Binaries: Reconceptualizing Gender and Its Relationship to Language in Computer-Mediated Communication." *Journal of Computer-Mediated Communication* 3(3). Retrieved September 10, 2008 (http://jcmc.indiana.edu/vol3/issue3/rodino.html).

Rogers, Thomas. 2008. "What the Pregnant Man Didn't Deliver." Salon.com. Retrieved September 5, 2014 (www.salon.com/2008/07/03/pregnant_man_3).

Ronai, Carol R. and Carolyn Ellis. 1989. "Turn-ons for Money: Interactional Strategies of a Table Dancer." *Journal of Contemporary Ethnography* 18(3): 271–298.

Rooney, David. 1997. "A Contextualizing, Socio-Technical Definition of Technology: Learning from Ancient Greece and Foucault." *Prometheus* 15(3): 399–407.

Ross, Craig, Emily S. Orr, Mia Sisic, Jaime M. Arseneault, Mary G. Simmering, and R. Robert Orr. 2009. "Personality and Motivations Associated with Facebook Use." *Computers in Human Behavior* 25(2): 578–586.

Rupp, Leila. 2001. "Toward a Global History of Same-Sex Sexuality." *Journal of the History of Sexuality* 10(2): 287–302.

Sanchez, Carleen D. 2010. "My Second Life as a Cyber Border Crosser." *Journal for Virtual Worlds Research* 2(5): 3–18.

Sanders, Clinton. 1989. *Customizing the Body: The Art and Culture of Tattooing*. Philadelphia, PA: Temple University Press.

Sandstrom, Kent L. 1998. "Preserving the Vital and Valued Self in the Face of AIDS." *Sociological Inquiry* (68)3: 354–371.

Sandstrom, Kent L., Daniel D. Martin, and Gary Alan Fine. 2006. *Symbols, Selves, and Social Reality: An Interactionist Approach to Social Psychology and Sociology*. Los Angeles, CA: Roxbury Press.

Santoni-Rugiu, Paolo and Philip J. Sykes. 2007. *A History of Plastic Surgery*. New York, NY: Springer.

Schiebinger, Londa. 1987. "Skeletons in the Closet: The First Illustrations of the Female Skeleton in Eighteenth-Century Anatomy." Pp. 42–82 in *The Making of the Modern Body: Sexuality and Society in the Nineteenth Century*, edited by Catherine Gallagher and Thomas Laqueur. Berkeley, CA: University of California Press.

Schlenker, Barry R. 1980. *Impression Management: The Self-Concept, Social Identity, and Interpersonal Relations*. Monterey, CA: Brooks/Cole.

Schrock, Douglas, Daphne Holden, and Lori Reid. 2004. "Creating Emotional Resonance: Interpersonal Emotion Work and Motivational Framing in a Transgender Community." *Social Problems* 51(1): 61–81.

Schwartz, Lori A. and William T. Markham. 1985. "Sex-Role Stereotyping in Children's Toy Advertisements." *Sex Roles* 1: 157–170.

Seale, Clive. 2006. "Gender Accommodation in Online Cancer Support Groups." *Health: An Interdisciplinary Journal for the Social Study of Health, Illness and Medicine* 10(3): 345–360.

Second Life. 2014. "What is Second Life?" Retrieved February 18, 2014 (http://secondlife.com/whatis/).

Segal, Howard P. 1986. "The Technological Utopians." Pp. 119–136 in *Imagining Tomorrow: History, Technology and The American Future*, edited by Joseph J. Corn. Cambridge, MA: MIT Press.

Shapiro, Eve. 2004. "Transcending Barriers: Transgender Organizing on the Internet." *Journal of Gay and Lesbian Social Services* 16(3/4): 165–179.

Shapiro, Eve. 2007. "Drag Kinging and the Transformation of Gender Identities." *Gender & Society* 21(2): 250–271.

Shapiro, Eve. 2013. "Social Psychology and the Body." Pp. 191–224 in *Handbook of Social Psychology*. New York, NY: Springer Netherlands.

Shaw, Heather, Lisa Ramirez, Ariel Trost, Pat Randall, and Eric Stice. 2004. "Body Image and Eating Disturbances across Ethnic Groups: More Similarities than Differences." *Psychology of Addictive Behaviors* 18(1): 12–18.

Shields, Rob, ed. 1996. *Cultures of the Internet: Virtual Spaces, Real Histories, Living Bodies*. London, England: Sage Publications.

Shih, Margaret, Todd L. Pittinsky, and Nalini Ambady. 1999. "Stereotype Susceptibility: Identity Salience and Shifts in Quantitative Performance." *Psychological Science* 10(1): 80–83.

Shilling, Chris, ed. 2007a. *Embodying Sociology: Retrospect, Progress and Prospects*. Oxford, England: Blackwell Publishing.

Shilling, Chris. 2007b. "Sociology and the Body: Classical Traditions and New Agendas." *Sociological Review* 55(1): 1–69.

Shilling, Chris. 2008. *Changing Bodies: Habit, Crisis and Creativity*. London, England: Sage Publications.

Shostak, Arthur B. 1999. *Cyberunion: Empowering Labor through Computer Technology*. New York, NY: M.E. Sharpe.

Smith, Marc and Peter Kollock. 1999. *Communities in Cyberspace*. New York, NY: Routledge.

Smith, Stephanie Ann. 2006. *Household Words: Bloomers, Sucker, Bombshell, Scab, Nigger, Cyber*. Minnesota, MN: University of Minnesota Press.

Snow, David A. and Leon Anderson. 1987. "Identity Work among the Homeless: The Verbal Construction and Avowal of Personal Identities." *American Journal of Sociology* 92(6): 1,336–1,371.

Snyder, Mark, Elizabeth Decker Tanke, and Ellen Berscheid. 1977. "Social Perception and Interpersonal Behavior: On the Self-Fulfilling Nature of Social Stereotypes." *Journal of Personality and Social Psychology* 35: 656–666.

Social Security Administrations. 2013. "RM 10212.200 Changing Numident Data for Reasons other than Name Change." Retrieved July 6, 2014 (https://secure.ssa.gov/poms.nsf/lnx/0110212200).

Soemmerring, Samuel Thomas von. 1796. *Tabula Sceleti Feminae*. Frankfurt am Main: Traiecti ad Moenum, Apud Varrentrapp et Wenner.

Soukup, Charles. 1999. "The Gendered Interactional Patterns of Computer-Mediated Chatrooms: A Critical Ethnographic Study." *The Information Society* 15(3): 169–176.

Spack, Norman P., Laura Edwards-Leeper, Henry A. Feldman, Scott Leibowitz, Francie Mandel, David A. Diamond, and Stanley R. Vance. 2012. "Children and Adolescents with Gender Identity Disorder Referred to a Pediatric Medical Center." *Pediatrics* 129(3): 418–425.

Spiegel, Alix. 2008a. "Two Families Grapple with Sons' Gender Preferences." *All Things Considered*. National Public Radio, May 28. Retrieved March 22, 2009 (www.npr.org/templates/story/story.php?storyId=90247842).

Spiegel, Alix. 2008b. "Q&A: Therapists on Gender Identity Issues in Kids." National Public Radio. Retrieved August 11, 2008 (www.npr.org/templates/story/story.php?storyId=90229789).

Staav, Yael and Tim Piper. 2006. *Evolution*. Toronto, Canada: Reginald Pike Films. Retrieved February 16, 2009 (www.campaignforrealbeauty.com/home_films_evolution_v2.swf).

Stanford, Jacqueline N. and Marita P. McCabe. 2005. "Sociocultural Influences on Adolescent Boys' Body Image and Body Change Strategies." *Body Image* 2(2): 105–113.

Steinmetz, Katy. 2014. "The Transgender Tipping Point: America's Next Civil Rights Frontier." *Time Magazine*, June 9.

Steward, Samuel. 1990. *Bad Boys and Tough Tattoos: A Social History of the Tattoo with Gangs, Sailors, and Street-Corner Punks, 1950–1965*. New York, NY: Haworth Press.

Stolberg, Michael. 2003. "A Woman Down to Her Bones: The Anatomy of Sexual Difference in the Sixteenth and Early Seventeenth Centuries." *Isis* 94: 274–299.

Stone, Allucquère Rosanne. 1991. "Will The Real Body Please Stand Up?: Boundary Stories About Virtual Cultures." Pp. 81–118 in *Cyberspace: First Steps*, edited by Michael Benedikt. Cambridge, MA: MIT Press.

Stone, Allucquère Rosanne. 1995. *The War of Desire and Technology at the Close of the Mechanical Age*. Cambridge, MA: MIT Press.

Stratton, Jim. 2007. "Largo Reaffirms Firing of Transgender Official." *The Orlando Sentinel*, March 24.

Strauss, Stephen. 2004. "Bradshaw + Blahniks = Tippiness Factor." *Globe and Mail*, March 24, p. R1.

Stryker, Susan. 2006. "(De)Subjugated Knowledge." Pp. 1–15 in *The Transgender Studies Reader*, edited by Susan Stryker and Stephen Whittle. New York, NY: Routledge.

Stryker, Susan. 2008. *Transgender History*. Berkeley, CA: Seal Press.

Sullivan, Nikki. 2005. "Somatechnics, or, the Social Inscription of Bodies and Selves." *Australian Feminist Studies* 20(48): 363–366.

Sullivan, Nikki. 2006. "Somatechnics, or Monstrosity Unbound." *Scan: Journal of Media Arts Culture* 3(3). Retrieved December 4, 2008 (www.scan.net.au/scan/journal/display.php?journal_id=83).

Summers, Leigh. 2003. *Bound to Please: A History of the Victorian Corset*. Oxford, England: Berg Publishers.

Sunden, Jenny. 2003. *Material Virtualities*. New York, NY: Peter Lang Publishing.

Swann, William B. Jr. 1987. "Identity Negotiation: Where Two Roads Meet." *Journal of Personality and Social Psychology* 53: 1,038–1,051.

Swann, William B. Jr. 1999. *Resilient Identities: Self, Relationships, and the Construction of Social Reality*. New York, NY: Basic Books.

Sweet, Nova and Richard Tewksbury. 2000. "Entry, Maintenance, and Departure from a Career in the Sex Industry: Strippers' Experiences of Occupational Costs and Rewards." *Humanity and Society* 2(1): 136–161.

Sweetman, Paul. 1999. "Anchoring the (Postmodern) Self? Body Modification, Fashion and Identity." *Body & Society* 5(2/3): 51–76.

"The Tattoo Fad." 1897. *Boston Morning Journal*, December 25, p. 3.

Thompson, Charis. 2005. *Making Parents: The Ontological Choreography of Reproductive Technologies*. Cambridge, MA; London: MIT Press.

Thompson, J. Kevin. 1999. "Body Image, Bodybuilding, and Cultural Ideals of Muscularity." *Mesomorphosis* 30: 1–6.

Thorne, Barrie. 1993. *Gender Play: Girls and Boys in School*. Buckingham, England: Open University Press.

Tolman, Deborah. 1994. "Doing Desire: Adolescent Girls' Struggles For/With Sexuality." *Gender & Society* 8(3): 324–342.

Tomlinson, Barbara. 1995. "Phallic Fables and Spermatic Romance: Disciplinary Crossing and Textual Ridicule." *Configurations* 3(2): 105–134.

Topp, Sarah S. 2013. "Against the Quiet Revolution: The Rhetorical Construction of Intersex Individuals as Disordered." *Sexualities* 16(1–2): 180–194.

Transgender Law Center. 2013. "Thomas Beatie Marriage Case." Retrieved June 4, 2014 (http://transgenderlawcenter.org/archives/3038).

Trivers, Robert L. 1972. "Parental Investment and Sexual Selection." In *Sexual Selection and the Descent of Man*, edited by Bernard Grant Campbell. Chicago, IL: Aldine.

Turbin, Carole. 2003. "Refashioning the Concept of Public/Private: Lessons from Dress Studies." *Journal of Women's History* 15(1): 43–51.

Turkle, Sherry. 1994. "Constructions and Reconstructions of Self in Virtual Reality: Playing in MUD's." *Mind, Culture, and Activity: An International Journal* 1: 158–167.

Turkle, Sherry. 1995. *Life on the Screen: Identity in the Age of the Internet.* New York, NY: Simon & Schuster.

Turkle, Sherry. 2011. *Alone Together: Why We Expect More from Technology and Less from Each Other.* New York, NY: Basic Books.

Turner, Bryan S. 1984. *The Body and Society: Explorations in Social Theory.* Oxford, England: Blackwell Publishing.

Turner, Bryan S. 1997. "What is the Sociology of the Body?" *Body & Society* 3(1): 103–107.

Turner, Bryan S. 2007. "Culture, Technologies and Bodies: The Technological Utopia of Living Forever." Pp. 19–36 in *Embodying Sociology: Retrospect, Progress, and Prospects,* edited by Chris Shilling. Oxford, England: Blackwell Publishing.

United Nations. 1992. "The Convention of Biological Diversity." Retrieved December 4, 2008 (www.biodiv.org/convention/convention.shtml).

United Nations Educational Scientific and Cultural Organization. 1985. "Technology Education within the Context of General Education." Working Paper presented at the International Symposium on the Teaching of Technology within the Context of General Education, November 18–22, Paris, France: Retrieved July 3, 2008 (http://unesdoc.unesco.org/images/0006/000664/066416eb.pdf).

van der Ploeg, Irma. 1995. "Hermaphrodite Patients: In-vitro Fertilization and the Transformation of Male Infertility." *Science, Technology & Human Values* 20(4): 460–481.

van Doorn, Niels. 2010. "The Ties that Bind: The Networked Performance of Gender, Sexuality and Friendship on MySpace." *New Media & Society* 12(4): 583–602.

Verlinden, Jasper. 2012. "Transgender Bodies and Male Pregnancy: The Ethics of Radical Self-Refashioning." Pp. 107–136 in *Machine: Bodies, Genders, Technologies,* edited by Michaela Hampf and MaryAnn Snyder-Körber. Heidelberg, Germany: Universitätsverlag.

Vidal-Ortiz, Salvador. 2002. "Queering Sexuality and Doing Gender: Transgender Men's Identification with Gender and Sexuality." Pp. 181–233 in *Gendered Sexualities,* Advances in Gender Research, Vol. 6, edited by Patricia Gagne and Richard Tewksbury. New York, NY: Elsevier Science Press.

Vidal-Ortiz, Salvador. 2008. "Transgender and Transsexual Studies: Sociology's Influence and Future Steps." *Sociology Compass* 2(2): 433–450.

Waggoner, Ashley S., Eliot R. Smith, and Elizabeth C. Collins. 2009. "Person Perception by Active Versus Passive Perceivers." *Journal of Experimental Social Psychology* 45(4): 1,028–1,031.

Wagner, David G. and Joseph Berger. 1997. "Gender and Interpersonal Task Behaviors: Status Expectation Accounts." *Sociological Perspectives* 40(1): 1–32.

Walker, Danna L. 2007. "The Longest Day: Could a Class of College Students Survive Without iPods, Cellphones, Computers and TV from One Sunrise to the Next?" *Washington Post Magazine,* August 5, p. W20.

Warin, Megan. 2009. *Abject Relations: Everyday Worlds of Anorexia.* New Brunswick, NJ: Rutgers University Press.

Waszkiewicz, Elroi. 2006. "Getting by Gatekeepers: Transmen's Dialectical Negotiations within Psychomedical Institutions." Master's Thesis, Georgia State University, Atlanta, GA. Retrieved September 5, 2014 (http://scholarworks.gsu.edu/cgi/viewcontent.cgi?article=1012&context=sociology_theses).

Weber, Max. 1947. *The Theory of Economic and Social Organization.* New York, NY: Oxford University Press.

Weber, Max. 2005. "Remarks on Technology and Culture." *Theory, Culture & Society* 22(4): 23–38.

Webster, Juliet. 1996. *Shaping Women's Work: Gender, Employment, and Information Technology.* London, England: Longman.

Weisbuch, Max, Zorana Ivcevic, and Nalini Ambady. 2009. "On Being Liked on the Web and in the 'Real World': Consistency in First Impressions across Personal Webpages and Spontaneous Behavior." *Journal of Experimental Social Psychology* 45(3): 573–576.

Wesely, Jennifer. 2003. "Exotic Dancing and the Negotiation of Identity: The Multiple Uses of Body Technologies." *Journal of Contemporary Ethnography* 32(6): 643–669.

West, Candace and Sarah Fenstermaker. 1995. "Doing Difference." *Gender & Society* 9: 8–37.

West, Candace and Don H. Zimmerman. 1987. "Doing Gender." *Gender & Society* 1: 125–151.

Wierckx, Katrien, Eva van Caenegem, Guido Pennings, Els Elaut, David Dedecker, Fleur van de Peer, Steven Weyers, Petra de Sutter, and Guy T'Sjoen. 2012. "Reproductive Wish in Transsexual Men." *Human Reproduction* 27(2): 483–487.

Williams, Simon. J. 2004. "Embodiment." Pp. 73–76 in *Key Concepts in Medical Sociology*, edited by Jonathon Gabe, Michael Bury and Mary A. Elston. London, England: Sage.

Wilson, Jenny L., Rebecka Peebles, Kristina K. Hardy, and Iris F. Litt. 2006. "Surfing for Thinness: A Pilot Study of Pro-eating Disorder Website Usage in Adolescents with Eating Disorders." *Pediatrics* 118(6):e1635–e1643.

Wilson, Robert E., Samuel D. Gosling, and Lindsay T. Graham. 2012. "A Review of Facebook Research in the Social Sciences." *Perspectives on Psychological Science* 7(3): 203–220.

Windsor, Elroi J. 2011. "Regulating Healthy Gender: Surgical Body Modification among Transgender and Cisgender Consumers." PhD dissertation, Department of Sociology, Georgia State University.

Windsor, Elroi J. N.d. "Enhancing Selves through Gendering Bodies: Comparing Surgical Body Modifications among Transgender and Cisgender People." Unpublished manuscript.

Wolkowitz, Carol. 2006. *Bodies at Work.* London, England: Sage Publications.

"Woman's Emancipation (Being a Letter Addressed to Mr. Punch, With a Drawing, by A Strong-Minded American Woman)." 1851. *Harper's New Monthly Magazine,* 3 (August), p. 424.

Wood, Elizabeth Anne. 2000. "Working in the Fantasy Factory: The Attention Hypothesis and the Enacting of Masculine Power in Strip Clubs." *Journal of Contemporary Ethnography* 29(1): 5–31.

Xavier, Jessica M., Marilyn Bobbin, Ben Singer, and Earline Budd. 2005. "A Needs Assessment of Transgendered People of Color Living in Washington, DC." Pp. 31–47 in *Transgender Health and HIV Prevention: Needs Assessment Studies from Transgender Communities across the United States*, edited by Walter Bockting and Eric Avery. New York, NY: Haworth Medical Press.

Yee, Nick and Jeremy Bailenson. 2007. "The Proteus Effect: The Effect of Transformed Self-Representation on Behavior." *Human Communication Research* 33(3): 271–290.

Yee, Nick, Jeremy Bailenson, and Nicolas Ducheneaut. 2009. "The Proteus Effect: Implications of Transformed Digital Self-representation on Online and Offline Behavior." *Communication Research* 36(2): 285– 312.

Zammuner, Vanda L. 1987. "Children's Sex-Role Stereotypes: A Cross-Cultural Analysis." Pp. 272–293 in *Sex and Gender*, edited by Phillip Shaver and Clyde Hendrick. Newbury Park, CA: Sage Publications.

Zhao, Shanyang. 2005. "The Digital Self: Through the Looking Glass of Telecopresent Others." *Symbolic Interaction* 28(3): 387–405.

Zipern, Andrew. 2001. "Technology That Aims To Do Good." *New York Times*, November 8.

INDEX

Note: 'n' after a page number indicates a note; 'f' indicates a figure.